NANTEOS:

A WELSH HOUSE AND ITS FAMILIES

NANTEOS:

A WELSH HOUSE AND ITS FAMILIES

edited by

Gerald Morgan

with chapters by

the late Capt. J.Hext-Lewes
Richard Moore-Colyer
Gerald Morgan
Caroline Palmer
A.J.Parkinson
Juliette Wood

GOMER

First Impression—2001

ISBN 1 85902 802 0

This book is published with the support of the
Arts Council of Wales.

Printed in Wales at
Gomer Press, Llandysul, Ceredigion

CONTENTS

Foreword and acknowledgements   vi

Note: The Nanteos Archive   viii

List of illustrations   x

1. NANTEOS: THE EARLY CENTURIES.   1
   Gerald Morgan

2. WILLIAM EDWARD POWELL AND HIS FAMILY CIRCLE.   45
   Caroline Palmer

3. W.E. POWELL AND REBECCA.   81
   Gerald Morgan

4. THE AESTHETE OF NANTEOS: GEORGE POWELL 1842-1882.   91
   Gerald Morgan

5. NANTEOS: A LANDED ESTATE IN DECLINE 1800-1930.   117
   Richard Moore-Colyer

6. THE LAST OF THE POWELLS.   145
   J. Hext Lewes & Gerald Morgan

7. NANTEOS MANSION.   153
   A.J.Parkinson

8. SOARING AMBITIONS IN THE NANTEOS DEMESNE.   183
   Caroline Palmer

9. NIBBLING PILGRIMS AND THE NANTEOS CUP: A CARDIGANSHIRE LEGEND.   219
   Juliette Wood

Appendix I: Nanteos Heraldry   *Michael Siddons*   255

Appendix II: Genealogy of the Llechwedd Dyrys and Nanteos families.   259

Contributors   260

Index   261

FOREWORD

THE genesis of this volume was a day-school organised in 1991 under the auspices of the Department of Extra-Mural Studies, U.C.W. Aberystwyth (as both were then known). Four papers were given, by Dr Richard Moore-Colyer, Mr A.J. Parkinson, Dr Juliette Wood and myself. It was then my intention simply to publish the four papers and be done. However, time's delays hindered this simple purpose, and in the meantime the volume began to grow, especially thanks to the invaluable interest taken by Dr Caroline Palmer, who has contributed two chapters, offered many useful comments on some of the other chapters, jointly read the proofs and spent much time on the choice of illustrations, though I bear the responsibility for the final choice. The process of editing a collaborative volume of essays was a revelation to me; I know that I have by no means solved all the inevitable problems of consistency which emerged, but I am responsible for all errors and omissions. There is a small degree of repetition which enables chapters to be read independently.

It is inevitable that a book like this can never be complete. Had it been published in 1991 as intended, it could not have included Ms Janet Joel's revelation of W.E. Powell's alternative family in London. Again, while the book was going through the press, Mr Thomas Lloyd kindly drew my attention to Evelyn Lewes's *Out with the Cambrians* (1934), which includes a print of George II's harper, Griffith Evans, who played every New Year at Nanteos, and was reputed to haunt the place. It is reproduced on p. 29, but it was too late to rewrite the text of chapter I.

During the book's gestation, Mr Gary Hesp, for ten years the owner of Nanteos, continued the restoration - indeed the resuscitation - of what had been a very sick house. To him all lovers of this delightful mansion and site are indebted for its present good health. Changes had obviously to be made; the house had to generate at least some income towards its upkeep, but it still retains much more than once was feared of its integrity and charm.

I owe numerous debts of gratitude: to Mr Hesp, to Graham and Sue Hodgson-Jones and their predecessors and successors in charge of Nanteos from day to day, to Mrs Loveday Gee of Llanllyr for permission to publish the essay in chapter six by her late father, Captain J. Hext Lewes, to Professor Andrew Wawn of Leeds University and to the Brotherton Library there; to the late Richard Brinkley of the Hugh Owen Library, U.W. Aberystwyth; to Mr John Hefin; to the staffs of the National Library of Wales, the Royal Commission on Ancient and Historical Monuments of Wales, and of the Ceredigion Library; to the National Museum of Wales, to Mr Timothy Gwyn-Jones the new owner of Nanteos, to Mr H. Rees Thomas, to my colleagues at the (then) Department of Extra-mural Studies at the University of Wales, Aberystwyth, and particularly to Gwasg Gomer. Especial thanks are owed to the contributors for their patience. I offer my apologies to others whom I may have neglected to include.

My thanks are particularly due to the following for permission to include illustrations and for help therewith: Mr Peter White and the staff of the Royal Commission on Ancient and Historical Monuments in Wales, the Librarian and staff of the National Library of Wales, Mr Thomas Lloyd, Mr Miles Wynn Cato, and to the Earl of Lisburne.

GERALD MORGAN,
Aberystwyth

NOTE: THE NANTEOS ARCHIVE

The Nanteos papers were deposited in the National Library of Wales in 1957 by Major and Mrs Mirylees, then owners of the estate. It is one of the largest Ceredigion estate archives in the Library, rivalling the Goginan and Trawsgoed (Crosswood) collections. A brief preliminary schedule was swiftly prepared, to be followed in 1989 by a two-volume schedule of correspondence, accounts, inventories, bank books, game books and rentals, the invaluable work of Mrs Kathleen Hughes. A separate schedule was provided for the collection of documents housed in the Library's Department of Maps and Prints.

In the Department of Manuscripts, some documents remain accessible only through the preliminary schedule. A thousand landed deeds and abstracts of title are to be found in several boxes, from 1621 into the twentieth century; they await detailed scheduling. As is usual in such cases, there are deeds which have no direct relevance to the Nanteos estate; for example, seventy-two deeds are the result of Mrs Mary Powell (nee Frederick) having been executrix of a will. The deeds include a number related to the lease of ground for the building of nonconformist chapels in Aberystwyth, Blaenplwyf and Moriah.

The rentals, scheduled in detail by Mrs Hughes in 1989, comprise two hundred and seventy volumes from the mid-eighteenth century onwards. The vagaries of agents mean that they are not easy to exploit, since there was no absolute consistency in the process of forming the rent books year by year; the estate was not treated as a single unit, but divided between the Nanteos estate, the Abbey estate, the Breconshire estate, and the other lesser units in Carmarthenshire, Pembrokeshire and Merionethshire which from time to time were in Powell ownership. There are unfortunately only a few game books, dating from 1854-6, and one gamekeeper's account book.

Accounts form a considerable section of the archive; they nearly all date from the nineteenth and twentieth centuries, covering a vast range of subjects: litigation, valuations, accounts of butter and cheese, statements of accounts and expenditure, an estimate of damage done by rabbits, tithe assessments, conditions of sale, lists of repairs, and so on. Allied to these are a large range of vouchers for payment, ranging from Sir Thomas Powell's fees for his knighthood in 1687 to payments for wines and spirits, harbour dues, destruction of rabbits, thatching, brewing, tenants' dinner, a new phaeton, election expenses, bookbinding, and George Powell's subscription to a Cardiganshire Scholarship in the Royal College of Music.

The lead mining archive is touched on elsewhere in this volume; it includes a vast range of nineteenth century correspondence as well as leases, account books, statements of profits, a list of miners employed in 1821, shipments of ore and an advertisement for the lease of mines. Lead mining was not the only commercial concern of the estate. One box includes railway material, particularly concerned with the Manchester and Milford Railway, which swiftly became part of the Cambrian Railways company. This part of the archive includes a printed Act for the railway from Llanidloes to Pencader, which was never completed, and records of the Vale of Rheidol light railway.

The history of the archive has raised complexities of referencing in this volume. Professor Richard Moore-Colyer's chapter was written before the 1989 schedule of letters, and comment is made in the notes thereto. References to the letters appear as N.L.W. N.L.+ number, while maps and prints are simply given their present schedule number.

GERALD MORGAN

LIST OF ILLUSTRATIONS

1. A New and Accurate Map of South Wales, 1760, by Emmanuel Bowen. (National Library of Wales) Frontispiece

2. The earliest published view of Nanteos mansion: S.R. Meyrick, *The History and Antiquities of the County of Cardigan* (1809) (National Library of Wales)   2

3. Nanteos and its park under snow viewed from Llechwedd Dyrys (Gerald Morgan)   7

4. Col. John Jones (d.1666), by an unknown artist (National Museum of Wales)   11

5. The memorial tablet to Sir Thomas Powell on the south wall of the chancel at Llanbadarn Fawr (Gerald Morgan)   22

6. Thomas Powell's sister Anne, wife of (1) Richard Stedman, and (2) Sir Herbert Lloyd. (Private collection: print by courtesy of Mr Thomas Lloyd)   26

7. Griffith Evans, the Nanteos harper (from print in Evelyn Lewes, *Out with the Cambrians*)   29

8. The Rev. Dr. William Powell (1705-80). Original at Nanteos; print from National Library of Wales   31

9. Thomas Powell (1745-1797); (private collection: print by courtesy of Mr Miles Wynn Cato)   35

10. Poster: Nanteos Lead Mines (National Library of Wales)   37

11. W.E.Powell (1788-1854) in costume of Lord Lieutenant. Mezzotint reproduction of the portrait which formerly hung at Nanteos. (Print by courtesy of Mr Thomas Lloyd)   50

12. Designs for nine new houses at Laura Place 1827. (National Library of Wales)   56

13. W.T.R.Powell (1815-78), by William Roos (By courtesy of Mr Peter Lord)   71

14. 'Confound these Midges': sketch by W.T.R.Powell (National Library of Wales)   73

15. 'Going to Tregaron Market'; sketch by W.T.R. Powell (National Library of Wales)   74

16. W.E.Powell in old age (National Library of Wales)   76

17. Rebecca Rioters as depicted at the time in the *Illustrated London News*   82

18. Election Poster, 1847 (National Library of Wales)   87

19. George Powell with Algernon Swinburne, from Herbert Vaughan, *The South Wales Squires*, 1926, (National Library of Wales)   92

20. George Powell in early adulthood (National Library of Wales)   94

21. Eirikur Magnusson, Icelandic scholar (National Library of Wales)   96

22. Jón Sigurdsson, Icelandic patriot (National Library of Wales)   97

23. The frontispiece to *Icelandic Legends* (1866); by J.D.Zwecker (National Library of Wales)   101

24. Algernon Swinburne (National Library of Wales)   103

25. George Powell in Moroccan costume (National Library of Wales)   107

26. Initial 'A'. Sketch by George Powell (National Library of Wales)   109

27. George White, Nanteos Butler. (Private collection, print by courtesy of Mr Thomas Lloyd)   131

28. W.T.R. Powell in his wheelchair (National Library of Wales)   133

29. Election Poster, 1859 (National Library of Wales)   135

30. Edward Athelstan Powell, 1870-1930 (National Library of Wales)   138

31. William E.G.P.W. Powell (National Library of Wales)   139

32. Lord Ystwyth at the unveiling of the the memorial at Southgate to W.E.G.P.W. Powell (National Library of Wales)   141

33. Mrs Margaret Powell (National Library of Wales)   148

34. Nanteos in 1888 (by courtesy of the Earl of Lisburne)   154

35. W.R.Coultart's 1841 elevation for twin wings at Nanteos. (National Library of Wales)   156

36. Nanteos: ground floor and first floor plans (Modified by A.J.Parkinson from the drawings in the National Monuments Record of Wales, (Crown copyright: the Royal Commission on the Ancient and Historical Monuments of Wales); redrawn by H.Rees Thomas)   158-9

37. Elevations and ground-floor plans of Castle Howard and Nanteos (A.J. Parkinson)   161

38. Nanteos: Main staircase 1997. (Crown Copyright: the Royal Commission on the Ancient and Historical Monuments of Wales)   163

39. Nanteos: Saloon / Music room 1967. (Crown Copyright: the Royal Commission on the Ancient and Historical Monuments of Wales)   165

40. Nanteos: Gallery and stairwell 1997. (Crown Copyright: the Royal Commission on the Ancient and Historical Monuments of Wales)   166

41. Nanteos: Stable entrance, 1948 (Crown Copyright: the Royal Commission on the Ancient and Historical Monuments of Wales)   169

42. Nanteos: Stable frontage 1993. (Crown Copyright, : the Royal Commission on the Ancient and Historical Monuments of Wales)   169

43. Nanteos: the Library 1967. (Private collection) 173

44. Nanteos: the Dining Room 1967. (Private collection) 173

45. Nanteos: the Lodge (Crown Copyright: the Royal Commission on the Ancient and Historical Monuments of Wales) from original by W.D.Lewis in National Library of Wales 178

46. Nanteos demesne: survey by John Davies 1764 (National Library of Wales) 184

47. 18th Century bridge in the lawn at the foot of Cottage Dingle (Caroline Palmer) 187

48. Plascrug, mapped by John Davies in 1764 (National Library of Wales) 189

49. The ruined façade of the 18th Century Eyecatcher Dog Kennel (Caroline Palmer) 192

50. Watercolour of Plascrug Castle by Thomas Martyn (National Library of Wales) 190

51. John Davenport's 1791 design for the Nanteos Demesne (National Library of Wales) 193

52. West elevation of Nanteos. Watercolour attributed to John Nash's assistant George S.Repton c.1812 (National Library of Wales / print by R.C.A.H.M.) 196

53. John Nash's design for an entrance lodge. Watercolour attributed to George S. Repton c.1812 (National Library of Wales / print by R.C.A.H.M.) 198

54. John Nash's design for Nanteos Dairy/Icehouse. Watercolour and plan attributed to George S. Repton (National Library of Wales) 200

55. William Crawford's survey of Nanteos demesne (National Library of Wales) 202

56. Crawford's demesne survey: detail (National Library of Wales) 203

57. The dovecote behind the mansion in 1948 (Crown Copyright: the Royal Commission on the Ancient and Historical Monuments of Wales) 205

58. 'Otter hunting in Cardiganshire' sketch by W.T.R. Powell. (National Library of Wales) 210

59. The hunt assembles at Nanteos (National Library of Wales) 211

60. Nanteos Cottage (Caroline Palmer) 212

61. The oldest sketch of the Nanteos cup, *Archaeologia Cambrensis*, 1888 (National Library of Wales) 220

62. The Nanteos cup with notes of attestation (Crown Copyright: the Royal Commission on the Ancient and Historical Monuments of Wales) 222

63. Strata Florida abbey, from Buck's *Antiquities* 1774 (National Library of Wales)   227
64. Another view of the Nanteos cup (Crown Copyright: the Royal Commission on the Ancient and Historical Monuments of Wales)   235
65. The icon of Elijah at St David's cathedral. (Gerald Morgan, by kind permission of the Dean and Chapter) p.238   238
67. Perhaps the oldest photograph of the (unrepaired) cup. (National Library of Wales)   243
68. A Powell funeral hatchment (Gerald Morgan)   255
69. Heraldic shield of Sir Thomas Powell, Llanbadarn Church (Gerald Morgan)   257

A new and accurate Map of South Wales (1760); showing the location of Nanteos.

N.L.W.

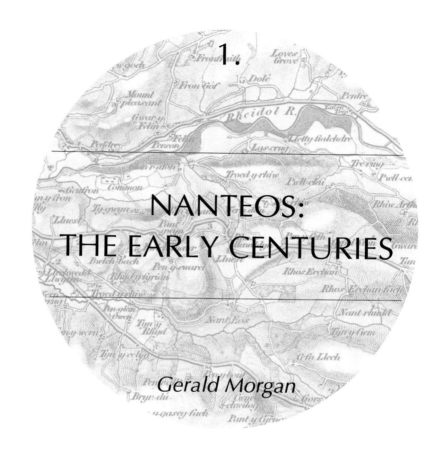

1.

NANTEOS:
THE EARLY CENTURIES

Gerald Morgan

The earliest view of Nanteos mansion (1809).
N.L.W.

THE EARLY CENTURIES

Few mansions and estates in Wales evoke more warm interest than Nanteos, three miles south-east of Aberystwyth. The name (meaning 'nightingale-stream') is poetic, the estate was for two and a half centuries associated with a well-known and influential gentry family; the house is beautifully situated in a sheltered suntrap, protected by hills and trees, and it has a fine southerly prospect. It is reputedly haunted, and has given its name to a widely-known healing cup. In its prime it was the centre of a thirty-thousand acre estate, and its squires were among the handful of leading men in Cardiganshire. Alas though for romance; several of those attributes are demonstrably either false or oversimplified. The attractive name, the association with the Powell family, and the Nanteos cup, are not entirely what they seem. The appearance of great wealth, too, was deceptive; the estate, like so many others, groaned almost continuously under a burden of debt. The cup, supposed by the credulous to be the Holy Grail, is the subject of a separate chapter, while the history of the Powells will shortly become clear, so let us first turn to the name Nanteos.

The stream which flows so picturesquely down the shallow valley to join the Ystwyth is the Paith; an unexpected name for a stream, meaning 'open country'. Nanteos is a sixteenth-century substitution for the site's original name, Neuadd Lawdden (Llawdden's Hall).[1] In the fifteenth century the Cardiganshire poet Deio ab Ieuan Du sang a *cywydd* describing his bardic journey through the county from south to north. When he reached the Aberystwyth area, he tells us:

> Llawdden oedd eu gwarden gynt,
> Hil Llawdden hael oll oeddynt.
> (Llawdden was once their warden,
> His race were generous every one.)[2]

Although the personal name is rare in medieval Welsh, Llawdden was a twelfth-century Welsh tribal patriarch in north Cardiganshire, and P.C. Bartrum's massive assemblage of genealogies shows a number of north Cardiganshire families descended from him.[3] It is not surprising therefore that there should have been a mansion called Neuadd Lawdden in this district; what is surprising is that the place changed its name. Neuadd Lawdden of the early sixteenth century had become Nanteos by the beginning of the seventeenth century, though we do not know who changed the name. The place-name Rhoslawdden still survives next to the little settlement of Moriah on the Aberystwyth-Devil's Bridge road, less than a mile from the mansion.[4] In Professor Ralph Griffiths's lists of office-holders in the Principality of South Wales in the later middle ages, north Cardiganshire is the only area where Llawdden occurs as a personal name.[5]

So Nanteos is not originally Nanteos but Neuadd Lawdden, and the first family we know of as occupiers of the site were not the Powells, but the Joneses; nor were they descendants of Llawdden, but of Elystan Glodrydd. Where they originally lived is not known, but it was not on the Nanteos site, as will be seen. Two men from the Jones genealogy, father and son, appear in Professor Griffiths's list of reeves of Creuddyn: Llywelyn ap Rhys ap Cadwgan (1466-67) and Ieuan Goch ap Llywelyn ap Rhys (1492-93).[6] This suggests that they were already small landowners, who had access to minor Crown office, and who took advantage of it, just as the early Vaughans of Trawsgoed did.[7] In 1539 Ieuan's grandson, Edward ap John ap Ieuan Goch, was the owner of hill farmland north of Cwmystwyth,[8] and in 1548 he and his brothers Thomas and Evan acquired Llety'r Cynydd in the commote of Creuddyn.[9] Later in the century Edward's son John married one Jane, heiress of Nanteos; it was then that the Jones family become known as 'of Nanteos', showing that this name had by then supplanted Neuadd Lawdden.[10] Jane's parentage is traceable only in her marriage settlement of 1592, where she is named as daughter of Richard ap Morris ap Jenkin, of whom nothing else is known.[11] Nor is it known how much land was attached to what would have then been the modest mansion of Neuadd Lawdden, but its heiress would certainly have been a catch for a man involved in the scramble to create an estate, a scramble which obsessed all ambitious men in late medieval and early modern Wales. Marrying an heiress was but one of a number of ways to create and increase a land-holding;

others were inheritance, outright purchase, lending money on mortgage to men who found themselves unable to repay, enclosing common land, gambling, and sheer theft. In addition, the holding of office under the Crown could be advantageous in gaining access to land confiscated by the government. Members of the Nanteos families were vigorously engaged in the hustle for land and influence which brought long-lasting advantage to some, while others suffered either through incompetence or simply lack of heirs. John ap Edward was busy in the land market during the two decades before his death.[12]

The Jones family of Nanteos were not of the first rank of Cardiganshire gentry. The Pryses of Gogerddan had already established a primacy which they never entirely lost, even though the Vaughans of Trawsgoed eventually managed to obtain a peerage, the first in the county. The main rival of the Pryses for local power at the end of the sixteenth century was Thomas Jones of Aberystwyth, grandson of Sir Thomas Jones (d.1559), of Abermarlais in Carmarthenshire, who was no relation of the Nanteos Joneses as far as I can tell. He had bought from Henry VIII the Abermarlais estate of his executed cousin Rhys ap Griffith. It is not clear to me how Thomas Jones acquired his Aberystwyth lands, including the original Penglais mansion, later sold to the Richardes family, but his son James at his death in 1678 was possessed of the estates of Penglais, Dolaucothi and Abermaed, with swathes of farms in both Cardiganshire and Carmarthenshire. His will survives in the Nanteos archives; Thomas Johnes of Hafod was his direct descendant.

Jane's husband John ab Edward ap John ab Ieuan Goch, owner of Nanteos in the right of his wife, might claim gentry status, but he got on with his farming, and with adding to his estate.[13] He made his will in January 1600, though he did not die until 1607.[14] Three facts suggest that either he died young or his marriage had been to a younger woman: his concern that his wife might be pregnant at the time of his death, his appointment of guardians for all the children, who were therefore under 21 at the time of his death, and that his eldest son survived him for twenty-nine years. John ab Edward's wealth and claim to gentry status are hinted at by his bequest of twelve pence to St David's cathedral rather than the usual yeoman's legacy of a groat. The children named in the will are two sons, Edward and Richard, and two daughters, as well as an illegitimate son. Edward, the eldest son, was still a minor at his father's death; probate was granted to the children's guardians. Edward inherited the bulk of his father's lands and wealth, including Nanteos, but Richard received three farms in the parishes of Llanfihangel-y-Creuddyn and Llanbadarn Fawr, and the two daughters were bequeathed forty pounds apiece as their dowries. Richard Jones became rector of Carew in Pembrokeshire, and another son, not named in the will but recorded in the genealogies as Owen, married Fortune, daughter of John Bowen of Crugbychan in the parish of Ferwig, near Cardigan.

All these facts imply that John ab Edward had established himself firmly among the competing, intermarrying parish gentry of Cardiganshire, and that he had been able to afford a good education for his sons. No schools are known to have existed in Cardiganshire; presumably the boys were either tutored, or sent to English schools. The inventory of John ab Edward's goods made at his death includes twelve oxen, seventy-one cattle and 160 sheep, outstripping local yeomen but by no means the largest in contemporary Cardiganshire inventories. Another of Edward's brothers, (named in the genealogies but not in his father's will) did well for himself. He was Evan Lloyd, who married Ellen Pryse daughter of Richard Pryse of Gogerddan, the county's leading family, and through his son Richard he was a founder of the Lloyd family of Ystrad Teilo and Mabws, Llanrhystud.[15]

In 1615 Edward Jones, squire of Nanteos in succession to his father John, was accused in the Court of Star Chamber of riot. One Thomas Lloyd of Aberystwyth complained to the court that Edward Jones of Llanbadarn, gentleman, along with the Thomas Jones named above and a band of other men, 'ranged up and downe the streets of llanbaderne seekeinge and enquiringe [for Lloyd] to assault, wounde, beate, hurte or murder [him]. They challenged Lloyd to 'a match of running', calling him a 'scurvy lob', and one of them attacked him with a knife.

No serious harm seems to have been done; prosecutions in Star Chamber seem often to have been born more of malice or acquisition of property than from injury. The roisterous encounters of the Cardiganshire gentry, less deadly than those of the Montagus and Capulets in Verona but just as noisy, are recorded (and ludicrously exaggerated) in the records of the Court of Star Chamber.[16]

Edward Jones's wife was Margaret Lewis, daughter of James Lewis of Abernant Bychan in south Ceredigion. The Lewis family was closely allied to the Pryses of Gogerddan and other leading county families, and among their descendants were the Leweses of Llanllŷr. This was a prestigious marriage for Edward Jones, bringing him nearer to the front rank of Cardiganshire gentry. By the early decades of the seventeenth century, with the Joneses well-established in Nanteos, the Powell family had come to

Nanteos and its park in snow viewed from Llechwedd Dyrys

live at Llechwedd Dyrys, which to this day is the name of the north-facing valley slope opposite Nanteos, though no trace of the house remains; the family's origins will be explained below. Elizabeth, sister to Edward Jones's father, had not looked far for a husband; in 1585 she had married David ap Philip ap Howell of Llechwedd Dyrys – the boy next door, so to speak – but she was not an heiress, so the Powells and the Joneses remained distinct families for two more generations.[17] Edward Jones himself can be traced in the Lay Subsidy Roll for 1627, when he was the largest contributor in the civil parish of Llanbadarn-y-Creuddyn, paying £3.12.0.[18] The genealogy thus far can be summarised as follows:[19]

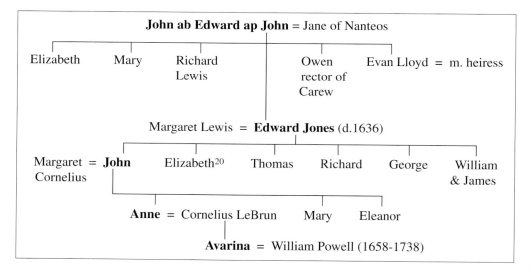

Other than the references to him in the Lay Subsidy rolls and Star Chamber records, Edward Jones hardly appears in the fragmentary documentation for Ceredigion history at this time. He certainly maintained and increased his inheritance, and gave his sons a good education, but did not command sufficient status to have been chosen as a Justice of the Peace. He made his will in 1636.[21] The inventory of his goods is brief, but he owned sixteen oxen, 138 cattle and 350 sheep, as well as sixty goats, all in all a modest increase over his father's stock, though too much emphasis should not be placed on these figures. His concern for his children, most of whom were still minors at the time of his death, is detailed, and his choice of their guardians interesting. He named his brother-in-law Sir John Lewis of Abernant Bychan, Rowland Pugh of Mathafarn (both men with close Gogerddan connections), and David Lloyd of Llangoedmor, a graduate and priest. In their care Edward left one daughter, Elizabeth, and six sons: John, Thomas, Richard, George, William and James. At the time of their father's death the two eldest sons were students. John was studying law at the Inns of Court in London, and his mother was instructed by the will to provide sufficient money for his books, maintenance and a chamber, while Thomas was at Merton College, Oxford, also studying law. Thomas spent much of the decade of the 1640s travelling on the Continent, but on his return to Oxford he submitted to the Parliamentary Visitors in 1649 before taking his M.A. degree. After leaving Oxford for the second time he practised law at Doctor's Commons, London, and died, apparently a lifelong bachelor, in the Great Plague of 1665. He published three Latin legal texts, which makes him one of the earliest Cardiganshire authors to have his work printed.[22]

Thomas Jones, then, was a younger son who took advantage of his education. Younger sons had to make their way in the world, and might find themselves apprenticed to a trade if they lacked ability, unless they could find heiresses to marry. Another of Edward's younger sons, George Jones, succeeded in gaining an estate by marrying Mary Vaughan, heiress of the small Rhoscellan estate, between Clarach and Borth. Richard Jones, another younger son, did nearly as well; he was the second husband of Eleanor Purcell of Montgomeryshire, and their son Edward Jones married Grace Phillips, daughter and heiress of John Phillips of Llethrneuadd in Carmarthenshire; his half-brother (through his mother) Daniel Gwyn bequeathed to him the Llanina estate and thus was begun the line of Jones of Llanina, New Quay.[23] The twists and turns of these genealogies may seem like a cat's cradle to our eyes, but they were of the very fibre of their society.

John Jones, the eldest son, was born about 1616. He achieved for the family a further step up the social ladder by marrying an Englishwoman, Margaret Cornelius, daughter of Jasper Cornelius of Freemantle, Hampshire; English marriages were generally seen to be advantageous. We know a little about the composition of the estate which Jones had inherited in 1636, thanks to the survival of his marriage settlement.[24] The document names fourteen farms as well as Nanteos; some of them can be identified as farms surviving in the area today, like Wernddu and Glanowen (now Penglanowen); he also owned Pencarreg in Ysbyty Cynfyn. These farms were not the whole estate, simply the part chargeable for an income in the event of Margaret being left a widow, probably representing a third of the whole.

John Jones was a substantial landowner with friends in high places, though only a little information survives. During the 1650s he had a long legal wrangle with Sir Richard Pryse of Gogerddan, whose influential father-in-law, the lawyer Bulstrode Whitelock, described Jones as 'a cunning and envious adversary'.[25] In the Civil Wars he played first on one team, then the other. With the king at Oxford in 1644, he wrote excitedly about happenings at the royalist court. According to his memorial in Llanbadarn church, erected long after his death, he raised a regiment of foot for the king, but was soon commanding four hundred men for Parliament at the siege of Aberystwyth castle in 1647. Later, struggling to avert the confiscation of his wife's Hampshire estate, he was to deny that he had ever fought for the Crown. Such tergiversation was commonplace among men of his class, many of whom were most reluctant to put principle before possessions. An anonymous account of the lives and characters of leading Cardiganshire gentry, apparently written in 1661, says of him:

> One that appeared in the first publique differences for monarchy, and much suffered by reason thereof; yet, in 1647, he assisted the reducing of Aberystwith, a garrison then holden for the king, it was thought upon a personall injury offered him; his principles being stedfastly fixed for monarchy, and the true heir thereof; for he was constantly imprisoned, on all securing payd a deepe fine in Goldsmith's Hall, decimated and grievously sequestered, declyned, though sometimes tendred publique offices whatsoever; the constant object of the phanatique hatred; but one of mean parts, only wise in that he is partly sensible of the meanness of them.

The writer also accused John Vaughan of Trawsgoed of helping in the parliamentary army's siege of Aberystwyth castle. In Vaughan's case there is no other documentary evidence, but John Jones of Nanteos appears prominently in the records of the Committee for Compounding.[27]

This Committee, created by the Parliamentary government, was responsible for levying fines on estate-owners who had supported Charles I in the Civil Wars. They had to pay sums equal to a fraction of their estates, depending on the degree of contumacy, in order to clear themselves of the guilt of having supported the King.

John Jones appealed to the Committee against the confiscation of his Hampshire property, Freemantle, which he held in right of his wife. Like other Cardiganshire squires, Jones had begun as a Royalist, and was even

Col. John Jones.
National Museum of Wales

accused before the Committee of having written a book defending the King's actions, and of having joined Prince Rupert, Charles's general of cavalry. As we shall see, his family was to claim in later years that he had raised a regiment of foot on the King's behalf, which is not unlikely; many common men followed their masters rather than a cause, and would change sides when their leader changed. However, in 1645 John Jones had fallen out with the royalist governor of Aberystwyth castle and been imprisoned, but escaped. He had joined the Cardiganshire County Committee established by the Parliamentary authorities, hoping to avoid prosecution, and claimed to have raised four hundred foot-soldiers for Parliament, arming them at his own expense. This was probably the same regiment as that raised for the King. In June 1646 he was able to plead that he should not be fined, following the Act of Grace for South Wales. However, in November 1647 it was decided to fine him £398, one-tenth of his whole estate, but in view of his services to the Parliamentary side, payment was suspended. If his estate was worth nearly four thousand pounds, as the fine suggests, then he had been doing well. He was almost certainly in London in September of that year, since his daughter Anne was born in London.[28] In 1651 Johnes appealed to the Committee for the benefit of the Act of Grace for South Wales, the general settlement of scores between Parliament and most delinquent Royalists following the levying of a general fine. However, the Committee for Compounding was told that John Jones was not an inhabitant of South Wales but of Hampshire (his wife's home county), and again his property was ordered to be sequestered. However, the following year he put his case forcefully to the Committee, giving us an invaluable, if naturally biased, autobiography.

Jones told the Committee that he had been born in South Wales and lived there till his thirteenth year. Between the ages of 13 and 25 he was first at Gloucester (presumably at school), then at Oxford and Lincoln's Inn. For a period of ten years, from his twenty-seventh year until 1653, he had been 'housekeeper' (i.e. head of house) of a family of between 12 and 16 persons at his hereditary demesne of Nanteos, and had never been anything other than a lodger in

England.[29] His appeal was eventually successful, but malice still dogged his steps; in March 1655 he was committed to custody on a charge of forging indentures, but he was released on bail.[30] How he spent the rest of the Commonwealth years until the Restoration in 1660, we cannot tell, but he certainly survived these upheavals. In 1659 he was appointed J.P., and in 1665 he was High Sheriff of the county. In 1664 he held a twenty-year lease for mining lead in Cwmystwyth, in partnership with Cornelius Le Brun of Cologne and London, who had become his son-in-law. This is the first known connection between Nanteos and the lead-mining industry, but it was not to be the last.[31] The squire of Nanteos played little further part in the industry, however; he transferred the Cwmystwyth lease to Le Brun, and in 1666 he died, aged about fifty.

John Jones made no will, suggesting that his death may have been sudden, but the inventory of his goods suggests a much more sophisticated lifestyle than that of his father and grandfather. Fourteen pounds' worth of silver plate is listed, as well as cushions, curtains, snuffers, playing tables, globes, a quadrant, Jacob staffs and books, swords and rapiers; Jacob staffs were black and white measuring rods for surveying, for which a quadrant might also have been used. His cattle were priced but not numbered, and fewer sheep (104) are mentioned, but there was much grain, stored at Nanteos and at four other farms. Edward Jones's sixty goats had shrunk to three kids, with no mention of their mothers. Probate inventories do not tell the whole truth about a person's possessions; John Jones's list mentions only two horses, but he left 'saddles, bridles, malpillions, curry-combs and a portmanteau-case', suggesting (what one would have expected in a man of his status) that Nanteos had well-filled stables.

The inventory gives us a shadowy impression of the house as it was in 1666. 'The chamber above the hall' is mentioned, as are the parlour and a little chamber. The kitchen was well-equipped with pewter dishes and other plate, glass bottles, brass and iron pots and pothooks, a tin dripping-pan, a chafing dish, iron fire-dogs, bellows, tongs, fry-shovels, spits, trivets, brandirons, bakestones and frying pans, as well as wooden vessels of all kinds.

Jones's memorial inscription, composed with a blithe disregard for the truth of his career, is still to be seen in Llanbadarn Fawr church:

> Here lie the earthly remains of John Jones of Nant eos in the County of Cardigan Esq. Lieutenant Coll. of a Foot Regiment raised there for the service of Kg Charles the Ist of Bld Memory who by the Grace of God was true to the Church in time of persecution, to the King in time of Rebellion when for doing good, he suffered much evil and after when it lay in his power he required none. Who in the midst of much business and tedious trouble was a great example of Learning Himself, and a Furtherer of it to others. A Loving Husband, a tender Father, and a faithful Friend, who lived to see this Kingdom restor'd, but was called to receive his reward in a better, in the year of our Lord 1666, of his own Age 32 [this must be a mistake]. To the pious and well deserved Remembrance of whom, this Memorial was set up in the year 1708 by his Daughter Anne . . .[32]

John Jones had three daughters by his wife Mary, the Hampshire heiress, so the inheritance was divided three ways among them, passing thereby into their husbands' families. Daughter Mary married John Lloyd of Gwernmaccwy and then Oliver Howells, and her sister Elinor married William Corbet, second son of Thomas Corbet of Nash in Pembrokeshire. The details of the division of lands escape us, but Nanteos itself remained in the possession of the third daughter, Anne Jones, who had married her father's business partner Cornelius Le Brun, an unexpected candidate for admission to the Cardiganshire squirearchy. Although he was so far from home, and although his wife was not, at least originally, the sole heiress, nevertheless Le Brun had done well for himself.

Le Brun had been born in Cologne in 1627, and died in 1703. Nothing is known of his early career, except that he must have been involved in mining in Germany, which was technically in advance of British mining. He would therefore have been a valuable business partner in the Cardiganshire lead and silver mines, and a natural visitor to the home of a Cardiganshire squire owning land in what had been, in the early seventeenth century, a boom area for the production of silver and lead. John Jones settled an income on Le Brun in 1664, deriving partly from the lordships and manors of Tregaron and Pennardd, partly from mortgages and debts owed to him.[33] On Jones's death in 1666, Cornelius Le Brun became squire of Nanteos, in the right of his wife the heiress Anne, of whom we know virtually nothing. Since they in turn had no son, their only daughter, Avarina, would bring the Nanteos estate to her husband. She, like her great-great-aunt referred to above, married the boy next door, William Powell of Llechwedd Dyrys, in 1690; the two were third cousins. Her father Cornelius did not die until 1703, aged 75, so William had waited some time for his heiress wife to inherit.[34] She was the first Cardiganshire bearer of the name Avarina, which continues in occasional local usage till the present day.

*   *   *

Who then were these Powells, and where was Llechwedd Dyrys? The latter question is easily answered; the house of Llechwedd Dyrys, the 'obscure or tangled slope', faced north towards Nanteos, and was itself a small mansion, which was allowed to crumble away to nothing when William Powell married Avarina and moved into his wife's home. The actual house-site is either close to or under the Aberystwyth-New Cross road. The origin of the Powells is a longer story. Edwin of Tegeingl (Flintshire) is said to have died in 1073. He was counted founder of one of the so-called Fifteen Noble Tribes of North Wales, but in the south the dynasty of Llywelyn Caplan, described as lord of Aberaeron and certainly an ancestor of Dafydd ap Gwilym, looked north to Edwin as its genealogical founder. We may of course feel sceptical about the further reaches of some of these family trees, but we are on sure ground with Llywelyn Caplan's grandson Llywelyn Llwyd, who was reeve of Anhuniog in 1327, while his great-grandson Gruffudd ap Llywelyn was beadle of Anhuniog in the 1330s and 40s.[35] Here, as in the case of the Joneses, we have minor Cardiganshire landlords able to take Crown office and benefit thereby. Gruffudd is the first man to be associated with Llechwedd Dyrys in the genealogies, followed by his illegitimate son Ieuan (in the absence of a legitimate heir, a bastard might easily inherit in Welsh society). Ieuan's son Howell and grandson Philip both married local heiresses. Despite the early link with Llechwedd Dyrys, Philip ap Howell, who died in 1589, is more closely connected with Ysbyty Cynfyn, where as we have noted the Jones family held Pencarreg. The genealogies do seem rather suspect, since four generations cover more than two centuries.

Philip ap Howell is a well-documented figure. A number of his deeds of land-purchase survive in the Cwrtmawr collection,[36] and a few in Cardiff. A Cardiff document suggests that he had a brother, Morgan, and that in 1575 the two brothers were at loggerheads over 583 acres of land in Ysbyty Cynfyn, Llanbadarn Fawr and Llanychaearn.[37] A Morgan ap Howell, vicar of Llanfihangel Genau'r-glyn, died in 1563 naming his brother Philip ap Howell as executor.[38] Either the disputant of 1575 or the vicar may possibly have been brother to Philip ap Howell of Ysbyty Cynfyn, but not both! It is feasible that Tŷ Mawr, Ysbyty Cynfyn, may have been the home of Philip ap Howell, for although it belonged to the Hafod estate in the 19th century, it is said by tradition to have been lost to the Johneses by the Powells as the result of a bet, suggesting that it may, before the first Nanteos rentals of 1771, have been part of that estate. Such bets were not unknown.[39] A map of Tŷ Mawr survives in the Nanteos collection in the National Library, from a survey of 1765.

During the 1570s Philip was acquiring land by purchase and by mortgage in Llanbadarn Fawr and Llanfihangel-y-Creuddyn, including many farms and mills still recognisable today, e.g. Tyddyn-y-cennant, Cwmmagwr, Llanddwy, Melin Bodcoll, Melin Ucheldre and Waunfyddai. He sometimes described himself as yeoman, occasionally as gentleman. In 1579 his eldest son Morgan married Elizabeth Lloyd Price, resulting in a settlement of these and other named properties.[40] In 1589 Philip made his will, leaving a number of named properties to his son Thomas, money and stock to his son David, and the residue to his eldest son Morgan.[41] Philip is described as being of Ysbyty Cynfyn, and he left two shillings to repair its chapel. The inventory to Philip ap Howell's will is witness to his wealth. Apart from a long list of debts owed to him (most of them being in corn or stock) he owned 126 cattle and six oxen, fifteen horses and six hundred sheep. These are the largest holdings of stock I have yet found in local wills of this period. Philip ap Howell was obviously a successful farmer and rentier from the hill country of Ysbyty Cynfyn, dealing in land and cattle, buying land in the more temperate Aberystwyth area, and claiming gentry descent, despite the illegitimate status of his grandfather.

The first of Philip's three sons to die was Thomas Philip Powell in 1604; he is described as being of Llanbadarn Fawr, but he desired to be buried in Ysbyty Cynfyn, to which like his father he left a bequest. He seems to have been either unmarried or a widower without a legitimate heir; he left a legacy to an illegitimate son, farm stock to his brother David and the rest of his property to his brother Morgan. Morgan was the next to die, in 1622, but not before he had drawn up an enormous will on huge vellum sheets.[42] His wife was Elizabeth, daughter of William Lloyd Pryse, a younger son of Richard Pryse of Gogerddan. He is described as being of Llanbadarn-y-Creuddyn, that shadowy and churchless civil parish which includes Llechwedd Dyrys (and Nanteos), although the Lay Subsidy roll of 1613 locates him in Cwmrheidol (which may have included Ysbyty Cynfyn). Like his father and brother, he desired to be buried in Ysbyty Cynfyn. Morgan had no legitimate child, but two women had borne him illegitimate daughters. One girl was fobbed off with a legacy of five pounds, but the other, named Elizabeth like his wife, was the object of her father's special care. The will is unusual in that it names all his landed property, including his capital messuage in Llanbadarn-y-Creuddyn, 'Tyddyn talken y Lanuawr being my nowe dwelling house and mansion', seventeen farms, four *lluestau* or summer dairy houses, two burgages in Mill Street Aberystwyth, and Ucheldre Mill, Llanfihangel-y-Creuddyn.

The reason for his naming all these properties seems clear in context. His heir at law was his surviving brother David, but Morgan wanted his widow to retain control of the whole of his estate for her lifetime, as he was free to insist. Normally the reversion of the estate after his widow's death would have gone to his legitimate heir-at-law, his surviving brother David. But Morgan bequeathed the reversion after his wife to his illegitimate daughter Elizabeth; if David the heir-at-law wanted the estate, Morgan demanded that he make a single payment of £700 to Elizabeth. The will is shaped, not by spite against his brother or any desire to see his daughter ruling the estate, but by the need to ensure a large wedding dowry for Elizabeth. Morgan Powell's view of his own status is confirmed not only by his description of himself as a gentleman, but also by the agreement of Thomas Pryse of Glanfread, a member of the Gogerddan family, to be tutor-guardian of Elizabeth, and by the presence as witnesses of a number of leading gentlemen of the area, including two of the Herberts of Hafod.

David Powell, the last of the three Powell brothers to die, made his will in 1635.[43] He certainly acquired his brother's estate, but on what terms is unknown. He, as we have seen, had married Elizabeth, sister of Edward Jones of Nanteos. David, like his father and brothers, desired burial in Ysbyty Cynfyn, but he was the first of the family to leave a legacy to Llanbadarn Fawr, for the poor of the parish. Like his brothers, he fathered an illegitimate child, but was the only one of the three sons of Philip ap Howell to beget legitimate children, a daughter Jane and a son, John, to whom he left his whole estate. John, of whom we know very little, had married Jane Pryse, one of the many daughters of Thomas Pryse of Glanfread, of the Gogerddan family. This was a social advance for the Powell dynasty. They had two daughters and a son, Thomas.

Thomas Powell was to prove the most distinguished member of the Powell dynasty, the only one to play a rôle, brief though it was, on the stage of national history. Born in 1631, he was the first Powell to be appointed a J.P. Of his sisters, Elinor's life is only known through her will; she died a spinster in 1699, leaving bequests to her sister Elizabeth (Pryse) and to Anne Le Brun, who witnessed the will. The simplified Powell genealogy for 1589-1700 is as follows:

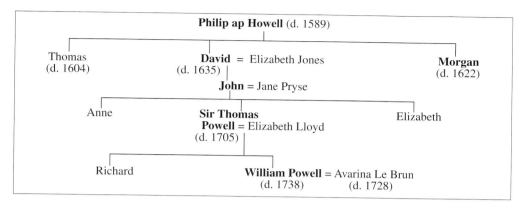

Thomas Powell had his legal education at Staple Inn, and moved to Grays in 1656. He became a serjeant at law in 1683 and a judge on the north-west Wales circuit in 1685; in 1687 he became a Baron of the Exchequer and was knighted. He was one of a number of Welshmen who gained promotion in the London courts; his contemporary Sir John Vaughan of Trawsgoed was another. Vaughan had been Chief Justice of the Common Pleas before his death in 1674. Powell was a judge of the entirely separate court of King's Bench, and sat with others on the bench in the appeal of the Seven Bishops. The seven had been imprisoned by James II for defying his authority; the court allowed their appeal on a majority vote, with Powell voting with the majority, and the bishops were released to rapturous welcomes from the anti-Catholic London mob. Strangely, although Sir Thomas had voted against the Crown in the trial, we are told on the authority of Edward Lhuyd that he withdrew from the Bench after the accession of William and Mary, and that he had Jacobite sympathies.[44] It must however be an indication of his popularity following the legal rebuke to James II that Newcastle-on-Tyne made him a freeman of that borough.[45] Following his brief period on the King's Bench he lived on until 1704. Sir Thomas's legal career is surely linked to the large collection of legal books kept in the Dark Closet at the old mansion, a list of which survives.[46]

Sir Thomas's chosen wife was a local heiress, Elizabeth daughter of David Lloyd Gwyn of Aberbrwynen, Llanychaearn, just south of Aberystwyth, which accounts for the family's subsequent extensive holdings in that parish. Although the genealogies suggest that the couple only had one son, William, the Nanteos correspondence in the National Library shows that there was an elder son, Richard.[47] Several letters survive from Thomas Powell, and from his other son William, addressed to Richard, who was a practising lawyer in London. The letters all date from the early 1680s, were written from Llechwedd Dyrys, and throw a brief but welcome personal light on family affairs. In 1681 Thomas wrote to his son that he hoped to meet him at Ludlow, obviously during a meeting of the Council of Wales and the Marches. In 1683 Richard had complained to his father that the city air in London did not agree with him. A few months previously, after asking Richard to act for him in a Chancery case, Thomas continued:

> I must now also desire you to cause an appearance to made for me in the high court of Chancery at the suit of Col. Edward Jones who lately served me with a suppona and I heare you are also made defendant in that suit, to what purpose I know not unless it be to beare company with our neighbours of Nanteos . . . (damaged) . . .
>
> I suppose tis either passion or ill advice that persuaded Col. Ned: Jones to trouble you and me in this busnes, and such infirmityes I would willingly pardon especially to all friends and relations . . .
>
> I have not received a line from you since I saw you tho I heare you have been kinder to others however I continue Yr Loving father T:P:[48]

This Edward Jones was the son of Richard Jones of Llanina, and therefore a male descendant of the Edward Jones of Nanteos who had died in 1636; in 1682 Nanteos was owned by Cornelius le Brun in the right of his wife Anne, daughter of Edward Jones's uncle, Col. John Jones. Presumably Edward regarded himself as the rightful male heir to Nanteos, wrongly deprived by female inheritance, though the Powells could hardly have been considered a threat, since there was at the date of the letter no marriage alliance between Powell and Le Brun.

Further brief but dramatic light on family affairs comes from one of William Powell's letters to his brother Richard, written in February 1682/3. William was 24 or 25 at the time; Richard was already a practising barrister:

there was a meeting lately at Llanbadarn between Mr Pugh of Mathavarn, Mr Lloyd of Castle Howell, and Mr Herbert of Cum y ddalva, in order to compose the difference between Ed: Jones and his Cousins of Nanteos, wch proved ineffectuall; the most remarkable thing there was the discretion of Mr George Jones, who without any the least provocation was pleased to be very abusive towards my father, by giving him the lye severall times, and by venting severall other more abusive words before all yt good companie, soe that it seems Baxter has at lenth [sic] drove him stark mad.[49]

The most interesting of this handful of early family letters is the slightly earlier letter from William to his brother, which tells us not about history but family tensions:

In my former I complaind to you of my fathers anger and the occasion of it, now I must lament at the continuance of it in soe high a degree, that neither my prayers, time or absence have been able to produce the least abatement of it. I was in good hopes that Ludlow would have afforded him that Liquor of a Lethean nature, wch might have defaced the image of soe innocent an offence, but it seems my misfortune is an antidote against the charms of absence: for at his return when I found the doggs to have better reception than my selfe, however I have nothing to complain of but my owne unhappinesse . . . Judge deare brother what a life I lead, and lend my your pitty if not yr councel . . . I protest he is the most akward [sic] man in the world, pray God preserve him there has been scarce a day since you saw him wherein my heart has been without sorrow or my Mothers eyes without tears in them what the reason is I know not I hope yr Companie will dissipate something of this cloud therefore that we may suddenly see you is the Earnest desire of Deare brother, yours faithfully and eternally, Will. Powell.

Richard Powell must have died before his father Sir Thomas, who left a will, mostly small legacies to kinsmen, and £15 a year to his daughter-in-law Avarina (Le Brun) in case she should be widowed; he also left her his best diamond ring, surely a rare object in Cardiganshire at that time. His son William Powell, born in 1658, now became possessed of Nanteos by his marriage to Cornelius Le Brun's daughter and heiress Avarina. The marriage had

The memorial tablet to Sir Thomas Powell on the south wall of the chancel at Llanbadarn Fawr Church.

taken place in 1690, when Avarina was about fifteen, and her husband thirty-two.[50] She died in 1728, while he survived her to die in 1738, in his eightieth year. Their memorial inscription in Llanbadarn church is worth repeating:

Near this place lie the bodies of William Powell Esq. Son of Sir Thomas Powell Knight & of Avarina his wife Daughter of Cornelius Le Brun Esq. She died January 9th 1728 aged 53 years, he May 8th 1738 in the 80th year of his Age, having lived together upwards of 31 years in uninterrupted Harmony and Affection. She among other excellencies possessed an understanding superior to most of her Sex, and for the good Conduct and government of her affairs, and family, left few Equals. He was Master of sound sense and prudence formed on Experience, and regulated by Temper and Moderation. His Duty to the best of Fathers, whose virtues and principles he inherited with his Fortune, was exceeded only by his Piety to his Creator. Both well discharged the several duties of Christians, Parents, Friends, and were remarkably eminent for their singular Benevolence and Hospitality. They had Issue three Sons; Thomas, John who died in Africa May 7th 1737, and William, and two daughters, Eliz. and Ann. Their Eldest Son, out of a pious regard to the memory of his dear parents, has caused this stone to be erected.

What then of William's son John Powell, who died in Africa? His father wrote a pathetic letter home to his wife from London on 20 July, 1720:-

Yesterday Poor Jacky Powell was forced to leav [*sic*] the town and follow the Ship that was gon befor to Gravesend as they usually doe befor they take in all their loading his brother and my selfe were resolved to see him on board, and 3 or 4 other friends would needs accompany us The place is 20 miles down the river Thames wher by Course of the tides we could not arrive befor Eleven of the clock last night, this morning we saw all his goods shipp'd, dined with him, and soon after parted with him to the Joy and Sorrow of my heart he is a brav Boy, and I hope understands his duty to God and man as well as most of his age and under his circumstances, soe that we have noe more to doe for him than to pray to Allmighty God . . .[51]

John Powell sailed for the Cape coast of Africa, where he died.

William Powell's marriage united the two estates of Llechwedd Dyrys and Nanteos. The Nanteos estate created by the Joneses is described in great detail in a covenant of 1718.[52] In outline, the Joneses had inherited or otherwise acquired a great deal of land in the parish of Llanbadarn Fawr, particularly in Cwmrheidol, Ystumtuen and the lower Rheidol valley; a number of farms in the Paith valley not far from Llechwedd Dyrys, in the administrative parish of Llanbadarn-y-Creuddyn; much land in and about Tregaron (including Fountain Gate, once home of Twm Sion Cati) and some holdings in Llanfihangel-y-Creuddyn, Llangeitho and Llanbadarn Odyn. Particularly interesting is the amount of land 'in the manor, town and liberties of Aberystwyth'. Despite later urbanisation, many of the names are still recognisable.[53]

It seems clear that whereas Sir Thomas Powell had followed a successful legal career, his son William used his marriage, which brought together his own Powell lands with the Nanteos estate, to live as a gentleman squire rather than pursue a career. This pattern can also be seen in the Vaughan family of Trawsgoed, where Sir John Vaughan (1603-1674) pursued a highly successful legal career, but his descendants lived on the proceeds of the family estates. The Powell genealogy continues:

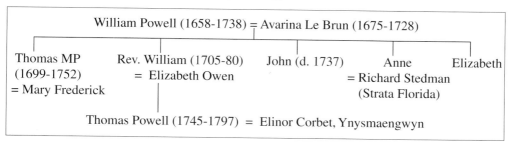

William Powell (1658-1738) = Avarina Le Brun (1675-1728)

Thomas MP (1699-1752) = Mary Frederick

Rev. William (1705-80) = Elizabeth Owen

John (d. 1737)

Anne = Richard Stedman (Strata Florida)

Elizabeth

Thomas Powell (1745-1797) = Elinor Corbet, Ynysmaengwyn

The next steps upwards for the Powell family were a parliamentary career and an English marriage. William Powell himself never stood for Parliament, but was inevitably involved in county political intrigue. Like the Pryses he was a Tory and a Jacobite, but he was nevertheless persuaded in 1710 to join with an anti-Jacobite, John Vaughan the first Viscount Lisburne, in supporting Sir Humphrey Mackworth, the Glamorgan industrialist and exploiter of the Cardiganshire lead-mines, against the Gogerddan nominee for the county seat, Lewis Pryse. Despite this powerful coalition of interests against him, Pryse won the day. In no wise downhearted, William Powell was involved in several further intrigues to secure sympathetic candidates for the county and borough seats.

William Powell was more successful in arranging a wealthy marriage for his heir, as is evident from the Nanteos archive. He had for some time been concerned about his son Thomas's lack of interest in the opposite sex. When therefore in 1720 Thomas mentioned to his father his interest in a Miss Mary Frederick, sister of Sir John Frederick and daughter of the wealthy London businessman Thomas Frederick of Westminster, William Powell lost no time. Although personally unknown to the widowed Mrs Frederick, he wrote to her in the most polished and diplomatic manner, begging permission to bring his son to visit her and her daughter with a view to marriage.[54] Mrs Frederick and her daughter must have been duly impressed, for the marriage ensued, bringing the Powells a great deal of money, which must have helped Thomas to fulfil the second family ambition by taking the parliamentary seat for Cardigan boroughs.[55]

Thomas's wife Mary left a will which gives a remarkable insight into the riches which she brought to her husband.[56] From it we learn that she had borrowed £2,700 to enable her husband 'to purchase the one undivided 3rd part of Nanteos Estate';[57] she gave back to her husband the £200 solitaire diamond ring he gave her at their marriage. The contents are much too detailed even to list her; she had her own collection of books, many rings, much china, and an organ given her by her brother, which was to be packed up and sent by sea back to him.

The tendency among many great families throughout the country was to confer together to avoid expensive electoral contests. The factional labels Whig and Tory meant little in local political life; loyalty was to individuals, to families and to 'interests'. Cardiganshire politics had been confused by the Jacobite loyalties of the Gogerddan family in 1715, and by the subsequent death of the head of the family, leaving a minor as heir. In 1725 after the death of Stephen Parry of Noyaddtrefawr, the sitting member for the borough seat, Thomas Powell was nominated by the Tory interest for the by-election, and defeated a Gogerddan nominee, Thomas Pryse of Dol.

At the general election of 1727 Powell was persuaded to yield the borough seat to the Gogerddan candidate Francis Cornwallis, who had been the county member for the previous five years. Instead Powell fought the county seat against John Vaughan, second viscount Lisburne, but there the Whig interest prevailed, and Powell had to wait for the by-election which followed the death of Cornwallis in 1728. He then fought his third election contest against Richard Lloyd of Mabws, who was both a descendant of Edward Jones of Nanteos and a kinsman of the Pryses. Powell used his influence in Tregaron to create eight hundred new burgesses, who did their drunken best to vote early and often. The vote was impressively large; Powell polled 1,224 votes and Lloyd 924. The ructions which surrounded the occasion were spectacular. A Powell supporter tried to bribe the returning officer at Cardigan, only to find that he had been outbidden by Lloyd. In the violence and disorder of the proceedings, which included a punch-up with the mayor, both candidates were declared elected, but in the subsequent investigation by the House of Commons Committee of Elections it was decided that Tregaron was not a borough and therefore did not form part of the constituency, so Powell was disqualified.[58]

This must have been a bitter blow to Powell, who did not stand again in the 1730s,[59] but in 1741 he tried again, this time for the county seat, and though he outpolled the Whiggish Walter Lloyd of Peterwell, the mayor of

Cardigan declared Lloyd elected. However, Powell appealed successfully against the result, and duly took his seat.[60] He sat until 1747, when replaced without formal contest by John Lloyd of Peterwell. No evidence seems to survive to explain why Powell was willing to resign his interest. Welsh members of parliament in the eighteenth and early nineteenth century were, by and large, not a politically ambitious or exciting group of men; there was no Welsh 'interest' in Parliament, and Powell was no different from the rest; he voted, but did not speak. The major purpose of most gentry in standing for parliament was not to share in government but to claim status at the head of the county gentry and to use their influence in London and locally on behalf of their family and friends.

Thomas Powell's sister Anne, who married 1) Richard Stedman, and 2) Sir Herbert Lloyd.

As well as involving himself in county politics, Thomas found time to spend his wife's money on building the present attractive Palladian mansion, beginning in 1739, soon after his father's death, and leaving no trace of the former house except possibly its cellars; nor does any picture of it survive. The architecture of the house is dealt with below in chapter 7. A useful list of rooms in the new house survives in a 1793 inventory of furniture.[61] The splendid gallery overflowed with:-

> 8 Family Pictures, 37 Historical Pictures, 59 Views in Wales, 24 Prints without Frames, 2 Long Prints with Frames and Glasses, 2 prints without Frames views in Wales, 4 Pictures Flowers with Frames and Glasses, 2 Family Pictures.

The Servants' Hall held three pistols, a blunderbuss and twenty-four javelins!

With money, the intermittent prestige of a parliamentary seat, and a new house, Thomas Powell was doing well, and before his sudden death in 1752 he brought off a remarkable coup for the Nanteos estate.[62] In 1723 his sister Anne Powell had married Richard Stedman of Ystrad Fflur. Earlier generations of Stedmans had been polyphiloprogenitive; the John Stedman who died in 1613 produced three sons and seven daughters; John's eldest son John produced three sons and a daughter; the eldest of the next generation, James, produced four sons and two daughters. But of the four sons only Richard, who died in 1703, had progeny, a single son, the Richard who married Anne Powell. The Ystrad Fflur estate had since the time of John Moel Stedman (d.1607) been one of the more important in North Cardiganshire. Its core was the monastic demesne of Strata Florida with other monastic lands acquired by the Stedmans in 1573 or earlier; it was increased by the marriage of John Moel's son John to Margaret Lloyd of Ystrad-ffin, a landed heiress of considerable character, judging by her remarkable will of 1617. The family married its daughters into the Gogerddan, Trawsgoed and Maesyfelin families. For several generations they had produced Justices of the Peace and high sheriffs of the county, though they were not at a level to produce parliamentary candidates. However, by the time of the last

Richard Stedman the Ystrad Fflur estate was heavily in debt, and the major creditor was Thomas Powell, Richard Stedman's brother-in-law. On Richard's death in 1744 probate was granted to Powell, and although the Abbey estate remained for a time in the name of Anne Stedman, who soon found a second husband whom she seems quickly to have regretted, the notorious Sir Herbert Lloyd of Peterwell, Thomas Powell established a controlling interest *force majeure*, in view of the money owed him. With Anne's death in 1778 the Abbey estate finally passed into Nanteos ownership,[63] though to judge from the surviving rentals, it was already being administered from Nanteos. The estate increased the Nanteos holdings by thousands of acres, mainly in the large parish of Caron.

Thomas Powell achieved many goals, but his marriage did not bring children, although according to William Morris he had an adult illegitimate son living at Nanteos and acting as leader of his mob of followers.[64] Thomas's death in 1752 brought the succession to his brother, the Rev. Dr. William Powell, who as a younger brother had chosen a church career.[65] He had married Elizabeth Owen, daughter and co-heiress of Athelstan Owen (1676-1731) of Rhiwsaeson, and his wife Ann Corbet of Ynysmaengwyn.[66] Thomas Powell had been an M.P.; as a clergyman William Powell was prevented from standing for parliament, but it did not prevent him playing an active role in the county's political and economic life. Within a year of his accession to the estate he was deeply involved in the Esgair-mwyn fracas which caused the Crown mines superintendent Lewis Morris such grief.

It was some years previously, in the 1740s, that Lewis Morris had become involved with mining in Cardiganshire, and in a letter he recounted the background to the conflict that Thomas Powell had with the Crown over a mine on common land at Bwlch-gwyn. Morris says that:

> Sr Thomas Powell the Grandfather of the Present Mr Powell I believe was one of the Co[mpany] of the mine adventurers, and was alive in the year 1693 as I find in a lease of a mine which he took and made over the Company . . . His son Mr Wm Powell was also one of the Co in the year 1698.[67]

Griffith Evans, the Nanteos harper who played there every New Year c. 1730-60.

When ore was discovered at Bwlch-gwyn, near Ystumtuen, in 1742, Powell claimed the mine on the grounds that, though on common land, Bwlch-gwyn was within the liberty of Pen-y-berth, a Nanteos farm, and he proved his claim through the courts. The dispute was not with any neighbouring landlord, but with the Crown, which claimed ownership of the wastes or commons. In 1746 the Crown appointed William Corbett as Steward of the county's crown lands, and he in his turn appointed Lewis Morris his deputy. Morris had already tried to help Corbett, but found obstacles in his way when he tried to prove that Bwlch-gwyn should be in the hands of the Crown:

I meet with great difficulties in getting any little light into the nature of this Lordship. No sooner than I speak with an old man who can give me some account of the antient usage, customs, &c. but Mr Powell or his soll[icito]r or friends Immediately stop his mouth, and I cannot get a word out of him, and he is afraid of comeing near me. Mr Powell & his sollr live on the spot, and are all guilty of encroaching and are men of Fortune here and have these poor people under their clutches.[68]

In 1751 Morris and Thomas Powell clashed again. Morris describes a meeting at Nanteos:

I had some business with Mr Powell the other day at Nanteos, when he and his brother the clergyman could not help complaining what a cruell thing it was of the Government to fall upon a private Gentleman as they had done upon him, and that it was wicked in me to be concerned against him . . . all the answer I made was, that I was but a servant of the Government's, and it was very hard the King should not have the same privilege of defending his right as a private man had. I asked him whether he allowed the King had any property in this Country, to which he replyed, that he had much less than I imagind.[69]

Morris had opened the old mine at Nantycreiau, but Powell sent his men to work there, only to be forced to withdraw. If not before, Powell was now Morris's bitter enemy, and the enmity was to be taken over by his brother William when Thomas Powell died childless in 1752.

In 1751 Lewis Morris's labourers discovered a good vein of ore at Esgair-mwyn, on the common between Ysbyty Ystwyth and Ffair-rhos. The common was half-encircled by small farms owned by ten different landlords, including Wilmot Vaughan, third viscount Lisburne, and Thomas Powell of Nanteos (the two men were co-lessees of Llwynymwyn and Esgair-mwyn).[70] Lewis Morris worked the mine successfully until February 1753, when he was arrested at pistol-point and imprisoned briefly at Cardigan, and the work was taken over by John Ball on behalf of the Rev. William Powell, now owner of Nanteos. Eventually through a series of compromises the Crown regained control of the mine, and Lewis Morris felt justified in crowing over his adversary:

> Powell had borrowed more than £1500 to carry the case forward, and hundreds are not easily had in this county for such games . . . He calls for his rent before hand, and curses the hour he ever meddled with this lawsuit.[71]

However, Lewis Morris was soon brought low, losing both his post as superintendent of mines and his collectorship of Customs at Aberdovey. Wilmot Vaughan, son of the third Viscount Lisburne, had sought William Powell's support for the county seat in the election of 1755, and was quick to repay the favour, writing to Powell in 1757:

> The Duke of Newcastle has desired me to assure you that no regard is payed to any representations made by Lewis Morrice, he having proved himself to the Conviction of the Treasury to be a very base & dishonest Fellow. Orders are issued to prosecute an Enquiry with the greatest Spirit & Exactness & he is immediately to be dismiss'd from his Employment in the Customs.[72]

Lewis Morris's feeble revenge was his savage comment on the death of William Powell's wife Elizabeth[73] in 1757:

Powell of Nanteos's wife Elizabeth, daughter to Mr Owens Ynys y Maengwyn, has died in childbirth, from bad enough stock, there was too much of a bad streak there already.[74]

It seems that Powell may have made some effort to mend the rift with Lewis Morris, but in vain.[75] Richard Morris's letters to Lewis reveal that William Powell became a member of the Cymmrodorion in 1760:

Amusing to see the Powell put five golden guineas in the poor box when he had the honour of being sworn a Cymrodor in our last meeting! Your brother Richard is great chums with Powell! What would you give for such an honour?[76]

When in 1760 it became clear that, in the complicated manoeuvres of Cardiganshire politics, Wilmot Vaughan was to be squeezed out of his Cardiganshire seat, Lewis Morris commented in almost untranslatable Welsh:

Nid oes un gwr pwysig o du'r Trawsgoed ond y Pwel, a hwnnw nid yw ond fal ffagl o wellt pys cric crac yn chwilboeth.[77]

Morris's legal involvement with Powell dragged on until Morris's death in 1765, and he described his opponent as *'Rogyn trwyddo, a hil Satan benlas'*.[78] However, Richard Morris regretted that the two could not be reconciled, and continued to appreciate Powell's attendance at the Cymmrodorion:

Powell told me in the meeting room that he had never, and would never, raise his tenants' rent by one penny. What a good heart! He put another gold guinea in the poor box the last time he was with us.[79]

The Rev. Dr. William Powell (1705-80).
N.L.W.

Powell outlived Lewis Morris, who died in 1765, by some fifteen years.

The best source for William Powell's later years is the series of letters he received from Wilmot Vaughan of Trawsgoed, fourth viscount and first Earl of Lisburne, although since Powell's replies have not survived, we learn more about Wilmot Vaughan than Powell.[80] Wilmot's first letter, written in 1755, is couched in the highly formal, courteous and flattering language of which he was a master, begging Powell's support for nomination for the county seat in that year's election. Powell noted his favourable reply on the back of the letter. Trawsgoed and Nanteos do not previously seem to have been close politically; Nanteos had tended to follow Gogerddan's Tory leanings. However, Trawsgoed needed friends; the two Wilmots, father and son, saw the Lloyds of Peterwell and the Johneses of Llanfair and Aber-mad as enemies, and cast around for support against them. Following Powell's favourable reply, the tone of Vaughan's letters became warmer. Wilmot, elected M.P., reported on several meetings with Powell's ten-year-old son Thomas, a pupil at Westminster School, gave a lively account of a Commons debate, and found a naval post for a friend of Powell's. Letters survive until 1783, and the last of them echoes the first – a request for support in a forthcoming election.

Wilmot Vaughan was ousted from the county seat in 1761, and there is a gap in the correspondence for several years. In 1769 Wilmot, now the fourth Viscount Lisburne and re-elected M.P. for the county the previous year, wrote to Powell at Nanteos in December concerning the candidacy for the borough seat at the next election:

> [Mr Pryse's] Idea & mine perfectly concurred, in leaving to yourself principally Mr Lloyd of Mabus & the Gentlemen at Cardigan the nomination of the Candidate [i.e. for the borough seat]. Your son, Mr Thos Powell, if he should be inclined to stand, was our first object and next, Mr Pryse thought of offering the Seat to either of Mr Campbell's Sons . . . In matters relative to the Borough I never attempt to interfere further, than by my honest & impartial Advice, when required. If Mr Thos Powell should offer, which I most cordially wish, who can be so agreable to me, as the Son of my best Friend?[81]

However, the nomination went to Ralph Congreve, presumably on the insistence of Pryse, and when an election was again in the offing in 1773/4, Pryse again brought forward his own nominee without consultation, this time his relative Sir Robert Smyth, who was however defeated on appeal by Thomas Johnes of Hafod, a remarkable setback for the Gogerddan interest. Wilmot had obviously been astounded by Pryse's choice, and by the lack of consultation, describing it to Powell as 'this sudden Event, for which I am in every respect little prepared', and referring to the 'Trouble & Embarrassment' caused by the lack of consultation.[82]

Wilmot must have been even more troubled and embarrassed by the behaviour of William Powell's heir, Thomas Powell. Wilmot had urged his candidacy for the borough seat on more than one occasion, without success. In 1783 Wilmot wrote to Thomas Powell asking for his support in the forthcoming election,[83] but discovered that Powell was actively canvassing for the nomination against him, although he was his father's old friend, and had been kind to him as a boy. Wilmot's letters to James Lloyd of Mabws vividly describe his electioneering efforts to cut the ground from under Thomas Powell's feet, which he managed successfully.[84]

*   *   *

Although William Powell visited London frequently, as the Morris letters show,[85] he paid some attention to the management of his estates. His lands were extensive, though without a schedule of the surviving Nanteos deeds it is not easy to trace their history in detail before the first surviving rentals. A solitary rental survives from 1756-57 for the Pennant estate in Merionethshire, but whether that was acquired with the later marriage of Thomas Powell to Elinor Corbet, or whether the document is simply a stray from the Pennant archive and was never in Nanteos ownership, is not clear. However, a fairly regular sequence of rentals survives from the 1770s onwards, and the estate's administrative divisions become clearer.

The core Nanteos estate in 1771 consisted of seventy-two tenancies in Llanbadarn Fawr, thirteen in Llanfihangel-y-Creuddyn, twenty-three in Caron, seven in Llanychaearn, and scattered properties in Llanfihangel Genau'r-glyn, Llansantffraid, Llangybi, Betws Bledrws, Llanfair Clydogau, Llanddewibrefi and Llanbadarn Odyn. The total of 133 properties (many simply cottages or houses) produced £616 in cash, with arrears owed of £129. In the same year the Abbey estate, acquired from the Stedmans, consisted of fifty tenancies, mostly in the Pontrhydfendigaid area but including some in Carmarthenshire; it yielded £675 in cash rent. The Breconshire estate in 1776, originally brought by Margaret Lloyd to Strata Florida on her marriage to John Stedman in the sixteenth century, consisted of seventeen properties giving £107 rent.

The Aberystwyth estate in 1772 was mostly town houses (some thatched) and plots, but included swathes of land on either side of the Rheidol, especially Pendinas and lands around Plas-crug; there were ninety-three tenancies producing £381 in rent.[86] Additionally the family had some small tithe investments, and some rents were still paid in butter;[87] there was also land in Llanbrynmair, Montgomeryshire.[88] Rent income fluctuated considerably from year to year, but was driven sharply upwards by the Napoleonic Wars; in 1815 the estate rental totalled £7,831.14.6.[89] The same source mentions an estimated additional income from farm produce, mine rents and royalties, and bark sold from the woods, of one thousand pounds annually. The estate employed ten regular servants and many more in casual labour.

In 1764 William Powell had commissioned from John Davies a survey and map of the Nanteos demesne, and in the following year Davies mapped all the farms; most of the maps survive in the National Library collections. Such a survey was convenient for the management of a large estate, particularly at a time when agricultural improvement was in the air. In particular the maps are a help in attempting to visualise the eighteenth-century landscape of north Cardiganshire. The uplands were vast sheepwalks with tiny fields close to the farm-houses. Lower down, the fields are sometimes very different in plan from what was mapped in the tithe surveys of the 1840s. Large and awkward fields of 1765 tend to have become divided by the 1840s, while the tiny medieval strips that still survived, often owned by other landlords, had usually disappeared during the same period, often as a result of property exchanges. Other maps in the archive show how different was the layout of roads in the district

Thomas Powell 1745-1797.

(Miles Wynn Cato Gallery, London)

around Nanteos before the turnpike roads to Devils Bridge and to Pontrhydfendigaid were created in the 1780s.[90]

William Powell died in 1780, and his son Thomas, inheriting at the age of thirty-five, did not succeed in his parliamentary ambition of defeating the Earl of Lisburne before he died prematurely in 1797. He had married another Ynysmaengwyn connection, Eleanor, daughter of Edward Maurice Corbet, who as the next chapter shows became a dreadful burden to the estate during her widowhood. Little correspondence survives from Thomas Powell's seventeen years of headship of the family. He certainly had ambitions for the estate; a magnificent parchment map in the National Library, drawn in 1791 by John Davenport, shows a planned development for the Nanteos demesne. The open land fronting the mansion was to become a large and splendid curved lake, complete with island. Woods and plantations with elegant walks were planned to spread in all directions, ornamented with a Gothic ruin, a rotunda and a tower, as well as 'Gothic seats'. The plan was surely intended to out-Hafod Hafod, and might well have succeeded, given the potential of the Nanteos site, its gentler climate and greater accessibility. Why it was not adopted remains a matter for speculation; Thomas Powell was certainly in debt at the time, but debt was no deterrent to conspicuous gentry expenditure. He was ahead of many Cardiganshire gentry in his willingness to grant land to Methodists, in his case for the building of Tabernacle chapel in Aberystwyth in 1785. He was a supporter of the Cardiganshire Agricultural Society, and laid the foundation of the Welsh School in London (later the Welsh Girls' School at Ashford, Middlesex).

Thomas Powell's early death, following his failure in county politics, and leaving as he did a debt-burdened inheritance to his juvenile heir, would obviously have been felt as a severe blow to his family. However, despite this difficult situation, Nanteos would soon enter into its period of greatest importance in the social and political life of Cardiganshire.

NOTE: The Nanteos Lead Mines

The Nanteos archive contains a great deal of material on the lead mines owned by the estate, and reference has already been made to mining activity in the seventeenth and eighteenth centuries. Although John Jones and Cornelius le Brun were partners in the seventeenth-century exploitation of the estate's resources, there is no further material about their activities in the archive, and not much more survives from the eighteenth century. For the period 1820-1930, however, there is too much! Most of it is of little apparent relevance; the

Poster: Nanteos Lead Mines

N.L.W.

sheaves of correspondence bear little relationship to the history of the estate itself, only to minutiae of administration, income and expense, while family members were most often involved in assenting to leases. There are wads of documents listing royalty payments, but their survival has been haphazard, and it does not seem possible to make a serious estimate of the total income to the estate except in the 1870s. A particular problem is to be sure which mine is which at any particular time, since they often changed name when the lease changed, probably in the hope of attracting new capital from naïve investors. Thus the Strata Florida mine became Abbey Consols, while Llwybrllwynog became, by translation, Foxpath mine.

It is not always clear how a particular mine came into Nanteos ownership. The estate's most profitable mine was Cwmystwyth, the vast extent of whose workings is forever etched on the landscape. However, according to the tithe map for upper Llanfihangel-y-Creuddyn, in 1845 Nanteos did not own the extensive site. This is in spite of the fact that in a deed of 1718 William Powell of Nanteos owned 'a piece of land called Craig y Mwyn or Moin in Cwmystwyth . . . all mines of lead and other minerals in the parish of Llanvihangell y Croythyn . . . all mines of lead and other minerals in the parish of Llanvihangell y Croythyn [and] Ystimtean and Llwibyr y Llwynog'.[91] The lands of Cwmystwyth had originally formed a grange of the Cistercian abbey of Strata Florida, and lead had already been extensively mined there before 1540. The Cwmystwyth grange had become the property of Trawsgoed by 1632. Not all the land remained in Trawsgoed ownership; John Vaughan sold a number of farms to the Herberts of Hafod Uchdryd. In 1845 a traveller from Cwmystwyth village passing up the valley towards Rhaeadr would have passed Pentre farm (owned by Thomas Bonsall), Ty'n-ddol (a Trawsgoed property), Nantyronnen (the representatives of Morgan Jones) and Tŷ Llwyd (Trawsgoed). The main mining area lay on Ty'n-ddol and Nantyronnen, which according to the tithe map were not Powell's lands. Mr Simon Hughes has made a heroic effort to trace the early ownership and leases on the mine, but unfortunately he does not cite his sources, and I cannot always follow his argument.[92]

However that may be, the Cwmystwyth mine certainly belonged to the Powells, as did a number of other mines, briefly listed herewith using the names in a rentals/royalties book of 1869-1907:[93]

> Abbey Consols, Blaencennant, Cwmystwyth, Ystumtuen, Nantyronnen, Ty'n-y-fron, Geufron, Strata Florida, Powell United (Ponterwyd), Rheidol.

During the eighteenth and nineteenth centuries many of the long-lived Nanteos mines were leased to some of the best-known of the Cardiganshire mining entrepreneurs, most of them outsiders. Thus in 1754 the Rev. Dr William Powell leased Ystumtuen and Cwmystwyth to Chauncy Townsend, while in the mid-nineteenth century the Taylors, father and son, worked most of the estate's mines.[94] Liaison between the mining companies and the Powells was usually through the estate's agents. As well as leasing out working mines, the Powells would issues licenses to prospect for lead on their farms, and rent out non-working mines for what was known as a sleeping or dead rent. Royalties varied considerably according to the nature of the mine and the state of the market for lead. Ore was carried down by packhorse to Aberystwyth or over the hills to Garreg (Glandyfi) for loading into small ships which took it away, usually to Neath or Swansea, for smelting.

As has been said already, calculating the estate's income from the mines seems to be an almost impossible task in view of the fluctuating market and the gaps in the record. However, a few observations are possible. David Howell has worked out the estate's income from the mines for the years 1783-90; it totalled £957.15.7.[95] In 1870 and for some time afterwards Blaencennant and Bwlchgwyn yielded £20 rent each per annum, but no royalties. Cwmystwyth yielded £462 in 1871; this declined to £74 in 1879, when the market collapsed, but unlike many other mines, Cwmystwyth recovered thanks to its reserves of zinc, and yielded £332 in 1904. Ystumtuen yielded £158 royalties in 1876, Nantyronnen and Ty'n-y-fron £45 in rent only. The Rheidol mine, which according to other sources must have been productive, only yielded trivial royalties in the 1870s, and the Strata Florida mine paid £83 royalties in

1874.[96] An additional complication emerges from the book of royalties and rentals; Powell United Mine (Ponterwyd) yielded on paper the sum of £120, but only £91 was paid.

From these and other figures for earlier years, and by guesswork, it may be supposed that between 1750 and 1875 the royalties and rents of the Nanteos mines may have yielded, depending on the market and the state of the mines, between £300 and £700 a year. Even in the first decade of the twentieth century Cwmystwyth continued to yield £200-£300 a year, but thereafter it shrank to almost nothing.

NOTES

[1] See e.g. N.L.W Cwrtmawr Deeds 1648 of May 1691, 'a messuage formerly called Neuadd Lowdden now called Nanteos'. P.C.Bartrum (*W.G.1400-1500*, vol.5, Aberystwyth, 1983) gives a third early name, *Y Plas yng Nghefn Uwch*, from N.L.W. Peniarth MS 183, f.457. The name of Llawdden actually appears in the Powell genealogy according to Burke's *Landed Gentry 1937* s.n., but not in other sources.

[2] A. Eleri Davies (ed.) *Gwaith Deio ab Ieuan Du a Gwilym ab Ieuan Hen*, U.W.P. (1992), p.27. The translation is mine.

[3] P.C.Bartrum, "Pedigrees of the Welsh Tribal Patriarchs", *N.L.W.J* XIII, 1963, p.135. P.C.Bartrum, *op.cit.* p.678.

[4] In 1691 a Llawdden Mill is recorded on the banks of the river Paith (N.L.W. Cwrtmawr Deeds 1648/9 of 5.5.1691).

[5] R.A.Griffiths, *The Principality of Wales in the Later Middle Ages*, I (Cardiff, 1972), 449, 450, 465 (Llawdden ap Rhys ap Llawdden).

[6] Griffiths, *op.cit.* p. 466.

[7] G.Morgan, *A Welsh House and its Family* (Llandysul, 1997) 24-6.

[8] Glamorgan Record Office CL/Deeds 1/1539; he acquired Lluest Blaen Nant Rees (now a mountain bothy near the source of the river Dilyw) and Gweirglodd y parke from John Morgan Dafid ap Ieuan ap Rees.

[9] N.L.W. Cwrtmawr Deeds 31.

[10] Francis Green, 'Genealogies of Cardiganshire . . . Families', *West Wales Historical Records*, I, 1910-11, 44, based on N.L.W. Peniarth MS 156. The marriage settlement is preserved in N.L.W. Cwrtmawr Deed 130.

[11] See Francis Green, *ibid.*, 44.

[12] E.g. N.L.W. Cwrtmawr Deeds 141, 802, 1067.

[13] E.g. N.L.W. Cwrtmawr Deeds 802 (with David Phillip ap Howell), 1067.

[14] Copies in N.L.W. Cwrtmawr Deeds 140 and Church in Wales St David's Probate Records.

[15] Lucy E. Lloyd Theakston & John Davies, *Some Pedigrees of the Lloyds of Allt yr Odyn* . . . (Oxford, 1913) 5.

[16] Dr Evan James kindly provided me with a copy of P.R.O. L. Stac 8 205/3.

[17] S.R.Meyricke, *The History of Cardiganshire*, 1907, 218.

[18] PRO E179/219/87. Edward ap John of Llanbadarn-y-Creuddyn paid 2s 8d in the Lay Subsidy of 1576 (P.R.O. E 179/263/37; both documents transcribed by Dr Evan James).

[19] Among the sources for the Jones and Powell pedigrees are the so-called *Old Pedigree* in N.L.W. Nanteos Deeds Box 20, drawn up about 1746, the family wills, Francis Green's 'Genealogies of Cardiganshire Families' in *West Wales Historical Records, I* (1910-11), 44-45, Meyricke's *History of Cardiganshire* (1909) 311-12, and N.L.W. MS 12021.

[20] She married Morgan Lloyd of Ffoshelyg, high sheriff of Cardiganshire in 1681; will 1688 (N.L.W. MS 12012, p.77).

[21] The wills of Edward Jones, Philip ap Howell and his three sons are all in the Nanteos Deeds collection in the National Library of Wales. A copy of Edward's will is also in the N.L.W probate collection, SD/1636/107. It was made in January and proved in April, 1636.

[22] *Oratio habita in Auditorio juridico . . .*; *De Judiciis, ubi de Persona & Officio Judicis apud Ebraeos & Romanos late disputatur*; *De Origine Dominii & servitutis Theses Juridicae*, published together at Oxford in 1660.

[23] N.L.W. MS 12,021, 85.

[24] N.L.W. Nanteos Box 21, unscheduled. Mary's father Jasper Cornelius is named as being of Clement's Inn, London.

[25] See the Index to Ruth Spalding (ed.), *The Diary of Bulstrode Whitelocke 1605-1675*, British Academy, 1990.

[26] See the index to Ruth Spalding (ed), *The Diary of Bulstrode Whitelocke 1605-1675*, British Academy, 1990.

[27] What follows is based on Mary Everett Green's *Calendar of the Committee for Compounding*, vol. II (1890) 1568-9.

[28] Nanteos Old Pedigree.

[29] He must have been born about 1616.

[30] M.E.Green, *Calendar of State Papers (Domestic) 1655*, ii, 1568-69.

[31] See W.J.Lewis, *Lead Mining in Wales*, Cardiff, 1967, 55.

[32] S.R.Meyrick, *The History of Cardiganshire* (1907) 305.

[33] N.L.W Cwrtmawr Deeds 728.

[34] It is fair to presume that Cornelius Le Brun spoke English on his hearth. His wife, or servants, may have taught their daughter Avarina some Welsh, and Welsh may have remained at least a second language of the Jones-Powell families till early in the 18thC.

[35] Ralph A. Griffiths, *op.cit.* 479, 484, 485.

[36] E.g. N.L.W. Cwrtmawr Deeds 2, 906, 942, 12, 182, 119, 946.

[37] Digests of the Cardiff documents are available in the Ceredigion Record Office at Aberystwyth. This one is DD/804/38.

38 N.L.W. Edwinsford Deeds 1300.

39 I am grateful to Mrs Delyth Morris Jones of Tŷ Mawr for this detail. For a similar tradition see Gerald Morgan, *A Welsh House and its Family: the Vaughans of Trawsgoed* (Llandysul, 1997) 35.

40 N.L.W. Cwrtmawr Deeds 946. She was d. of William Lloyd (Price), N.L.W. 12021, p.99.

41 N.L.W. Cwrtmawr Deeds 728.

42 The wills of the brothers are in N.L.W. Nanteos Box 21. Documents attached to Thomas's will show that he was a monoglot Welsh-speaker, who had to have the priest's copy of the will read back to him in Welsh.

43 David Philip Howell paid three shillings in the Lay Subsidy of 1613, the largest contribution from Parcel Paith (but compare his brother Morgan's contribution of five shillings in Parcel Cwm Rheidol, and John Stedman's contribution of twenty shillings for Ystrad Fflur). In the Lay Subsidy of 1627 David Powell contributed £1.4.0, but the subsidy that year was a much heavier one. My colleague Dr Evan James transcribed PRO E/179/219/84 for 1613 and PRO E179/219/87 for 1627.

44 N.L.W. N.L.45. Edward Lhuyd, known to the Powells through his aunt, Jane Pryse of Glanfread, designed a monument with inscription for Sir Thomas Powell.

45 N.L.W. Nanteos Box 20 (unscheduled).

46 Listed in an 18C hand in N.L.W. Nanteos Box 20. Perhaps it was Sir Thomas who adopted the family coat of arms: argent a cross flory engrailed sable inter four Cornish choughs. The motto is *Inter hastas et hostes* – between the spears and the enemy.

47 The Old Pedigree names the godparents of the Powells born after 1690; as might be expected, they include grandparents, the Bishop of St David's and an assortment of county gentry and ladies. Places of birth are sometimes given; the children of the Rev. Dr William Powell were born at Strata Florida, Cardigan, Ynysmaengwyn and Nanteos. W.E.Powell was born at Shrewsbury. Powell wives were peripatetic.

48 N.L.W. N.L.17, dated 25.5.1682. As we have already seen, George Jones was another of John Jones's younger brothers, squire of Rhoscellan.

49 N.L.W. N.L.25, dated 13.2.1682/3.

50 N.L.W. Cwrtmawr Deeds 324, 1625.

51 N.L.W. N.L.60.

52 N.L.W. Cwrtmawr Deed 203.

53 E.g. Tir dan y Dynas (Pendinas), Pen Maes Glas, Park Heol y Wig (Pier Street), Ffynnon y Garreg (the chalybeate well), Pen y Perkydd (Penparcau), Tir ywch r' Anchor (Penyrancor).

54 N.L.W. N.L.61.

55 At her death in 1730 Mrs Frederick left Mary £1000 in the East India Company, and (perhaps of more questionable value) £2000 in the South Seas Company (N.L.W. Nanteos Box 21).

56 N.L.W. Nanteos Box 21.

57 I am not clear to what this refers.

58 P.D.G.Thomas, 'Eighteenth-Century Elections in the Cardigan Boroughs Constituency', *Ceredigion*, V (1967), pp.404-08. See also *The History of Parliament: The House of Commons 1715-1754*, I (1970), 373-74, and Vol.II, 364; also P.D.G.Thomas, *Politics in Eighteenth-century Wales* (Cardiff, 1997).

59 Although lacking a seat, he spent time in London; he is recorded as having soothed an angry audience at Drury Lane, persuading the manager to return the entrance money. *The Earl of Egmont's Diary*, Historic MSS Commission, I, 216.

60 P.D.G.Thomas, 'County Elections in Eighteenth-Century Cardiganshire', *Ceredigion*, XI, 3 (1991), 239-58.

61 The inventory (N.L.W. Nanteos Deeds Box 20) lists the following rooms (I have added a few of the most interesting contents): Best Hall, Dining Parlour (9 family pictures), Dining Room Closet, Drawing Room, (11 pictures), Little Parlour (8 pictures), Little Hall, Servants' Hall (3 pistols, one blunderbuss, 24 javelins), Butler's Pantry, Best Staircase, Housekeeper's Room, Still Room, Laundry, Best Gallery, Saloon (pianoforte), Mrs Powell's Room, Dressing Room, Mackcaw (sic) Room, Room over the Kitchen, Best Room, Tent Room (?), Pink Room, Common Staircase, Housekeeper's [Bed]Room, Servant Men's Room, Gallery, Room over the Mackcaw, White Room, Check Room, Master Powell's Room (33 Framed Pictures, 26 Pictures without Frames), Green Room, Miss Powell's Nursery, Little Lodging Room, Mr Powell's Dressing Room (30 Pictures and a Frame, A Biddy [?], Garrets, Kitchen, Passage, Store Room, Cellar, Brewhouse, Dairy, upper Kitchen and Malt Room (95 Pounds of Hops).

62 He died of an apoplectic fit in the street, 17 Nov. 1752 (*Gentleman's Magazine*, 1752, p.536).

63 See the copy of *Lloyds Evening Post & British Chronicle* for August 10-12, 1778, in N.L.W. Nanteos Deeds Box 20.

64 M.L.I,p.216; 17 September 1752.

65 Ordained deacon 1732, priest 1732; curate of East Hanningfield, Essex, 1734, of Llanfihangel Genau'r-glyn 1735. St John's College Oxford informed his father that William had 'taken his degree very creditably, being honour'd with the title of Optime by the Proctor'.

66 She is the subject of one of the best-known ghost stories of Nanteos, that of the jewellery which she is fabled to have hidden from her detested husband before her death, and to which her apparition is supposed to return.

67 ALMA, I, p.136, dated 16.11.1744.

68 ALMA I, p.164, dated 6.7.1745. The same letter tells us that Powell's solicitor was Thomas Parry, squire of Llidiardau.

69 ALMA, I, p.204, dated 1.2.1750/1.

70 N.L.W. Box 3, unscheduled.

71 M.L. I, p.306.

72 N.L.W. N.L.138, 24 February 1756.

[73] She was the daughter of Athelstan Owen of Rhiwsaeson, Mont., and Ann Corbet of Ynysymaengwyn, Merion.

[74] M.L. I, 461, dated 9.3.1757.

[75] M.L. II, p.30.

[76] M.L. II, p.187.

[77] M.L. II, p.176, 24.2.1760. 'No one is on Vaughan's side but Powell, and he is nothing but a bundle of pea-straw crackling in the fire.'

[78] L.M. II, 259. 'An utter rogue, a very son of Satan'.

[79] M.L. II, p.364.

[80] See Gerald Morgan, *A Welsh House and its Family: the Vaughans of Trawsgoed* (Llandysul, 1997), chap.4.

[81] N.L.W. N.L.149, subscribed "From my Bed Thursday morn 5 oclock".

[82] N.L.W. N.L.156.

[83] N.L.W. N.L.158.

[84] Gerald Morgan, *A Welsh House and its Family*, ch.4.

[85] He was a founder-member of the Royal Society of Arts in 1754; see F.R.Lewis's letter N.L.W. Nanteos L.4775-6.

[86] The Aberystwyth properties included two in Church St, 16 in Weeg St, 9 in Castle St, 14 in Bridge St, one in Nightingale Lane, three in Penmaesglas, 20 in Trefechan and 28 in Plas-crug.

[87] N.L.W. Nanteos R3 (for Nanteos and Aberystwyth in 1772); R1 for Abbey estate in 1771; R15 for Breconshire.

[88] This *may* have come with the marriage of the Rev. Dr. William Powell to Elizabeth Owen, co-heiress of Athelstan Owen of Rhiwsaeson, Montgomeryshire. The Llanbrynmair lands were sold in 1828 to one John Conroy for £18,250 (N.L.W. Nanteos Preliminary Schedule, p.1).

[89] N.L.W. Nanteos R45.

[90] N.L.W. Nanteos Maps 301, 342 and 354.

[91] N.L.W. Cwrtmawr Deeds, 203. Craig-y-mwyn is the prominent crag above the main mining site.

[92] S.S.J.Hughes, *The Cwmystwyth Mines*, a monograph of the Northern Mine Research Society (1981), 7-10.

[93] N.L.W. Nanteos, box 6 (unscheduled).

[94] N.L.W. Nanteos, box 7 (unscheduled).

[95] D.W.Howell, *Patriarchs and Parasites: the Gentry of South-west Wales in the Eighteenth Century* (Cardiff, 1986), 106.

[96] R.Burt, P.Waite, R.Burnley, in *The Mines of Cardiganshire* (Univ. of Exeter, n.d.), bravely attempt to bring together figures for separate yields of all the mines where sources allow; the figures for Rheidol are particularly confusing. (p.81).

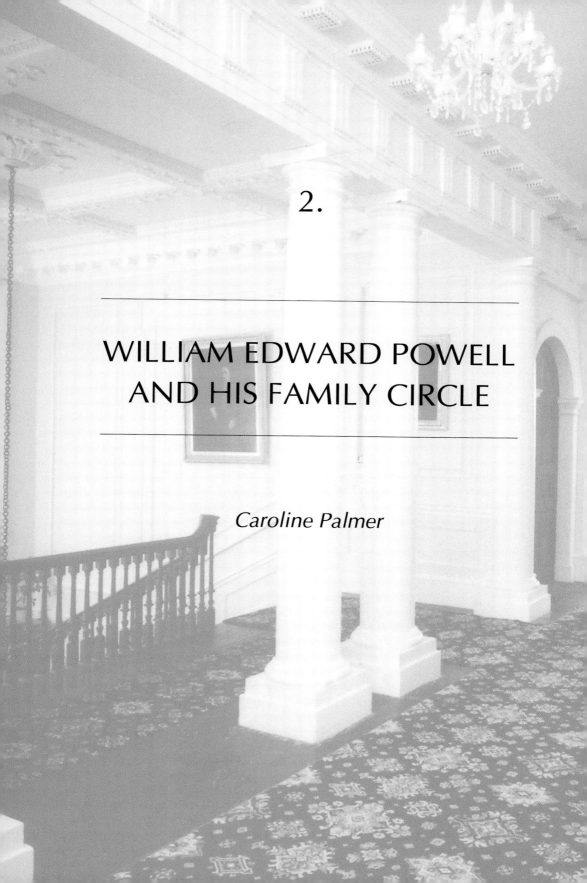

2.

WILLIAM EDWARD POWELL AND HIS FAMILY CIRCLE

Caroline Palmer

W.E. POWELL AND HIS FAMILY CIRCLE

THE personal history of William Edward Powell, seen in the context of his grandparents, parents, wives, mistress and extensive kin provides a colourful insight into the behaviour and preoccupations of a gentry family of the early nineteenth century. As has been shown in chapter 1, William Edward's father, Thomas Powell, was born in 1745, and in middle age married a young wife, Eleanor Corbet, his first cousin once removed, daughter of Edward Corbet of Ynysmaengwyn, Merionethshire. Five children were born between 1788 and 1797, three boys and two girls; one of the boys died in infancy. When Thomas Powell died on 14 April 1797,[1] William Edward, his eldest, was nine years old, and his youngest, Anne Corbetta, just seven months of age.[2]

Losing his father at a tender age, William grew up in the certain expectation of inheriting his patrimony, with its attendant status and obligations, on attaining twenty-one years of age. He entered adult life at the time which has been captured so entrancingly by the pen of Jane Austen, and, like the variously eligible young gentlemen in her novels, he moved from public school and Oxford to the glamour of the military and the social life of Bath and London. He rapidly acquired a young wife, Laura Phelp, as poor in substance and rich in younger sisters as Eliza Bennett. Sadly for her, Powell proved to be no Mr Darcy, and his political and material success must be balanced by a record of marital neglect, convoluted debt obligations, ill-tempered disputes, and sexual peccadilloes. His impetuous marriage led swiftly to two further alliances with the Phelp family from Leicestershire, bringing much English blood into this predominantly Welsh lineage. Though little remembered today, Phelp relatives played a large part in Nanteos affairs for much of the nineteenth century.

The widowed Eleanor Powell had been left with four young children and the debt-encumbered estate. She was herself an only child, her father and her mother having divorced, and her father had married again.[3] Her mother, Hannah, had been co-heiress with her sister Mary to the estates of their father, John Chambre of Petton, Shropshire. While Mary had been married advantageously to the second son of the first baronet of Hawkstone, Hannah's share had been sold by her husband to a Liverpool merchant, and subsequent to the divorce she lived in Aberystwyth, renting Crynfryn House from Sir Thomas Bonsall.[4]

It is thus not surprising that Thomas Powell had little faith in his father-in-law. In his will he had appointed three executors and guardians of his young children: his widow Eleanor, the Aberystwyth lawyer Thomas Morgan, who had dealt with his affairs in his lifetime, and John Hill of Prees, husband of Eleanor's mother's sister Mary, and brother of the second baronet of Hawkstone. The three were to receive legacies of £100, £100 and £5000 respectively.[5] Clearly Thomas Powell pinned his confidence on John Hill.

John Hill of Prees was a family man, whose sixteen children included cousins of similar age to the two young Powells. Correspondence amongst the Hill letters indicates that the young William Edward often spent holidays at Prees, and later at Hawkstone, when John Hill, on the death of his brother, became third baronet. The responsibilities of executor weighed heavily on John Hill, and occasioned many visits to Cardiganshire, and much correspondence, for Eleanor Powell at the time of her widowhood was already living in London. The agent, Thomas Robson, occupied Nanteos and was responsible for the care of the estate. Thomas Powell had left debts as well as dependents, and money needed to be raised from the estate. In 1797 Hill estimated that the debt of £12,000 'could be rubbed off in six years, the estate yielding £4000 a year, and the annual outgoings, after this year, should be £2000'.[6]

The principal preoccupation of the executors during the two years following Thomas Powell's death was in the matter of raising additional income by letting the house along with a small amount of land, on a ten-year lease to a suitable gentleman. Such an arrangement would make the house available again by the time William Edward reached twenty one years of age. Hill was eager to advertise the property in May 1798, 'as the bathing season is now coming on, People may have an opportunity of seeing the place and knowing particulars'. The phrasing of particulars occasioned some difficulty, 'the house being furnished, though we cannot say elegantly'.[7] He suggested 'we have a right to ask £100 a year for the house and furniture, pleasure grounds and etc, the land at a fair valuation'. However structural repairs would be necessary:

> the saloon floor being of sycamore wood is so much decayed (by what I believe is called dry rot) that it will scarcely bear to be trod upon, and some of the boards are actually broken through.[8]

While he resisted Eleanor's demands for additional money from the estate, Hill did not allow cost considerations to deter him from strongly advising her to send William, then ten years old, to Westminster School, not back to Mr Carr's at Cheam. 'I wish you had said he was going to Westminster, that being the school I believe that was pointed out by his father and I am convinced that if a Boy is to go to a public school he cannot well do it too soon, and let his expectations be what they will, to fight his way up in common with other boys'. Westminster had been Thomas Powell's school.

By October 1798 several potential tenants for Nanteos had been identified, but to Hill's consternation, Eleanor's father also wished to rent it.[9] To prevent this eventuality Hill and Morgan suppressed the advertisement in favour of seeking a private contract and wrote to Eleanor:

> I assure you, as a sincere wellwisher to you and yours I am happy to hear there is a prospect of your becoming on good terms with each other, but I cannot but observe that I hope he has no intention of interfering in the management of the concerns left by your late worthy husband to yourself, Mr Morgan, and myself. Poor Mr Powell well knew how your father managed his own affairs and what a husband and parent he was, or he would not have put the concerns of those that were most near and dear to him into other hands, in short it is impossible for Mr Morgan or myself to act with Mr Corbet, of which I doubt not your own good sense will convince you.[10]

A year later, Nanteos was still not let, but two gentlemen, John Hill's candidate Sir George Murray, Bart, and Eleanor Powell's candidate Captain Pocock, appeared

W.E. Powell (1788-1854)
in costume of Lord
Lieutenant

willing to pay £300 per annum. In the event, Eleanor Powell seems to have been more worldly-wise than her co-trustees, for on 22 October, John Hill had to confess himself entirely deceived by Murray:

> I am very happy to find your penetration was deeper than mine as thereby we have escaped from the tricks of the *Worthy Baronet*, you have seen most of his letters to me, and I dare say are not surprised at my having been taken in for the moment ... the Baronet's first note being dated Birmingham it appears to me that he is connected with one Freeman, a notorious swindling attorney at that place, who I have this day heard has frequently been concerned in taking houses and purchasing furniture on credit, and then dispensing of it to the loss of the landlord and tradesmen. I therefore congratulate you upon our deliverance from *my respectable friend*.[11]

The bad baronet having been avoided, the house was let to Captain Pocock, who was in residence by summer 1800, and appears usually to have been on time with the rent, and to have carried out some repairs. Pocock was clearly not perceived as a social equal; John Hill wrote to Eleanor Powell: 'Mr Morgan and I breakfasted at Nanteos, the Ladies were as polite as they seemed *to know how to be*, the Capt was in London. I hope he is, as you are informed, a man of fortune or I am sure he will never make one by farming. Robson is on good terms with the family, he however, is determined to have a watchful eye on their proceedings.'[12] Similar misgivings about this non-hereditary tenant are reflected, with great tact, in Malkin's tour of 1804.[13]

Letters from John Hill do not survive beyond 1801, but during these first four years of her widowhood Eleanor Powell appears to have moved to a good address, 38 Mortimer Street, Cavendish Square. For her children she was allowed £100 a year for her older daughter's education and £80 a year for each of the younger children until they should go to school. William Edward's bills from Westminster were sent directly to the trustees Mr Morgan and Mr Hill, and he usually holidayed at Prees with his friend and cousin Edward Hill, a pupil at Charterhouse school. John Hill wrote of his ward, 'a sweeter tempered conformable good lad cannot be'.

From Westminster, William went to Christ Church, Oxford, and thence into the army in 1807. He purchased a commission in the Royal Horse Guards (the Blues). He was not entirely happy with this choice and corresponded with both his solicitor Edward Horne and with J. Dorrien at Windsor on the subject.[14] They dissuaded him from a change, and in December 1807 the estate forwarded him £700 for the purchase of a company, and his consequent elevation to the rank of Captain.[15] In 1808-09 he was in England, at Ropley, Alresford, and at Bath. Here he received letters from his agent Hugh Hughes at Aberystwyth, and his sister Ellen Elizabeth, who, with her mother and siblings, was exiled by debt, in Dublin. All looked forward to his coming-of-age on 16 February 1809. Nanteos needed attention and all agreed that a Mrs Southern should be employed as housekeeper, being 'a fit person to put the furniture of Nanteos in proper order after the destruction Mr Pocock made there'.[16] Ellen and her mother had picked out 'a dinner service in imitation of old Indian china which we all think much more handsome than the one we saw at Wedgewood's.' At eighteen guineas, they urged him to have it, commenting, 'Blue and white china is so vulgar now'.[17] Mrs Powell was also eager to have furniture, linen, sherry and claret shipped from Ireland and proffered much advice from the gentlemen of her acquaintance. Hugh Hughes was adamant that the shortage of money and differing excise duties made this imprudent but was equally keen on throwing a fine party. He wrote: 'You have an amount of Wine here at Nanteos – I hope you can afford, and have the will to have some champaigne in your cellars', but recommended that it be obtained from London via the Shrewsbury Waggon.[18]

In the January preceding the party, Powell himself was still in Bath and evidently entertaining company. Having desired woodcock to be sent to Bath from Nanteos, he was implicitly blamed by Hughes for the accidental death of Petit the gamekeeper, who shot himself when returning, carrying his loaded gun, from executing this commission.[19] Hughes was also keen to keep Powell informed as to the gossip which had reached him: 'Mr Rice Williams has reported within these five days that you are already or will be married by the 16th so that we shall have a Birthday and a wedding visit on the same day. The Young lady is beautiful, *one* out of a numerous family, but whose father or grandfather was a Clothier – but her brother is *An Officer*.'[20] This sounds very much like the family of Phelp.

Her unpaid debts prevented Mrs Powell, her children and attendant beau from returning to Nanteos for the party, and Powell was soon back at Bath, leaving the estate in the care of Hugh Hughes and his son James. This was evidently a mistake, for in May 1809 came a letter from his maternal grandfather Edward Maurice Corbet:

> The distress and misery that may be the most certain and immediate consequence of your inattention to your concerns are the urgent and forced reasons for my addressing this serious and important alarm to your heart – come down to Nanteos, receive your own rents and inspect the proceedings. Your Agent Hugh Hughes is declared insane and incapable of all Business and has not appeared since the 16 of February. Your woods were sold under value and you confirmed that sale by Letter of Attorney tho' my only request to you (upon your appearance) was as forcibly and affectionately made as my utterance was capable of. 'to sign no paper until your affairs in Chancery were settled and confirmed'. *At all hazards at all events, come down* and *preside* at your Rent Day which is at hand. *Let not an hour be lost as warned and advised.*[21]

Powell's mother's and younger siblings' debts in Ireland were pressing. In March his solicitor Robert Appleyard had informed him that bills for his mother's debts had been filed against him, and in September of that year she was in fear of going to gaol for debts of £3,300 and a further £2,500 borrowed. Appleyard again paid from the estate, and informed William that 'she is now free to return to England without fear of imprisonment, whenever she pleases'.[22] Appleyard knew that William's sister Ellen Elizabeth would soon be due her portion of £5000, at age 21 or at marriage, whichever should happen first, and the younger Powells would similarly soon be claiming their inheritance.[23] Such financial prospects recommended financial stringency to his lawyers, but not, perhaps, to a young man who, since the age of nine, had been waiting to take hold of the reins of power.

Immediately upon attaining his majority, Powell assessed his assets. In March of 1809 he obtained from the goldsmiths Makepeace and Harker a valuation of the Nanteos plate, consisting of a cutlery service of 24 place settings (barring a few losses), and large items such as a punch-bowl, candlesticks, candelabra, epergne, tea urn and coffee pot. The whole weighed an estimated 1757 ounces and was valued at £527.6.10.[24] He was also probably responsible for commissioning William Couling's large roll map of The Town and Burgh of Aberystwyth, completed in October 1809. The only known copy is in the Nanteos archive and on it W.E. Powell's lands are shaded in blue.[25] He commissioned a similar estate survey by Couling showing his lands in Llanbadarn Fawr.[26]

In February 1810 Powell obtained the nomination for Sheriff of Cardiganshire, an honorary post likely to involve considerable expenditure for the holder (even though it only lasted a twelvemonth), and Appleyard was seriously alarmed. His letter of 6 February suggests:

> I see by the papers you have been nominated for Sheriff of Cardiganshire for the coming year – now as it will be impossible for you to serve in your present weak state – let me hear by return of post that you wish to get off and I will immediately apply to Mr Percival to get him to nominate another gentleman in your room. And you must by the same post write to your Surgeon and the Physician and Apothecary who attended you *at the first* desiring they will each transmit a Certificate to Mr Percival of the accident which happened to you and of the total impossibility of your being in a fit state to take the Sheriff or do Business of any kind.[27]

The opportunity of a 'sick note' was apparently declined for *The Gentleman's Magazine* records in March 1810 that Powell had been appointed Sheriff for 1810. In May, Powell was commended in the same journal for 'raising an emolument offering premiums of 27 silver cups for improvement in the various branches of agriculture. Such spirited conduct in a young gentleman, just come into possession of his estates gives the fairest promise of his becoming a real blessing to his county, a patriot in the truest sense of the word.'[28] Thomas Johnes was not the only landowner to show some interest in promoting agricultural improvement.

Powell also lost no time in getting married, at St Nicholas, in the Diocese of Llandaff, on 4 October 1810,[29] to a girl of his own age, Laura Edwina, eldest daughter of Col. James Phelp, of Cottrell House, Glamorganshire and Coston House, near Melton Mowbray in Leicestershire.[30] It may have been through the regiment, or through the social life of Bath, that William Edward Powell had become acquainted with the Phelp family, who were numerous and relatively impecunious. They were probably the very family to whom gossip had already married him the winter before. Although not themselves designated by *Burke's Landed Gentry* as a landed family, Col. James Phelp was of similar social status to Powell, a deputy Lieutenant of the county of Leicestershire, a magistrate, and squire of Coston House. Mrs Ellen Phelp came from a landed family, the O'Briens of Blatherwycke Park, Northamptonshire. At this time Col. Phelp apparently rented Cottrell House, St Nicholas. It may be speculated that this substantial and ancient Welsh residence contributed to the impression that Laura would be a wealthy bride. If so, Powell must have been fully disabused of the belief before the marriage took place. Robert Appleyard's letter of 13 July 1810 spelt out the bleak reality.[31] Laura's dowry of £3000 would not be payable until Col. Phelp's death, and in the meantime Powell must pay the interest on a mortgage of £3000 obtained on Phelp's already debt-burdened estate. The marriage would bring in less than one of his own sisters' dowry requirements, or than his mother's recent debt.

Notwithstanding the delayed settlement, Powell, in anticipation of his marriage, settled land in the parishes of Llanbadarn Fawr (which embraced Aberystwyth), Llanfihangel y Creuddyn and Llanychaiarn in the hands of trustees on 14/15 September 1810. The administrating trustees were his cousin John Lewis of Llanaeron, and Laura's uncle John James Beddingfield of Ditchingham Hall, Norfolk. The pre-nuptial settlement was to hold the land to the use of Powell, and, following the marriage, of Powell and his wife Laura. In June and July 1810 Powell had begun an active programme of leasing plots for building in Weeg Street (Pier Street), Bridge Street and Castle Street in addition to re-leasing existing houses. All such developments subsequent to September 1810 recite this deed. New agreements were in the form of 60-year leases of building land.[32] In some cases the contract specified the demolition of a pre-existing property, in most a vacant plot was sold. All purchasers were obliged to build within a year, maintain and insure their leasehold properties, which would eventually revert to the Nanteos estate. Powell took an active interest in the design of the developing Aberystwyth and usually included detailed elevation drawings in the lease agreements.[33]

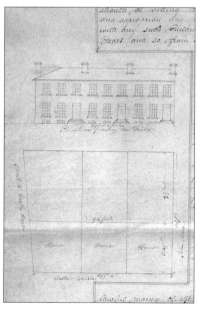
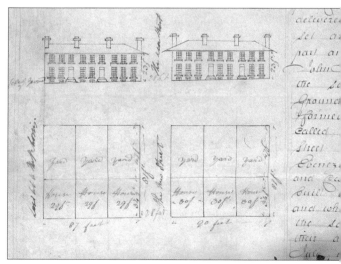

Designs for nine new houses at Laura Place 1827. Nanteos building leases at this time often included elevations and plans in cameo.

N.L.W.

Following their wedding, Powell and his bride disappear from view. A letter of 27 November 1810, from Robert Appleyard to Powell at Nanteos is rich with innuendo:

> I think I *may* venture (without being considered an intruder on Happy Moments) to felicitate Mrs Powell and yourself on an Event which I hope will contribute as much to your future Happiness as it promises to do. An Event however of which you kept me pretty much in the Dark, as I heard it first from a total Stranger, and then did not write to you not being certain where a letter would reach you. I shall however now be very glad of a line from you to say where you have been and that you enjoy yourself and Friends in your new Character.[34]

This 'event' cannot be the marriage, for Appleyard was fully involved in the arrangements for this. It is hard to avoid the inference that Laura married pregnant. However there is no subsequent evidence of a child, and the marriage was announced a second time, as having occurred 'lately', in *The Gentlemans Magazine* of February 1811.[35] An infant death may be presumed, but cannot be confirmed.[36]

Relations with grandfather Edward Corbet of Ynysmaengwyn were strained in December 1810, apparently because the new bride had not been introduced, and Corbet had omitted to communicate his goodwill. On Christmas Eve he wrote to Powell:

> Your letter describing 'the Friends and Relations' that sent to you conveys no direct insinuation but plainly intimates that I did not . . . If you chose to renew any claim to the consanguinity I expect you to present yourself and Lady here – knowing my situation and feeling that I am yr Grandfather.[37]

In 1810, Laura's brother, Edward Tufton Phelp wrote to the dowager Eleanor Powell requesting the hand of Powell's sister, Ellen Elizabeth, and defending his lack of wealth. 'I have had myself so much experience in the world to know that money does not entirely purchase happiness and that "gilded roofs" cover as many (if not more) aching hearts as cottages.'[38] Although Mrs Powell had misgivings about the match, the marriage took place in 1811, thus claiming on Powell a mortgage greater than the dowry owed on behalf of Laura. Soon Edward and Ellen were able to announce the birth, at Coston, of a son and heir, Cecil on 30 January 1813,[39] and a daughter, Ayliffe Julia on 31 May 1814.[40] That year Col. James Tufton Phelp died.

Rather than ameliorating the situation, Phelp's death bound the two families in an increasingly complex and indissoluble web of debt, bonds and obligations. Edward Phelp now became head of the family, master of a seriously dilapidated estate, and responsible for his widowed mother and young siblings, Julia, Fanny, Octavia, Eleanora and Cecil. W.E. Powell and his sister Ellen Phelp appear to have maintained over many years a most open and cordial correspondence, but in the wake of her father's death Ellen wrote from Coston in the most pressing terms to her brother:

> to entreat that you will use every exertion possible to induce Mr Edwards to settle the difference between Laura's fortune and mine, viz £2000, it being absolutely necessary to our present and future comfort that we have it *immediately*. You are, I daresay aware that she [the widowed Mrs Phelp] personally is subject to all Col Phelp's debts and we must purchase a considerable part of it to enable us to remain here——and in the event of our being disappointed of it she would be obliged to dispose of the furniture, stock etc. etc. by auction and we should be completely without a home.[41]

Edward Tufton Phelp also wrote desperately to Powell requesting bonds which would enable him to carry out repairs on Coston and, as soon as the estate was put to rights, to sell it.[42] His mind was also preoccupied with the possibility of his imminent death, being about to leave for Europe to fight in the Napoleonic war, and he requested: 'will you be so good as to look out for what would be useful in the campaigning way – such as a Hammock and Canteen for me'.

While Ellen and Edward Phelp's first three years of marriage had been crammed with incident, and fruitful of two adored children, Laura's early years of marriage were lonely ones. In November 1811 Powell had left the Royal Horse Guards and sought Col. Johnes of Hafod's support to take command of the Royal Cardiganshire Regiment. For more than two years Major Powell toured Ireland with his regiment, receiving increasingly despairing letters from his lawyers, Hopkinson and Sons, at successive addresses in Dublin, Limerick, Monkstown and Loughrea.[43] His debts were soaring, his estate was ill-managed, and Hopkinson insisted he enlist some reliable gentleman to take his affairs in hand. It was thus that Col. John Edwards of Bloomsbury became involved at Nanteos, and, with occasional deference to Laura's preferences, supervised improvements to the estate.[44] Even when the regiment returned to Porchester Castle near Portsmouth in late 1813 Powell seemed in no hurry about coming home. Ellen warned her brother: 'you are so remiss in writing that if your *cara sposa* or any of this party were apt to be fanciful it might be imagined that you had an intention of *cutting the concern* —— I now earnestly request in the name of this *august assembly* that till you come you will be more punctual in writing as your deficiency in that respect makes your little wife miserable. I really am not joking.'[45]

Laura seems to have divided her time between Nanteos and Coston during these years. The two widowed mothers were out in society parading their unmarried daughters, Eleanor Powell with Anne, and Ellen Phelp with Julia and Fanny. Powell eventually returned to his wife, and on 4 October 1815 his heir, William Thomas Rowland Powell, was born at Swansea.[46] His arrival was acknowledged in a letter to Powell from his grandfather Corbet: '[I] congratulate you on the birth of your son as I did upon that of his father . . . I was apprehensive that too much care and too much attention might have been paid to the young Spark, but after repeated enquiries I find he is hearty, well and jumbled about with great propriety. We all desire our congratulations to Mrs Powell.'[47] Powell now devoted his energies to becoming an important figure in the county. In 1816 he became Lord Lieutenant of the county, and M.P. for Cardiganshire; he also began angling for a baronetcy but in this he was not successful.[48] His new senior status kept him much in London where he cultivated aristocratic friendships, and attended levees at Court. While he resided in lodgings, most often at Limmer's Hotel, Hanover Square, Laura usually remained in the country.

In 1817 a younger Phelp sister, Eleanora, not yet sixteen years of age, attracted the eye of William George Cherry Esq., of Buckland, Hereford, lately captain in the Royal Horse Guards, and a close friend of Powell's. The proposal was approved by the widow Eleanor Phelp, and by the girl herself, but was referred to her guardian Alex Macleod, of Muravon House, Linlithgow, who wrote to Powell as Cherry's nominated particular friend. Cherry, it appeared had £700 a year, rising to £1000 a year at his father's death. The marriage took place on 29 March 1817,[49] and Cherry was to act for some ten years as a trustee of Powell's estate. A further attempt was made by Edward Phelp to solve his intractable financial difficulties at this time, allowing £2000 for each of his sisters, and £3000 for Cecil, but the arrangement depended upon the repair and sale of Coston.[50] Probably the feared auction of its contents and assets had already taken place, for by now Phelp and his wife Ellen were living in Aberystwyth, apparently renting Castle House in 1817, Penglais in 1818, (from where their twin children Frances Ellen and William Edward were christened on September 10 1818),[51] and the Vaughan property of Gelli in 1820.

On 8 February 1817, on her birthday (which Powell had evidently forgotten) and pregnant with her second son, Laura wrote to her husband from Nanteos describing her visit, accompanied by Harriet Maurice and the two-year-old W.T.R., to shop and visit with Ellen and Edward Phelp in Aberystwyth.

> 'I am sorry to tell you I am far from well, have scarcely closed my eyes the last two nights which makes me feel low spirited and weak. I trust you will either contrive to get a house shortly or will come down here yourself. I sleep by myself as I prefer it to having Harriet for a bed fellow. We are much pressed to go to Llaniron [Llanaeron], and if I get a little better perhaps we shall go for two or three days.'

The same letter also describes the deceit of servants in selling Nanteos hares in Aberystwyth, and ordering themselves linen and clothing at local shops at Powell's expense.[52]

The winter of 1817 had been a time of great hardship for the poor, both as a result of terrible weather and of agricultural depression in the wake of the Napoleonic war. While little evidence remains of Powell's political activities, it appears that his efforts to alleviate local hardship were appreciated by David Williams of Bronmeurig, secretary of Lord Seymour's committee to alleviate the distress of the poor in west Wales, who declared that 'you have already been of more service than any who have had the Public Interest of the said county confided in them for ages.'[53]

In June Laura was advanced in her pregnancy, impoverished and looking ahead to her confinement. She wrote urgently to her husband from Bath:

> Notwithstanding I don't think myself at all equal to encounter the fatigues of the passage without a gentleman with me the necessity of my no longer delaying the time of my being settled for good has determined me to set off from here on Saturday after the post comes in if I get a remittance from you which must be from £10 to £15 pounds, I mean to go as far as the passage [i.e. the Aust ferry across the Severn] the first day and have the carriage taken over either that night or early the next morning whichever time the tide serves best . . . Pray do not delay coming down as my time draws so near I have taken it so strongly into my head you will not be with me it quite prays on my spirits . . . Be sure you write by return of post as my situation is awkward. Pray come down soon, kind regards from the family. I think you had better send me £15 as what should I do if I had not enough for the road.[54]

On 25 July 1817 the baby Cornelius was born, also at Swansea, and apparently Powell did go there for her accouchement.[55] Several family members allude to her subsequent illness but in no specific detail. Both boys were later christened (in W.T.R.Powell's case, for a second time),[56] at Llanbadarn Fawr on 19 August 1819.[57]

Laura's life at Nanteos did not improve over the next few years; Powell returned to London, while both her brothers concerned themselves in Powell's affairs. They were in no doubt that Barber the agent, and Powell's lawyer Appleyard, served him ill. Cecil's advice to Powell was that 'nothing but force will ever, in my opinion make this knot of lawyers and rascals do you justice'.[58] Laura, oppressed by her own ill-health and Cornelius's serious attacks, found herself in a difficult position as Powell fell out with yet another agent. She wrote to him:

I have had a letter from Mr Armstrong enclosing a copy of one to you in answer to one he shewed me from you yesterday which he asked me to explain the meaning of, which you are aware was not in my power to do – being ignorant of your plans I may not be competent to advise but I should *certainly* recommend Mr Armstrong's being treated with civility and *temper* by those persons you employ to settle your affairs as I am quite certain it is neither to your advantage or credit to make enemies of every agent you dismiss witness Mr Barber.[59]

Notwithstanding this counsel, Armstrong and Appleyard were both sacked by the irascible Powell in 1820. His financial situation was becoming desperate as he exhausted all possible sources of money. His relationship with his brother-in-law and trustee William Cherry was becoming strained, and his 77-year-old grandfather Corbet wrote emphatically complaining at his failure to pay interest on loans, and demanding full repayment of his money.

In Aberystwyth Powell continued his programme of selling leases of building land in the town on the land held in trust for himself and Laura. On 26 March 1819 he had begun the development of an undeveloped field east of the castle, and adjoining Uvedale Price's Castle House. Eager to provide the growing resort town with fashionable Public Rooms he issued a lease in respect of a plot of land near St Michael's Chapel, for the purpose of constructing Assembly Rooms.[60] The lessees were local gentry: Pryse Pryse of Gogerddan, John Jones of Derry Ormond, John Nathaniel Williams of Castle Hill Llanilar, John Lewis of Llanaeron and George Bonsall of Glanrheidol. The agreement placed an obligation upon Powell to lay out and maintain an associated pleasure ground between the Rooms and Castle House. Powell himself apparently employed and paid George Stanley Repton, formerly chief assistant in John Nash's office, to prepare the elevations and estimates for the rooms, which were then funded by subscribers under a committee.[61] The design for the pleasure ground, though not completed until a decade later, may also have been by George Repton. The newly erected public rooms were duly opened on 11 July 1820. Ninety-four people attended the opening ball, and William Lewis of Llanaeron (who had subscribed just £20) danced the first dance with Laura Powell, having first dined at Nanteos.[62] Correspondents to the *Oswestry Herald* wrote warmly of the Rooms and other facilities now available at Aberystwyth, including a newly-opened theatre and a range of 'proper Baths, calculated for every kind of warm and cold sea bathing, shower, vapour and other baths'.[63]

Powell did not himself attend the opening of the Assembly Rooms, and Laura's correspondence of 1820 indicate his attention was fully occupied elsewhere. On 4 May 1820 she had written to her husband, from Buckland, where she was staying with her sister Eleanora, and her husband William Cherry. She was painfully conscious that her husband was moving in a quite different and more glittering world:

> Of course you have seen *Mary* ere this I hope you said everything kind for me I ought to have written to her but of late my spirits have not enabled me to write letters about nothing. How is she looking? Is she as fascinating as you used to find her? . . . Tho' last, most interesting to me is how is Mama looking, also my sisters I hope you will contrive to call upon them often as I know it will gratify them very much. Remember to look about you and bring us accounts of the fashions. Cornelius is well my bulletin of today announces. I shall reserve my few commissions till I am *quite* sure I have *remembered* them all I almost envy your peep at the gay world but lament less every day as the country improves in beauty. I enclose a list of the people I am anxious you should pay out of the Curzon Street money. Talking of Curzon Street I should think if the coronation really takes place early in August we might get a very great rent for the whole month of July. All here unite in love . . .[64]

Laura probably did not know that Powell was himself in arrears on the rent owing for the townhouse in Curzon Street which he kept furnished but seldom occupied himself.[65] Her next letter from Buckland shows real desperation for money:

> You will think yourself the most persecuted of men when even your own wife begins to *drive* you but I am under the necessity of begging you will try to get the two hundred pounds *I* lent you out of my building money as the house

will come to a standstill if I have it not directly which would make bad worse. I have just had an application for the payment of slates which doubles all I at present possess – I have sent ten pounds to Mrs Southern to pay part of the dairymaid's wages. I had a letter from Mr Armstrong today in which he says he has not a farthing to pay the remainder. We are going to spend tomorrow at Leominster. I return on Tuesday. Julia and Eleanora unite in love with your affectionate wife.'[66]

In June, Laura was back at Nanteos, where she found her situation insupportable, and believed herself about to be supplanted in her own home:

I have just received your letter in which you say the Committee you are on may not be finished for a fortnight before which time I must certainly *run away* unless you can contrive to send me some money as the scenes I am obliged to go through are distressing and humiliating to the greatest degree. You may have thought it advisable to act towards me as you have done and perhaps I deserve it. I however find some comfort in not being aware that I do so. Richard[67] wrote to Ellen to ask if the chaise was to be sent today, not receiving any answer he did not send it but we fancy there has been some mistake as the *Carter* has brought word from Aberystwyth today that he saw Edwin James, who told him the servants were discharged at Gelly and that Mrs Phelp was going to live at Nanteos, the servants here are all aware of my perfect ignorance about it all which is very *gratifying* to my feelings. I do think you might have said something about it in your letter, but I conclude that your *fears* for *Mrs* Weston's non arrival engrossed all your thought as it must be a thing of wonderful consequence in comparison with my respectability – indeed you have been very unkind in keeping me in such perfect ignorance about all your plans and if I have expressed myself too warmly about you may impute it to the unhappy state of mind I am in. I have only 5/6d in the house and claimants I grieve to refuse every hour for money. The late dairymaid came back again here the day I returned and it was with difficulty I could persuade her I had it not in my power to pay her the money due to her or to go away without it. The woman who nurses Mary the housemaid's child[68] has been here for the seventh time this morning in the greatest distress for four pounds owing to her besides several others equally pressing. If you could send me fifty pounds by return of post, or even twenty it would relieve some of the people who are so much distressed. I must beg to hear from you by return of post to know how I am to conduct myself whether I am to consider myself Ellen's visitor or she mine. I remain your affectionate wife.[69]

Powell evidently sent £25, and reassured her that he was not installing his sister and her brother in Nanteos in her stead. Laura's letter, of 13 July 1820, two days after she danced at the newly opened Assembly Rooms, is an effort at reaffirming wifely sentiment:

I have just received your letter which was most welcome on two accounts first that I find by it that you were not the planner of the sudden taking possession of Nanteos by Edward and his family and secondly the 25 pounds is really a *godsend* as you can have no idea how very distressing my situation has been and I fear I wrote my second letter to you more under the dominion of passion than so *sweet tempered* a personage should have done ... Cornelius is very much better today and has recovered his spirits and his appetite in some degree but I fear you will think him much altered for the worse in his looks. If Williams will take charge of him now I have the wherewithall he shall go when she does to Llandrindod. I hope the things my sister got for me have been sent off as William is quite in distress for a frock and his brother for several articles of dress contained in my commission. John Lewis wrote word he was coming here today but the rain is so incessant I dont expect him at all. The men of the Cardiganshire Militia are very anxious to see the Major. I fear Mr Lozon will leave Aberystwyth before you arrive unless you write and ask him here. I am sure any attention we can pay him is due out of gratitude. With the united love of this party I remain your affectionate wife.[70]

Other correspondents throw some light on the circumstances of Laura's distress. Mrs Southern appears to have been responsible for the misunderstanding or malice which fuelled the crisis, but neither Ellen nor Edward Phelp speak kindly of Laura in their letters to Powell. Ellen wrote to her brother:

I regret extremely that Laura was not open and ingenuous enough to mention the subject which appears so much to have annoyed her to me when she saw me, by which all misunderstanding must have been prevented, but indeed where there is no disposition to be on affectionate or even friendly terms, an excuse for a breach is too readily and easily caught at.

She explained that she and Edward had planned 'to go together to Nanteos, not to take possession as Mrs Southern (I imagine without foundation) represented to Laura, but under the idea of Edward's exertions enabling *you* to continue to live there with comfort to yourself.'[71] Edward wrote similarly:

> you must recollect that it was you yourself that asked Ellen in the first place to come and stay at Nanteos during your projected absence . . . to have kept you steady in a plan to eventually save your property and by that means your own comfort and respectability and your sons' after you. I as I can appeal to Ellen, did it with very little hope of getting the better of the eternal cabal of Laura etc., who for God knows what purpose has this life taken every underhand means of either injuring or mortifying us, and knowing unfortunately that you have the failing of being indecisive and being reserved and suspicious towards your best friends and letting people abuse your confidence of whom you ought to be suspicious . . . Tell Laura as she has succeeded in getting rid of me etc. etc. the less we have to do in future with each other the better and that tho' I bear no resentment, I will not consent to be the subject of these sort of unpleasant occurrences perpetually . . . and since the affair of Mrs Southern's letter to Buckland I have made up my mind that Ellen had better not have any further communcation with her.[72]

That they wrote to him in such frank terms implies they expected he would sympathise with their view of Laura. Edward Phelp withdrew thereafter from involvement in Powell's affairs and proposed that Powell's bond to him should be transferred to Cherry, Mrs Phelp and the Phelp sisters in lieu of their claims upon the Phelp estate. Cherry however continued to pursue Phelp vigorously to obtain his wife Eleanora's share of money. As Ellen put it: 'Nothing will satisfy Mr Cherry but our immediate annihilation.'[73] Soon debt would force them to move to France.

At the end of 1820, Powell's younger sister, Anne, married Roderick Eardley Richardes of Penglais at Llanbadarn church. Her dowry (if it was ever paid) would have cost the estate £5000.[74] The witnesses were Henrietta Maurice, Richard Owen Powell and Nanteos agent George Warbrick. In London, Powell's maternal grandfather, Edward Maurice Corbet died, aged 79.[75] Another Phelp girl, Octavia also married, a Major Archibald Crawfurd of the East India Company's Artillery. Her life was not long, for by 1826 her sister Fanny alluded to the news that 'we hear from Mrs Crawfurd that Archibald is now at St Thomas' Mount near Madras with his little boy, and as he is not likely to be called into service again. He says the dear child is the image of its poor mother in appearance and disposition, and so remarkably healthy that there is no intention of sending him to England.'[76]

Less than two years later, her sons just seven and five years old, Laura Powell died on 8 September 1822, aged 35 and was buried ten days later at Llanbadarn Fawr.[77] The possibility that her death was at least part self-inflicted is hinted in a paragraph from W. E. Cherry to Powell at Curzon Street on 12 August 1821: 'We are much concerned to hear so bad an account of Laura. Mr Tupper I apprehend is a competent judge of her case, and I should hope that jointly with Sir Wm Knighton he will set her up again. I hope she does not owe her suffering to any violent medicines which have been administered.'[78]

So what was Powell up to while his wife ailed and feuded, fretted about her total impecuniosity, and died? Janet Joel has identified the existence of a parallel family, that of Mary Selina Gennet, of Brittania Street, London (just off Gray's Inn Road), whose four children born 1816, 1819, 1825, and 1830 were all baptised as children of William Edward Powell.[79] Laura's letter of 4 May 1820 acknowledged, cordially, a Mary, of whom she wrote 'is she as fascinating as you used to find her?' Sadly for the marriage, it appears he found her even more so, but insulated by 200 miles of countryside, he held his wife in ignorance of the situation, at least for a while. However he may have treated his mistress little more generously than his wife. In 1825 he was being pursued by the Parish Officers of

Camberwell for the support of 'Mrs P' and her children, who had been receiving parochial relief for their support. On 4 August S. Allen of Bayswater wrote to Powell at his club, the United Service Club, Regent's Street:

> My Dear Sir, I am just returned from seeing Mrs P. who informed me she had been before the Parish officers of Camberwell three times and had sworn the children to you and had actually received Parochial relief for their support. The Overseers will not apply to you before Friday next in order to give the Attorney an opportunity of settling the affair and he is to endeavour to see you today and to adjust the business if possible without its going any further. She told me that the landlord had consented to wait till the 12th of this month for the Quarters rent amounting to £5-5-0 and if this is not paid on that day her goods are to be taken in distress, she is likewise in daily expectation of being annoyed for £4-9-0 for the Attorney's Bill for the Marshalls – a business – altogether she appears in a very woeful plight indeed. P.S. pray don't avoid seeing the officer from the Parish on Friday or a Warrant will be issued.[80]

This 'Mrs P.' could be Mary Gennet. Four years later, on 15 March 1829, Powell further acknowledged this second family by christening his three illegitimate sons, Edward William, Frederick James and Henry William under the surname Gennet or Powell, at St Leonards, Shoreditch.[81] The boys would have been 13, 10 and 4 years of age at the time.

Powell's finances had lurched from bad to worse during the last years of Laura's life. A letter of 1821 from W.G. Cherry contains his categorical refusal to get his personal finances in any way embroiled as security for Powell loans, but he does suggest one or two remaining assets which could be mortgaged, namely the furniture at Curzon Street, and the freehold of the mines.[82] Powell's mother Eleanor was also desperate for money. In 1823 the sheriff's officers were at the Nanteos door, and only the sale of unentailed lands in Montgomeryshire averted Powell's bankruptcy.[83]

Following Laura's death Powell seems to have taken but perfunctory interest in his children, whose progress is principally charted by the letters of their doting maiden aunts, Julia and Fanny. Mrs Phelp senior also took an interest in her grandsons' conduct and the Nanteos housekeeper Ann Southern found herself under attack. She replied extremely defensively to Mrs Phelp's allegation concerning young master Powell's language:

> In reply to your enquiry respecting Dear Master Powell I have no hesitation in saying that I never heard him make use of *any words* unbecoming to a child of his consequence, therefore whatever impressions Mrs M may have contracted, it must have been *since* he went to school, and I am surprised Mr Pollard should insinuate to the contrary. I can further say that the Elegance of his address and Manners were much spoken of by several Ladies (who travelled in their own carriage) with whom he got acquainted . . . indeed one Lady in particular told me that she *never* met with *so elegant* a mannered boy in her life, and that his Parents must be very proud of him.[84]

W.T.R. Powell was now at school, at Totteridge, not far from Hadley, Barnet, north of London, where Mrs Phelp and her unmarried daughters resided, when not visiting the O'Briens at Blatherwycke or the Cherrys at Buckland; it seems that the Phelp women took over care of the two boys. On October 1 1824 Julia Phelp wrote:

> William went to school in good spirits, we gave him five shillings and he seemed to think himself in great luck to get as much. Cornelius is very well, his nose a little more stuffed than usual . . . The five pounds you sent – there is a little left after paying the lodgings and the shoe bill, washing, and twelve shillings to Nathaniel who poor man was quite powerless to recommend what we think of spending upon shoes for Cornelius. I am sorry to say his wants are rather prominent – he must have a new hat and great coat and a set of clothes the latter had better be like William's. Eleanora has kindly offered to get him a few things out of her private purse and run the risk of having payed again so we have begged her to send him some pantaloons and new collars to his shirts which will be a great help to us.[85]

For the next two years Julia's regular letters to Powell express care and affection for her nephews. In summer 1825 Powell had the boys at Nanteos, and Julia wrote: 'I am very glad to find you are so comfortable and happy and of course very gay as Aberystwyth season has begun. I am rejoiced to hear the dear Boys are so well, I quite long to see Cornelius again all his ideas will be so changed . . . I can fancy Nanteos looking beautiful, I should indeed like to see it again but I fear the remembrance of past happy days would make me feel most melencholy'.[86]

The following summer, having rejected the matrimonial advances of a Mr Dickens, Julia wrote to say how much they looked forward to their forthcoming visit to Nanteos, but expressing disquiet about William's personal and material well-being: 'William came to us on Thursday and stayed till Sunday, he came with the same borrowed *old* cap we were obliged to get him a hat, he was a very good boy but dull, and in my opinion *too quiet*. He talks of his holidays and hopes to spend them at Nanteos, – his clothes are getting very shabby.'[87]

That summer at Nanteos cannot have been tranquil for just as Julia and Fanny and their mother arrived at Nanteos, Powell quarrelled with William Cherry, who was soon displaced as trustee, and replaced by James Hughes of Glanrheidol. Much unpleasantness ensued as an attempt was made to disentangle suspect dealings of the past. On August 8 1826 Powell received from Eleanora Cherry a stirring defence of her husband and a description of his wounded feelings.[88] She also wrote to her sister Fanny at Nanteos, stating 'In all probability, I shall now never see Nanteos again . . . I little thought that all my husband has done would be met with such a return'.[89] Both Fanny and Mrs Phelp also wrote to Powell urging a reconciliation with Cherry. One of the bones of contention, the Nanteos plate, was at Buckland at this time, and according to Eleanora was being returned, by instalments to Nanteos. The slur is there that Cherry may have sought to appropriate it.

From 1828, two years after the rift with Cherry, there survive a bundle of letters from Mrs Southern to the lawyer Victor Lozon, itemising her and other peoples' recollections (in some cases posthumous ones) of items which Cherry may have acquired at too favourable a price from a sale at Nanteos in 1820, and whether they had been sold at open auction or not.[90] This rift, with Cherry, as

W.T.R. Powell 1815-78
by William Roos.

bitter as that which had opened between Laura and her brother Edward five years before, seems once again to have been fanned by the contribution of Mrs Southern. Edward and Ellen by this time lived in exile near Dieppe with their children, mixing with many other impoverished gentry fugitives to vanquished France. Ellen was on hand to deal with the clearing up of affairs upon her mother Eleanor Powell's death at Calais in 1826; her social circle on the Normandy coast included many Cardiganshire names, the Boultbees, Roderick and Anne Richardes, and even Mr Ramsay, Anne's former suitor.[91]

From 1827-29 Powell resumed his policy of developing assets in Aberystwyth, leasing for sixty years land for gentlemen's townhouses on the east side of Castle field (now Laura Place), and modest workers' plots in New Street (now

High Street), Market Street and Castle Lane. He had already, in 1824 leased a plot of land to his brother Richard to build a dwelling south of Castle House, and undertaken to protect the views from this and the Assembly Rooms.[92] The new leases for nine new houses carried an undertaking on Powell's part to lay out by 1 June 1829 a pleasure ground on the north and west side of the former field, and contiguous with the castle grounds, for the use of the residents of the houses and the Assembly Rooms. Possibly it salved his conscience to name it Laura Gardens (now Laura Place). At Nanteos there was still a Phelp kinsman looking after the usually absent William Edward Powell's affairs, but now it was Lieutenant Cecil Phelp R.N., who reported on the game and advised what instructions should be given to the new agent Mr Pughe. Cecil even indicated a brief flirtation with the urge to earn his own living, asking Powell if he could procure him a situation suitable for a gentleman such as himself, possibly in Customs and Excise.[93]

"Confound these Midges" October 22 1872: One of the many humorous sketches executed by W.T.R. Powell in later life and preserved in his scrapbooks.
N.L.W.

October 22ⁿᵈ 1872 Confound these Midges *W.T.R. Powell Aant. 803*

It is a rare ray of cheer in the years of debt and acrimonious correspondence that on 25 March 1829, the fourteen year old W.T.R. Powell wrote to his father from school at Totteridge: ' I am very well and hope you are the same. I am very much obliged to you for the 10s that you sent me. There is now a master at Mr London's that can draw most beautifully, so there I hope that I may begin to learn to draw.

Mr and Mrs London are both very well, will you be so kind as to write soon and tell me whether I am to come home for the Easter holidays or no. Give my love to Aunt Fanny.'[94] In 1830, at the advanced age of 15 W.T.R. Powell was admitted to Westminster School. Unlike his father he remained only two years and did not go on the Oxford, but enlisted as an Ensign in the 37th Regiment of Foot, eventually retiring as Captain seven years later.[95] This far from prestigious education indicates how little his father was willing or able to pay.

W.T.R. Powell did indeed learn to draw, very creditably, and has left to posterity three scrapbooks embossed with his father's initials, in which are pasted pen and ink impressions from his experiences with the 37th Regiment in Madeira and the West Indies, and from his wheelchair-bound middle age when, even while holidaying in Europe, it seems Cardiganshire, Nanteos and foxhunting were seldom far from his thoughts.[96] These books have a dedication in their frontispiece 'to entertain the ladies of my, that is, the Welsh nation' and contain an ingredient, humour, undetectable in any of the other Nanteos papers. Particularly appealing are his pictorial representations of his sleeping brain whirling with images of plays and pantomimes viewed during Christmas in town, or of his beloved Nanteos overrun with every imaginable form of poacher whilst the keeper sleeps peacefully beneath a tree. They may be viewed as a redeeming feature in the light of the poor character which posterity, and particularly his rather peculiar son George, bestowed upon him.

By the end of the decade, William Edward Powell's financial situation had improved from the nadir at around the time of Laura's death, when even his mother and his younger brother Richard were pursuing claims against him. His mother was now dead, and in 1828 his younger brother Richard Owen Powell, (who had also been applying to all possible relations for money), married, quite wisely,

Going to Tregaron Market. Cardiganshire

Sketch by W.T.R. Powell dated 1866 in his New Book of Nonsense. Sketches subtitled "Jenny Jones and Betsy Evans mounted astride on Gallant Gray on their way to Tregaron Market. Hughkin Thomas, in attendance, would like bigamy abolished!"

N.L.W.

Harriet Ann, third daughter of William Wynne Esq., of Peniarth.[97] They resided in Richard's new house at Laura Place and christened their children Eleanor Laura on 14 October 1829 and Athelstan John on 4 June 1832 at St Michael's.[98] [Richard Powell's second son, William Beauclerk Powell, was eventually to inherit Nanteos from aesthete George Powell in 1882, while Cornelius' son Cornelius le Brun Powell at the same time inherited Sunny Hill, Tregaron.][99] For the hard-pressed Edward Phelp and his wife Ellen, things had yet to take a further turn for the worse. Cecil had found, not a job, but a Miss Knight willing to marry him, and had in consequence led her family to believe he was in certain expectation of his £5000. His elder brother, proprietor of a bankrupt estate, stared ruin in the face, and, as he wrote from France to his brother-in-law Powell:

> a dozen people are all in jeopardy because Mr Cecil Phelp is to be handsomely provided for – I am sure no conduct of

mine or Ellen can deserve the ruin and spoilation inflicted upon us. However as we must both, as well as the Children contend now with comparative poverty, I should wish you to see my friend Cragg to consult as regards your sister what is best to be done. Of course I have no means to support my present establishment. We must even pledge to sell all the valuables we can muster to enable us to get rid of the said establishment, and furnish us with the means of retiring to such a state of life as befits us. I am willing to conform to the wishes of Ellen or as my friends think best, if to come to England, it will be necessary for me to go through the Ordeal of Prison etc. etc. – which, as it attaches no blame or dishonour to me, I care nothing about – if I had nobody to care for but myself I should have long ago left these affairs to themselves, but have hitherto struggled as in duty bound, for my wife and children, having really no personal interest myself being long ago perfectly sacrificed.'[100]

It was a middle-aged William Edward Powell who returned to live permanently at Nanteos in 1830. The last of Powell's children by Mary Selina Gennet, a daughter christened Emma Mary, was born that year. The Gennet family eventually emigrated to New Zealand.[101] At Nanteos, Powell occupied the rôle of Lord Lieutenant and improving country gentleman, and undertook many alterations to his estate. He also promoted another surge of building in Aberystwyth, selling leases in Little Darkgate Street (now Eastgate), Market Street and Marine Terrace.

In the light of the antipathy which had accompanied W.G. Cherry's resignation as his trustee, it may not have pleased Powell that his son and heir W.T.R. Powell married, in May 1839, Rosa Edwyna Cherry, the elder daughter of his former friend, though the fact that Rosa Edwyna was co-heir of Cherry's estate must have sweetened the pill. In any case Powell was soon to follow his son's example, marrying, in 1841, very probably for money, Harriett Dell Ackers, widow of George Ackers Esq. of Moreton Hall, Cheshire.[102] When W.T.R. Powell's daughter was christened in 1844, she was given the names of her step-grandmother and of her mother, Harriet Edwyna.[103] She died in 1857 to be survived by her brother George.

Following William Edward Powell's second marriage, architects Coultart and Haycock were both busy at Nanteos and the house, grounds and gardens were well maintained. Powell died in 1854, aged 66, a highly respected man, father of two legitimate sons, Member of Parliament and Lord Lieutenant of the County for thirty-eight years. His widow, Harriet Dell Powell, erected a handsome memorial to him on the south wall of Llanbadarn church. It extols his many virtues: 'Philanthropy, integrity and consistency marked his public career. Charity, gentleness and kindness were the qualities that in private life gained him universal love and esteem'. There is a far more modest memorial to

W.E.Powell in old age
N.L.W.

Laura Powell high on the east wall above the altar. It offers no remarks upon her character, and was possibly erected long after her death to accompany a slightly smaller plaque commemorating her grandaughter, the thirteen year old Harriet Edwyna.

The fate of Edward Phelp is unknown, but Ellen lived to a very great age and was corresponding from Cheltenham with her nephew W.T.R. Powell in her own only slightly shaky hand in 1875.[104] Her second son William Edward Phelp, though raised half his childhood in France, became a Major in the Leicestershire Militia and later reappeared in Cardiganshire as the wheelchair-bound W.T.R. Powell's able-bodied agent. For many years he lived at Sunny Hill, Tregaron, and received £250 a year for managing the Nanteos estate. The two elderly double-cousins may be pictured at Nanteos in 1875, hosting a highly acclaimed fancy dress ball at which the dance music was played by the band of the Leicestershire Militia, and the guests supped at midnight in the long gallery on the first floor, and went home at dawn.[105] They both died aged 62, William Thomas Rowland Powell, on 18 May 1878, and William Edward Phelp on 5 December 1879, and were buried at Llanbadarn Church.

NOTES

1 *The Gentleman's Magazine*, 1797 (i) 439.

2 *The Gentleman's Magazine*, 1796 (ii) 787.

3 Burke, J. *History of the Landed Gentry*, 1838.

4 N.L.W. Bonsall Deeds 111.

5 N.L.W. N.L.165.

6 N.L.W. N.L.167.

7 N.L.W. N.L.174.

8 N.L.W. N.L.175.

9 N.L.W. N.L. 176.

10 N.L.W. N.L.177.

11 N.L.W. N.L.188.

12 N.L.W. N.L.191.

13 Malkin, B.H. 1804 *The Scenery, Antiquities and Biography of South Wales*.

14 N.L.W. N.L.686, 779.

15 N.L.W. N.L.802.

16 N.L.W. N.L.1059.

17 N.L.W. N.L.1060.

18 N.L.W. N.L.786.

19 N.L.W. N.L.787.

20 N.L.W. N.L.1060.

21 N.L.W. N.L.664.

22 N.L.W. N.L. 271.

23 N.L.W. N.L. 269.

24 N.L.W. N.L.5343.

25 N.L.W. Nanteos Map 79.

26 N.L.W. Nanteos Map 78.

27 N.L.W. N.L. 266.

28 *The Gentleman's Magazine*, 1810 (i) 479.

29 N.L.W. Bishop's transcripts: diocese of Llandaff.

30 *The Gentleman's Magazine* 1810 (ii) 382.

31 N.L.W. N.L.269.

32 NLW Nanteos A1, manuscript boxes 3,16,22 .

33 Palmer, C.D. *in prep.*

34 NLW N.L.273.

35 *The Gentleman's Magazine* 1811 (i) 182.

36 No bishop's transcripts survive, and Llanbadarn Fawr parish records appear incomplete.

37 N.L.W. N.L.665.

38 N.L.W. N.L.195A.

39 *The Gentleman's Magazine* 1813 (i) 179.

40 *The Gentlemens Magazine* 1814 (i) 621.

41 N.L.W. N.L.1063.

42 N.L.W. N.L.1074.

43 N.L.W. N.L.763-773.

44 See chapter 8.

[45] N.L.W. N.L.1062.

[46] Bishop's transcripts, parish of Llanbadarn Fawr.

[47] N.L.W. N.L.667.

[48] D.Gorman. 'William Powell of Nanteos and Public Affairs in Early Nineteenth Century Cardiganshire', *N.L.W.J.* XXIX, (i) 1995, 119-123.

[49] *The Gentleman's Magazine* 1817 (i) 370.

[50] N.L.W. N.L.1078.

[51] Bishop's transcripts, parish of Llanbadarn Fawr.

[52] N.L.W. N.L.1133.

[53] N.L.W. N.L. 1249, 1253.

[54] N.L.W. N.L.1134.

[55] N.L.W. N.L.1077.

[56] International Genealogical Index.

[57] Bishop's transcripts, parish of Llanbadarn Fawr.

[58] N.L.W. N.L.1042.

[59] N.L.W. N.L.1135.

[60] NLW Nanteos A1.

[61] H.Colvin, *A Biographical Dictionary of British Architects* (Yale, 1995), 801b; NLW N.L.970.

[62] Lloyd Evans, M. *Llanerchaeron,* Y Lolfa 1996

[63] *Oswestry Herald*, 18 April 1820, 21 August 1821.

[64] N.L.W. N.L.1136.

[65] N.L.W. N.L.750.

[66] N.L.W. N.L.1137.

[67] 'Richard' i.e. R.O.Powell, her brother-in-law.

[68] Laura Powell's obligation to pay 'the woman who nurses the housemaid's child' might suggest a claim of paternity, rather than a household exceptionally generous even *in extremis*.

[69] N.L.W. N.L.1138.

[70] N.L.W. N.L.1139.

[71] N.L.W. N.L.1064.

[72] N.L.W. N.L.1086.

[73] N.L.W. N.L.1065.

[74] R.J. [Moore-] Colyer: 'Roderick Eardley Richardes and Plas Penglais, Aberystwyth'. *Ceredigion* X, 1984, 99-103.

[75] *The Gentleman's Magazine* 1820 (ii) 572.

[76] N.L.W. N.L.1091, Octavia's sketchbook, chiefly of European scenes, survives, N.L.W. Nanteos 119.

[77] Bishop's transcripts, parish of Llanbadarn Fawr.

[78] N.L.W. N.L.545.

[79] Janet Joel, *Nanteos*, privately published, 1995.

[80] N.L.W. N.L.249.

[81] International Genealogical Index.

[82] N.L.W. N.L.547.

[83] See Chapter 5.

[84] N.L.W. N.L.1187.

[85] N.L.W. N.L.1046. Julia Phelp's letters are incorrectly scheduled as being by 'Cecily' Phelp, the error having arisen from a misreading of Julia's name, which she was in the habit of writing backwards!

[86] N.L.W. N.L.1047.

[87] N.L.W. N.L.1051.

[88] N.L.W. N.L.654.

[89] N.L.W. N.L.665.

[90] N.L.W. N.L.1510,1511, 1512.

[91] N.L.W. N.L.1066-1069.

[92] This building is now divided between a private home and the offices of the U.W.Aberystwyth Department of Continuing Education.

[93] N.L.W. N.L.1043.

[94] N.L.W. N.L.1144.

[95] Westminster School Records.

[96] W.T.R. Powell's scrapbooks N.L.W. Nanteos 45,46,47.

[97] *The Gentleman's Magazine* 1828 (i) 44

[98] Bishop's transcripts, parish of St Michael's Aberystwyth.

[99] *Burke's Landed Gentry*, 1937.

[100] N.L.W. N.L.1089.

[101] Janet Joel, *op.cit.*

[102] *The Gentleman's Magazine* 1841 (i) 648.

[103] Bishop's transcripts, parish of St Michael's Aberystwyth.

[104] N.L.W. N.L. 2634

[105] Carmarthen Journal 17 September 1875

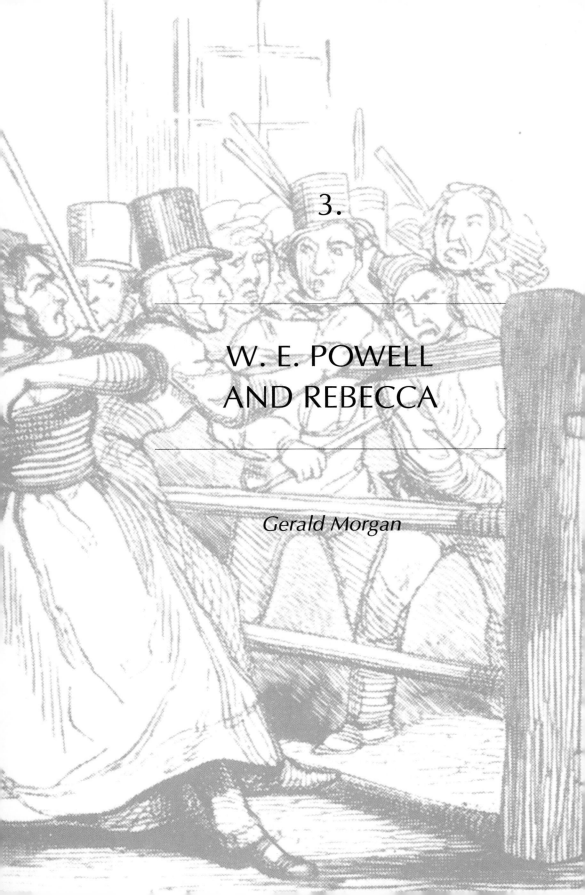

3.

W. E. POWELL
AND REBECCA

Gerald Morgan

*Rebecca Rioters as
depicted at the time in the
Illustrated London News.*

W. E. POWELL AND REBECCA

ALTHOUGH only one of William Edward Powell's forebears, his great-uncle Thomas (1699-1752), had been a Member of Parliament, and that only briefly, the family had a century and more of political involvement within the county. By this is meant, not involvement with a political party as such, because no such thing existed at a local level, and is not really recognisable (in modern terms) at national level. Rather, local politics meant 'interest', the concern of the wealthiest and most influential families to secure the highest offices available, namely the Lord Lieutenancy and the county and borough representation in parliament. Elections were to be avoided, since they were so expensive, and a parliament might be brief; instead, a prospective candidate cultivated the families of influence to secure, if possible, an unopposed election. This did not mean an absence of labour or expense. When in 1784 W.E.Powell's father, Thomas, sought to displace the first Earl of Lisburne from the county seat, there was a great flurry of letter-writing and canvassing, which involved some costs, before the Earl could rest easy.[1] It may be that Thomas Powell realised that the disenfranchisement of the borough of Tregaron in 1731 meant that it was futile to attempt the borough seat, but it was equally futile for him to have contemplated displacing the Lisburne interest in the county.

W.E.Powell avenged his father's defeat by taking the county seat unopposed in 1816 following the death of Thomas Johnes of Hafod, the sitting member.[2] John Vaughan of Trawsgoed, second son of the first Earl of Lisburne, was already the borough member, and when he withdrew in 1818, he was replaced by Pryse Pryse of Gogerddan. The Vaughan family was in some disarray; the second earl of Lisburne was a certified lunatic in the care of guardians, and his younger brother, although *de facto* head of the family, could not pay off the growing burden of debt which lay on his estate, and which he had increased by gambling. This meant a power vacuum in county politics, and Powell, having taken the county seat, was able to fill that vacuum. He was appointed Lord Lieutenant of Cardiganshire, a Crown appointment which he held, along with his unopposed tenure of the county seat, thus achieving for the first time the primacy of Nanteos in local affairs. It was unfortunate for the estate that his responsibilities were expensive; entertainment at Nanteos was a frequent duty, as was giving money to numerous charities.

When not in London, Powell took his responsibilities seriously, being a member of most bodies involved in local government. The lord lieutenancy involved him in the appointment of magistrates and deputy Lieutenants. He also played a prominent rôle in the Royal Cardigan Militia. He provided land in Aberystwyth for the second St Michael's church (replaced by the present building in 1890) and provided a new Corn Market building in 1832. He was briefly a town improvements commissioner, but the gentry were already being squeezed out by the growing merchant class in the town, typified in the figure of Thomas Jones, junior (1803-80), shipowner, timber merchant and minor industrialist.[3] Powell resigned from the House of Commons and the lord lieutenancy a few months before his death in 1854. He had always been recognisably a Conservative; for example, he voted for agricultural protection in 1846.

Like most M.Ps, Powell was little concerned with day-to-day House of Commons politics, but his position as Lord Lieutenant of Cardiganshire meant that when trouble broke out in south Wales in 1843, he was in direct contact with Government. Virtually all the counties of Wales had experienced unrest at some time or another during the previous half-century. There were riots in Aberystwyth in 1795 and 1816, enclosure riots on the Mynydd Bach in 1814, and in Llansanffraid and Cilcennin parishes in 1816. Augustus Brackenbury's new house, Waun Las, was destroyed by rioters in 1820, and the 'Rhyfel y Sais Bach' (War of the Little Englishman) disturbances continued into 1821, and flared up again in 1826, when Brackenbury finally gave up the struggle and sold his land.[4]

Prior to the outbreak of the Rebecca Riots in 1843, Powell had already gained some experience of dealing with Government at a time of unrest. In 1819 the civil turbulence which followed the Napoleonic Wars had not died down. The shortage of land and the rapidly increasing population exacerbated unrest to such a degree that in that year Powell appealed to the Home Secretary for military assistance. Troops had previously been used in Aberystwyth as recently as 1816. In 1819 Powell was urged by the Home Secretary to persuade the gentry of Cardiganshire to form a corps of yeomanry.[5] However, although bodies of yeomanry still existed in some counties, their day was over; within a few years counties would begin to feel the pressure to establish county police forces, as W.E.Powell was to find. In 1820 Powell took the depositions of Augustus Brackenbury complaining of the mob which had burnt his house, and forwarded the complaint to Lord Sidmouth, the Home Secretary.[6] I can trace no further direct involvement of Powell in the Brackenbury affair.

The Rebecca riots were the outcome of a period of general rural distress and a number of particular grievances, especially among tenant and small freehold farmers. Changes to the Poor Law were widely resisted. The narrow class allegiance of the magistracy came under criticism. Farmers were upset by the commutation of tithes, which meant the imposition of financial charges often felt to be unfairly levied. However their loudest single complaint was against the proliferation of turnpike or toll roads, with their inevitable bars, gates and charges. This process had begun in Cardiganshire in 1780, but the generation which saw the improvement or creation of roads had died, while the multiplication of tolls cost farmers much of the profits they made at fairs and markets.

The Rebecca disturbances in Cardiganshire were petty compared with such outbreaks as the Scotch Cattle in Monmouthshire, the Merthyr riots of 1831, or the Newport rising of 1839. Nor indeed did Rebecca have anything like the impact within Cardiganshire that she had in Carmarthenshire. However the practice of the *ceffyl pren*, that riotous communal disciplining of recalcitrant folk, was well established in the south of the county, and was seen both at the time, and by the historian of Rebecca, as a source of the rioting.[7] Prior to the outbreak of Rebecca rioting in 1839 (in Pembrokeshire) there had been disturbances in Cardigan in 1837 and in Llangoedmor in

1838, which caused the magistrates to beg London for help from the metropolitan police.

The 1839 outbreak of tollgate-breaking did not provoke imitation in Cardiganshire. However, in October 1842 arson at Llanllŷr caused the government and the magistrates to offer large rewards for information, but in vain. Rebecca became active again in Carmarthenshire and Pembrokeshire, and in May 1843 the Teifi valley saw the breaking of gates at Pont-tyweli and Troedrhiwgribyn. In June gates were destroyed at Newcastle Emlyn and Felindre Siencyn; troops arrived at Carmarthen, dragoons were sent to Newcastle Emlyn, and marines sailed from Pembroke Dock to Cardigan.

Rebecca and her daughters were not deterred. On June 21 they broke three gates on the Newcastle-Cardigan road, and two nights later they demolished two gates in the town of Cardigan. Edward Crompton Lloyd Hall, a lawyer in Newcastle Emlyn, was in the confidence of the local farmers, and in September he wrote to the Home Secretary claiming that Rebecca was pulling down toll-houses 'almost nightly' – referring to the situation in south-west Wales generally. The Misses Walters of Perthceraint, near Penbryn in the south of the county, complained to Powell of a terrifying demonstration at their home by Rebecca's followers, who had demanded the payment of a debt of one pound to a local widow due twenty years earlier; this is local evidence of a tendency to use Rebecca's complaints as an excuse for paying off old scores.[8]

On 15 September Sir James Graham at the Home Office wrote to W.E.Powell expressing sympathy with the farmers' grievances, particularly against rent charges and bars on side roads. Although Colonel J.F.Love, in charge of the troops, reported to Powell that all was quiet in Cardiganshire, Edward Lloyd Williams of Gwarnant Park wrote that he had been threatened by the daughters of Rebecca if he did not reduce his rents. He claimed to have made peaceable agreements with farmers and labourers.

Hitherto Rebecca had confined her activities to the Teifi valley, but on 15 September 1843 rioters struck in Llan-non, destroying a toll-gate there. Two months later an English lad who had been working at Gwern-llaeth farm denounced the farmer's son, Isaac Evans, to the authorities. Evans was arrested and brought before the magistrates in December. However, the magistrates acted foolishly in confining the witness, for his own safety but against his will, in Cardigan gaol; the youngster refused to testify and the case against Evans collapsed.

In October 1843 Powell wrote to the Lord Chancellor asking him to appoint additional magistrates, enclosing a list of suitable names, and the following month he received a favourable reply; at the same time (12 October), Major-General Sir George Brown sent a number of Metropolitan Police to be under Powell's command, while the following

---

TO THE
Gentlemen, Clergy, Freeholders, And other Electors
OF THE COUNTY OF CARDIGAN.

GENTLEMEN,

An early dissolution of the present Parliament being generally expected, I again take leave to solicit your suffrages for my re-election as your Representative.

This distinguished honor having been confided to me for more than thirty years, renders unnecessary a declaration of the principles which animate me in seeking its continuance.

Though recent events have dissevered parties, and given rise to conflicting opinions with reference to our Domestic Policy, be assured of my continued firm attachment to the Monarchy, and Protestant Institutions of the Country, with a great anxiety to promote the just interests of every class of our fellow subjects, and to encourage and aid in effecting your local improvements and prosperity.

I have the honor to be,

GENTLEMEN,

Your faithful Servant,

Nanteos,
17th July, 1847.

W. E. POWELL.

J. COX, PRINTER, PIER STREET, ABERYSTWYTH.

Election Poster, 1847.
N.L.W.

day 'all posts in Cardiganshire [were] to be occupied by troops the next day'. The Cardiganshire magistrates demonstrated their sense of priorities by refusing, on 17 October, to establish a rural constabulary, fearing the permanent expense; instead they agree to swear in special constables. However, the excitement of those responsible for law and order seemed to be self-generating: on 19 October General Brown wrote:

> I have desired Colonel Love to reinforce the Company of Infantry at Aberestwith and Aberayron, so as to enable it to furnish the Ports at Llanrhystid, Llanarth and New Inn. The Marines from Cardigan will furnish the [?Boat] at Blaunporth and as they will have several other Detachments to furnish on the Pembroke side a portion of Cavalry from Newcastle will be sent to Cardigan. Finally a Company of Infantry is moving on Lampeter with directions to furnish Detachments for Tregaron, Ystrad and Llandyssil.[9]

Powell was faced with several dilemmas. The government was under pressure to put the rioting down, even though the justice of the rioters' main complaints was privately admitted, and they expected Powell's cooperation and leadership in the county. The presence of troops and police involved cost to individuals and to the county purse; the magistrates over whom he presided were unwilling to establish a police force, especially after the apparent restoration of order by December 1843. Powell himself was a turnpike trustee; his father had used his influence in order to close the old road past Nanteos mansion, replacing it with the present road from Southgate to New Cross.[10]

Rebecca was not dead in Cardiganshire, however, but merely resting. On the night of 26 March, 1844, a gate at Pen-parc, Cardigan, was destroyed. Powell received two accounts on successive days from W.C.Freeman. The first reported the incident, discovered by Inspector Partridge of the Metropolitan Police. Next day Freeman wrote again, regretting that the malefactors had not been traced:

> An old woman and her daughter are the only two who apper to have seen any body that morning, they two came to the gate on the Aberayron side and had been in Cardigan

watching a corpse till between 3 and 4 oclock, when they returned home, and whilst undressing they observed from the window some half a dozen people dressed as women pass down towards the gate, and after the lapse of half an hour return with the gate on their shoulders, which they carried to the beginning of the Common and there destroyed.[11]

This had happened despite the presence of forty marines in the town. When Sir James Graham heard the details, he wrote to Powell pointing out that the gate had been so situated that travellers to Ferwig and Mwnt had to pay even though they only used fifty yards of the turnpike road. Graham invited Powell to use his influence to rectify the problem and have the gate moved. This was the last appearance of Rebecca in Cardiganshire. However, the magistrates had already yielded to the pressure to establish a police force, and on 2 January 1844 the Quarter Sessions agreed to appoint a chief constable, a superintendant and sixteen constables, who were sworn in on 5 March.[12]

Rebecca's work was done. Tollgate breaking was replaced by public meetings; the government was anxious to remedy the turnpike grievance once order had been restored, and eventually South Wales was better off for toll-free roads than much of the kingdom. The other main effect of the riots in Cardiganshire had been the creation, sooner than the magistrates had been willing, of a regular police force.

NOTES

[1] Gerald Morgan, *A Welsh House and its Family: the Vaughans of Trawsgoed* (Llandysul, 1997) 119-21.

[2] Although unopposed at the poll, Powell had had to canvass vigorously to achieve the nomination; for this, and Powell's local activities, see D.Gorman, 'William Powell of Nanteos and public affairs in early nineteenth-century Cardiganshire', *National Library of Wales Journal* XXIX, i (1995) 119-24.

[3] Gerald Morgan, 'Thomas Jones, Shipowner', *Maritime Wales* 15 (1995) 28-50.

[4] See David Jones, *Before Rebecca: Popular Protests in Wales 1793-1835* (London, 1973) passim.

[5] Ibid., p.183.

[6] David Williams, 'Rhyfel y Sais Bach', *Ceredigion* II, 1 (1952) 41.

[7] David Williams, *The Rebecca Riots* (Cardiff, 1955) 56. This authoritative work, and the Nanteos archive, are the sources of what follows. Rather than include endless footnotes, I refer the reader to the N.L.W. Nanteos Schedule, vol.I, nos. 1271-1346.

[8] Francis Jones, 'Walters of Perthceraint', *Ceredigion* VI, 2 (1969), 185.

[9] N.L.W. N.L.1306.

[10] N.L.W. Cardiganshire County Road Book A1, 9 February 1789.

[11] N.L.W. N.L. 1324.

[12] W.E.J.Williams, 'History and Development of the Cardiganshire Police Force 1844-1958', typscript dated March 1970 in Ceredigion Record Office ADX/165.

4.

THE AESTHETE
OF NANTEOS:
GEORGE POWELL
(1842-1882)

GEORGE POWELL

THE most extraordinary figure in Nanteos history is that of the artistic dilettante George Ernest John Powell, for four years squire of Nanteos, whose remarkable behaviour has not hitherto been examined in detail, save for his interest in art.[1] Who after all would have expected the son of a Tory Cardiganshire squire to have promoted Icelandic literature and financed the Icelandic independence movement, to have made the acquaintance of Wagner, Offenbach and Clara Schumann, and to have befriended Algernon Swinburne, to have corresponded with Longfellow, to have cultivated the memory of the Marquis de Sade and to have fed roast monkey flesh to Guy de Maupassant?

Little is known of George Powell's childhood. Born on February 10, 1842, he was educated at home by his mother before being sent to Eton in 1855, and it is reasonable to suppose that his adult interest in flagellation began at that brutal school. In 1860 he went up to Brasenose College, Oxford, but did not graduate. In that and the following year he published three volumes of verse best described as juvenilia: *Quod Libet* and *Poems First Series*, both printed in 1860 by John Cox of Aberystwyth, the latter under the pseudonym Miolnir, and *Poems Second Series* under the same pseudonym in the following year, also from Cox's press. Powell would certainly have paid for these publications himself. The poems are more remarkable for the fact of their being the work of the son of Nanteos than in showing any literary merit. The sentiments expressed are banal, the techniques unimpressive, the results forgettable, although one or two of his loyal friends proclaimed him the equal of Swinburne and Browning. Nevertheless, the very likelihood of a son of any nineteenth-century Welsh squire publishing volumes of teenage verse must have seemed remote, though his father was unusual enough in that he sketched prolifically and dabbled in comic versifying. George Powell's mid-Victorian adolescent swooning verses were however of a very different brand.

Powell's choice of pseudonym is more interesting; Mjolnir is the Icelandic name of Thor's hammer, and demonstrates that by 1860, at the age of eighteen, Powell had encountered the Icelandic legends in whose

Opposite: George Powell (left) with Algernon Swinburne.

N.L.W.

93

George Powell in early adulthood.

N.L.W.

dissemination to a wider audience he was to play an important part. European scholars had demonstrated an interest in Icelandic and Norse literature as early as 1636, and by the time of George Powell's adolescence some knowledge of the subject had been long established in English through the poetry of Thomas Gray and H.W.Longfellow, the translations of Bishop Percy and the writings of Thomas Warton, Samuel Laing and Thomas Carlyle. Even as Powell's youthful interest grew, Matthew Arnold and James Russell Lowell were writing poetry inspired by Norse material. George Powell's adolescent interest in Icelandic culture grew remarkably in the next few years.[2]

GEORGE POWELL

That same year of 1860, incidentally, was the year of his mother's death, while in 1863 his coming of age was celebrated at Nanteos. His mother had been for some years separated from his father, and according to his close Icelandic friend Eirikur Magnusson, writing many years later, George would express the tenderest feelings for his mother, and rage at the wrongs inflicted on her by his father, W.T.R. Powell. However, despite Magnusson's evidence, it seems that in 1860, George was on reasonable terms with his father, so it is not easy to decide when this breach between father and son occurred, nor exactly why. An affectionate letter to his father from Brasenose College, Oxford, about the time of his mother's death, shows that the alienation must have occurred later.[3]

In 1862 Powell travelled to Iceland for a short tour, and either then or during the following year he sent a parcel of books to H.W. Longfellow, to whom he had dedicated one of his volumes of verse, thus initiating a correspondence with the American poet. On the return voyage he met Eirikur Magnusson, a prominent Icelandic scholar, who was on his way to London to see through the press a revised Icelandic edition of the Bible for the British and Foreign Bible Society. Magnusson told Powell of a review he was writing of a collection of Icelandic legends by Jón Arnason, and translated some of the stories for him. Powell was excited, and proposed to Magnusson that they should jointly prepare a volume of English translations.[4] He invited his new friend to Wales, and they spent Christmas 1862 together at Nanteos. In 1864 *Legends of Iceland* was published in London by Bentley, probably at Powell's expense. The illustrations are dramatic; they are unattributed in the volume, but I believe that one or two may possibly have been Powell's own work though most were the work of Powell's friend J.B. Zwecker. George's only surviving sketchbook shows him to have been a competent draughtman of the human figure, but a single illuminated letter is in the style of the Icelandic illustrations. The contents of this and a subsequent volume were Icelandic folktales, not sagas, and they should have appealed to a public already familiar with the work of the Grimm brothers in Germany, but nevertheless both sold

*Eirikur Magnusson,
Icelandic scholar and
friend of George Powell.*
N.L.W.

badly. Powell persuaded Magnusson to begin work on an Icelandic dictionary, promising his help. But as Magnusson wryly put it in a letter to George Eyre Evans years later:

> Other interests intervened one after another. His intense love of music and of art generally caused him to spend much of his time in travel, and sustained sedentary application to the somewhat dry work of lexicographical interpretation was not congenial to his ardent spirit.[5]

In 1863 Powell went to Copenhagen, where Jón Sigurdsson, the leading Icelandic patriot, was being persecuted by the Danish authorities, from whom the Icelanders were seeking to be liberated. Magnusson described Powell as:

> [being] full of the most sympathetic enthusiasm for the cause of Icelandic Homerule and Jón Sigurdsson's classical

patriotism. "I have decided to defeat the Danes," were Powell's words, "by enabling Sigurdsson to attend to his parliamentary business in spite of them."

In early 1865 Powell planned to relieve Sigurdsson of his financial embarrassment. According to Magnusson in 1905, he gave £1,100 to Sigurdsson, an astonishingly generous sum, expressing the hope that in return he might write the history of Iceland. However, a letter of Sigurdsson to Magnusson at the time expressed joy at the possibility of receiving £400.[6] This was certainly a generous gift, and involved Powell in the sale of shares. He was 22 at the time, obviously in charge of his own money, and extremely generous in his patronage. Sigurdsson had not published anything, despite passionate promises, when Powell wrote

Jón Sigurdsson,
Icelandic patriot
N.L.W.

to the Icelander in 1872 asking about progress, but Sigurdsson, though he had accumulated much material, never produced the promised work. To this day he is regarded as the father of Icelandic independence, and the national day (June 17) is named for him.

In 1866 Powell and Magnusson published the second, larger volume of Icelandic legends, and announced plans to publish their collaborative translations of two sagas, but though the work may have been largely completed, it was never printed. Powell is also likely to have subsidised the production of the second volume, particularly in the provision of illustrations. It is a sizeable book, with a 150-page introduction by Magnusson, and 664 pages of text.

Magnusson remained in correspondence with Powell during the years 1867-72. The Icelander was often desperate for money, though eventually he gained employment in the Cambridge University Library, but was apparently not well-paid. Powell made him gifts or loans during the late sixties, but in 1872 Magnusson sold an old Icelandic Bible to the University Library for five pounds, which he sent to Powell in reply to what must have been a letter begging for repayment.[7] Had Powell overreached himself in his enthusiastic generosity? The sources are unclear. By 1868 Magnusson had found another collaborator in William Morris, of whom he wrote enthusiastically to Powell:

> It is a pity that you don't know Morris, he is as good a fellow as ever I met, with tastes very much like yours only he is a pre-raphaelite in his views about art, yet with a very good judgment . . . He is beside a Welshman like yourself.[8]

Today William Morris's work on Icelandic literature is remembered, particularly in Iceland, while Powell's is forgotten, although his near-contemporary the Icelandic dramatist Matthias Jochumsson (subsequently author of the Icelandic national anthem) dedicated one of his plays to him. Icelandic culture benefitted immensely from Powell's support during the 1860s, both financial and moral, for Eirikur Magnusson and Jón Sigurdsson. Powell did not abandon his Icelandic interests suddenly; during the late 1860s he worked on an English version, still not published, of Havardr's Saga, and wrote to Magnusson that he was translating a selection of their previously-published legends into French, for private publication, but nothing came of it.[9]

The early 1860s must have seemed to George Powell, in later life, to have been his best days, when he had money to spend, before the rift with his father. The extreme nature of their breach was first made public by H.M.Vaughan:

> He was wont to speak of Nanteos as 'my beautiful but unhappy home,' and indeed there could have been little concord there. Amongst other things, George had an aversion to shooting, which particularly annoyed the old squire. So one day Colonel Powell presented his son and heir with a gun and cartridges, and with paternal arrogance bade him take the gun and not return to the house till he had shot something. George silently obeyed, and gun in hand proceeded to the park, where he deliberately aimed at and killed one of his father's most valuable bullocks . . . The story found its way to literary circles in London, where it caused amusement, and was partly utilized by George du Maurier for an incident in his novel of Peter Ibbetson.[10]

Whether the story is true, and if so, the year of its occurrence, are not known. Early in 1865 William Phelp had written in a state of panic from Nanteos to George, who was in Algiers. W.T.R. Powell, a widower since the death of his wife in 1860, was to be sued for breach of promise by Miss Margaretta Lewis and financial ruin stared him in the face; would George make the necessary sacrifices? Miss Lewis was sister to W.T.R.'s secretary Sylvanus Lewis, and to Anna Maria, wife of W.B. Powell, who was eventually to inherit Nanteos.[11] George wrote two long letters to Phelp to attempt to calm him down, and to his father:

> I am very glad . . . that you are bearing up well and brightly, under all the bother of this Lewis affair . . . I cannot tell you how grieved I am that this affair should have come into open court . . . Anything more injudicious and more injurious to your own case, than the bringing forward and then withdrawing a groundless accusation against Miss Lewis, I really cannot conceive. Who on earth suggested such an idea to you? The story current about Miss M.L. and captain Fraser was, like all Cardiganshire stories, a vicious bit of tittle-tattle . . .[12]

The young man affectionately offered to come home, at the same time urging his father to come out to Algiers for a rest and change. Soon, however, George's attitude had become completely negative, and remained so. In 1866 he was lodging at a house in Penllwyn, east of Aberystwyth. He wrote to Magnusson:

> All sorts of mischiefs are brewing at NantEos, and the villainous lawyer Cooke has lately appeared upon the scene. I am formally forbidden the place, which seems rather absurd, as I have not the faintest inclination to set foot in it henceforth and for ever. The Chief [i.e. his father] is going to stand again for the county; where the money is to come from, even though the election be not a contested one I am at a loss to imagine. The idea of that stuffed dummy sitting once more among the legislators of the land! He is about as useful in the House of Commons as a straw effigy of Guy Fawkes would be in the same place, and as for his votes – he votes at random, and in favour of the party which has toadied him the most. It makes me sick to think of it.[13]

The evidence for their mutual detestation is further supported by the fact that W.T.R.Powell forbade Swinburne from staying at Nanteos when George brought the notorious poet, laureate of 'Our Lady of Pain', to Wales in 1866. It was hardly to be expected that the hunting squire would be enamoured of a son whose every instinct was diametrically opposed to the family's bucolic traditions. In any case, from 1866 onwards every reference to W.T.R. Powell by George and his friends is hostile, often savagely so:

> Col.P . . . will go on living in spite of the whiskey (!) and the doctors! . . . I can fancy no greater benefit to humanity than his death, and even strangers to whom I had not imparted a word of my sentiments have said the same thing.[14]

It was the publication of the second volume of *Legends of Iceland* in 1866 that had brought Powell into close contact with Swinburne. Late in 1865 Powell had asked the poet for his permission to dedicate the volume to him;

GEORGE POWELL

The frontispiece to
Icelandic Legends *(1866);*
by J.B.Zwecker

N.L.W.

Swinburne was pleased to agree, and sometime before the summer of 1866 the two met. In October Swinburne visited Aberystwyth, staying at the Queen's Hotel. For some years they wrote enthusiastically to each other, and the editor of Swinburne's correspondence was moved to comment unfavourably on Powell ('not altogether an appealing figure') and his supposedly bad influence on the older man (Swinburne was five years the elder).[15] Readers of the numerous biographies of Swinburne may prefer to think that Powell was led on by the older man's cult of homosexuality and flagellation, not to mention heavy drinking and other excesses.

Swinburne's visit to Aberystwyth, where he enjoyed swimming against the advice of beach lifeguards, had displeased George's father, and the poet wrote to George after his visit, 'With regard to your parent I think you are right to abjure his grounds until the day when he shall relieve them and the world of his benignant presence' and again:

> As to your father, forget his existence – especially during an English November . . . Certainly during his too long life I think in your place I would *not* set foot in grounds which are his – until they become yours and regain their native attraction. (*Letters*, I, 213-4).

Nothing could better illustrate at second hand the son's ill-feeling towards his father.

The surviving letters of George Powell to Swinburne have not been published, but deserve some brief attention.[16] The first, dated August 1866, expresses Powell's sympathy with his new friend, whose *Poems and Ballads* had come under the lash of reviewers, who found the volume 'not fit to be put into Ladies' hands'. His comment tells us a good deal about the man himself:

> I have only to say that twenty of *my* lady-friends have seen and read it, and admired its beauties (in their superficial, feeble way) without discovering that anything was amiss.

> They looked upon 'Anactoria' and the 'Laus Veneris' as upon hymns to the Virgin.

Powell's complicity in Swinburne's obsession with flagellation is obvious from their correspondence. Powell sent his friend copies of two of the Marquis de Sade's letters, on which Swinburne commented by way of thanks:

> My copy of his monstrous offspring is still in the hands of an Eton friend, who having been incessantly whipped during the rosy years of boyhood – rosy in bottom as in face – takes, I fear, a voluptuous interest in the Titanic flagellations which crown its pages. (*Letters* I, 216)

As well as the Sadean letters, Powell gave Swinburne a birch used at Eton, and a photograph of the school's whipping or swishing block. Swinburne enjoyed a vigorously decadent life-style, as may be discovered from any recent biography, or from his letters.

In 1867 the two friends were planning a journey to Munich to see Wagner's new theatre, and to witness a performance of parts of the *Ring* cycle, but the plan fell through. Powell took a house at Etretat on the Normandy coast, and Swinburne visited him there, writing enthusiastically to his mother:

> Powell has got the sweetest little old farmhouse fitted up inside with music, books, drawings, etc . . . There is a wild little garden all uphill, and avenues of trees about. The sea is splendid.[17]

However, Swinburne forbore to mention that Powell had christened the house *La Chaumière de Dolmance*, a name derived from de Sade's *La Philosophie dans le boudoir*. Lurid details of the establishment are provided by Guy de Maupassant.

Maupassant had not apparently known either Powell or Swinburne before an occasion at Etretat in 1868, when Maupassant was only eighteen. Swinburne had swum too far out to sea, and got into difficulties from which he was rescued by a fisherman. Maupassant had offered his assistance, and was rewarded with an invitation to lunch. Years later he described the occasion, and subsequent visits, to the brothers Goncourt:

GEORGE POWELL

*Algernon Swinburne,
from a photo owned by
his friend George Powell.*
N.L.W.

A strange house . . . containing some very beautiful pictures . . . and a great monkey gambolling about inside. The lunch! I didn't know what I was eating; all I remember is that it was something like fish. I asked its name. The proprietor told me with a strange smile that it was meat, and it was impossible to find out any more about it. There was no wine, they only drank spirits . . . from time to time Powell tickled his monkey, who escaped his fingers to tap the nape of my neck, when I leaned forward to drink.' After lunch the two friends brought out gigantic portfolios of obscene photographs, taken in Germany, life-sized and all of masculine subjects. Among others, I recall an English soldier masturbating himself at a window. Powell showed me that [when] completely drunk, from time to time sucking the fingers of a dried hand, which served, I believe, in that house as a paper-weight.[18]

According to the Goncourts, Maupassant paid other visits:

They live together, satisfying themselves with monkeys or with young servants of fourteen or fifteen, who are sent out to Powell every three months or so, serving-boys of exceptional cleanliness and freshness . . . During the whole of lunch we talked about art, literature, humanity, and the opinions of those two friends cast over everything a kind of disturbing, macabre light, for they had a way of seeing and understanding that made them seem like diseased visionaries, drunken with a poetry magical and perverse . . . Messrs. Powell and Swinburne were delightful in their fantasy and lyricism. They recounted Icelandic legends, translated by Mr Powell, of a gripping and terrible novelty.

According to Maupassant, who eventually wrote his own account of his first meal at La Chaumière, Powell was short and fat, with a blonde moustache, and light of gait.[19] Maupassant claimed that the monkey had been killed by an infuriated negro servant, who was then driven from the house by Powell at pistol-point. The two friends had obviously made a remarkable impact on the sensitive young Frenchman, though presumably the story did not suffer in the retelling.

The relationship between Powell and Swinburne remained affectionate, though they did not again share the same address. In 1869 Powell, himself living at 41, Mornington Crescent, helped Swinburne find new accommodation in London, and dealt with his landlord. In 1874, when Ralph Waldo Emerson was reported in the press as referring to Swinburne as a sodomite, Swinburne persuaded Powell to circulate a letter denying this, and caused it to be published in the *New York Times*. Prior to this occasion Swinburne had been making strenuous efforts to establish a reputation as a heterosexual. He frequented a brothel in St John's Wood, referring to it as 'the Grove of the Evangelist', and invited Powell there, though it is not clear whether he accepted.

The late 1860s were not a good time for Powell. He seems often to have been short of money, and the generosity of his early twenties had of necessity faded, perhaps as a result of his father's problems. In 1869 he wrote to Magnusson in reply to a pressing letter that he could only send a small cheque, since he was being hounded by tradesmen. A single letter survives from the year 1870, written from Mayence in France, which is quite startling in its implications:

> Every farthing of my extra resources has been spent upon these hopeless wounded, whom I am allowed to visit in the hospitals and at the stations.[20]

In other words, he was visiting casualties of the Franco-Prussian war.

As well as allowing his friendship with Swinburne to become less heated, Powell slowly drifted away from Magnusson and his other Icelandic contacts. At the same time the flow of letters from artists and musicians, quite steady in the 1860s, dwindles to the merest trickle. The first intimation we have of his interest in music is the affectionate letter of c.1860 to his father, referred to above. Powell had gone to Broadwoods to buy a piano; 250 guineas was too much to pay for a grand, so he bought a 'cottage piano', and instructed his father that no-one was to be allowed to tune it, that it must be kept in a room with a fire during winter and spring, and be covered by green baize when not being played.

Apart from Swinburne and Magnusson, George Powell had numerous correspondents whose warm affection for him is quite striking. He remained unmarried until 1881, and seems to have enjoyed his bachelor life greatly. He travelled to Leipzig, Copenhagen, Spain and Algeria, and spent long periods in France, where among other contacts he interviewed the artist Gustave Doré.

The surviving letters from friends and acquaintances include many in French and a few in German. His friend the artist Zwecker wrote to him: 'you are a Will O the Wisp, here there, everywhere, Nobody can follow, now in a hollow, quick on the top of a tower or in a Maidens bower, Now in Algeria, now in Spain, in the twinkle of an Eye in Paris again.' He was frequently invited by friends and acquaintances to dinner or to stay, to drink chocolate, to the theatre, to art galleries, to the London Zoo, and was a member of the Bach Society; he himself also enjoyed entertaining others. But some among the company of his friends were decidedly louche. He received many letters from the homosexual artist Simeon Solomon and his sister Rebecca; Solomon, according to Swinburne in a letter to Powell, had 'done things amenable to law such as done by a sane man would make it impossible for any one to keep up his acquaintance and not be cut by the rest of the world as an accomplice.'[21] As the Welsh saying has it, Satan chastises sin.

Powell's musical interests were, like all his involvements, dilettante, but they seem to have lasted most of his adult life. There are apparently no detailed accounts of his interviews and other meetings with Wagner, Offenbach and Liszt, and there is certainly no truth in the often-repeated story that Wagner came to Nanteos, or that his opera *Parzifal* was inspired by the Nanteos cup; the supposed connection of the cup with the Grail had not yet been invented! David Lewis Jones avers that George Powell, a few days before his death, said: 'It is one of the privileges of my life to have been favoured with private interviews with Wagner, in the quietness of his room.' Unfortunately he does not cite his source, nor have I been able to trace it.[22] However, Powell wrote to Swinburne from Bayreuth in September 1876:

> I have just had a long conversation (over tea at the Wagners house) with Madame Cosima Wagner, about your works, which has resulted in my offer to send her all your writings. I dine with them today (*Great Master*, Cosima, Big dogs and all). I must tell you by word of mouth all about this *wonderful* time.

Powell had already attended the first complete performance of *The Ring* in August of that year.

As a pianist, Powell was a good enough amateur to have been invited by Sir Thomas Lloyd, Bronwydd, to give a concert for his local church. He collected musical manuscripts, and John Stainer thanked him for the loan of a Cherubini score, and of Schumann's songs, 'which have been a source of immense pleasure to me.'[23] In 1871 Powell presented Clara Schumann with an ivory comb as proof of his admiration of her husband's music, and she replied: 'I hope I shall find time at the end of this month to play to you some of my husband's works.'[24]

One of Powell's more frequent musical correspondents was Sir Frederick Ouseley (1825-89), an important figure in the world of Victorian church music, professor of music at Oxford and founder of the College of St Michael and All Angels, Tenbury. Ouseley was involved in the Oxford Movement; St Michael's was the first collegiate church to be established in England since the Reformation, and under Ouseley's influence became a model for Anglican choral services, especially cathedral worship. He wrote to Powell on matters of musical technique, as well as expressing his gratitude for Powell's gift in 1863 of £300 towards the college. He also wrote for Powell a letter of introduction to S.S. Wesley, saying that 'he is an enthusiast for the higher order of Music'. Another church musician who corresponded with Powell was Sir George Elvey (1816-93), composer, and organist at St George's Chapel, Windsor from 1835 till 1882; Powell made a present to Elvey of a volume of Lapland legends.

George Powell had a number of harmless habits. One was to send people copies of his photograph; he received a number of replies expressing thanks, and regret at the writers' inability to reciprocate. One correspondent was sent an album full of photographs of Powell in various costumes and attitudes, apparently in narrative form. Another interest was collecting autographs.[25] He met more than his match in the Ouseley family; Sir Frederick informed him in 1861 that his sister had a collection of over 3,000 holograph letters, and that she would willingly exchange a list of duplicates with a similar list of George Powell's. In 1872, however, George offered to sell some of his collection (which included the signatures of two kings of France) to Ouseley, who graciously declined. Powell was still pressed for money; the numerous gifts, large and small, which he had made in his early twenties (including gifts to Joseph Parry's musical academy in Swansea) had by this time quite dried up.

George Powell in Moroccan costume
N.L.W.

Apart from autographs, Powell collected books, and left some four thousand five hundred volumes to the library of the University College of Wales, Aberystwyth, including Dr Johnson's copy of Warburton's 1747 edition of Shakespeare, containing Johnson's notes. His library was particularly strong in English and French literature, and in early Icelandic texts. His other manuscripts included a medieval Dutch service book and some eighteenth-century oriental works; these too he left to the College library. Naturally he collected music, including holograph works by Mendelssohn, Benevoli and John Blow, and letters from Offenbach, as well as an early performing copy of Handel's *Messiah*, and some three hundred volumes of printed music. The music collection was originally bequeathed to Joseph Parry's Musical College of Wales, but when that institution closed, the reversion came to the College library. Powell's interest in art is described below.

Some of Powell's friends felt able to reprove him gently for his lax style of life. The artist, Simeon Solomon, who as we have seen was no paragon of virtue, wrote: 'I am extremely sorry to hear that your health is so queer, but I must candidly say that you ought hardly to be surprised – for you live so irregularly in the way of meals etc and lay yourself so open to catching colds.' He advised Powell not to drink during the day.

We may speculate as to why Powell did not marry until 1881; his apparent homosexuality would not have been a barrier to his doing what was expected of the heir to an estate. He certainly enjoyed the relaxed freedom and irresponsibility of the bachelor life, and his estrangement from his father and his home would have made it difficult for him to establish a suitable *ménage*. Nothing seems to be known of the woman he eventually married, Dinah Harries of Goodwick, Fishguard, though he may have met her when convalescing at Goodwick in 1877;[26] it is said that she was a hotel chambermaid, and indeed, comparatively little is known of the brief period between W.T.R.Powell's death in 1878 and his son's demise in 1882, when Dinah swiftly remarried and went to America. However, one of George's letters to Swinburne, of May 1880, reveals that he had taken his friend Kumpel to Nanteos for six months in the hope of prolonging his life.

Despite the hostility between father and son, and his own frequent travels, George Powell did not entirely neglect his home district. He had made a valiant if clumsy effort to endow Aberystwyth with a museum and art gallery to which he was willing to give his own collections. The affair has been described in great detail, and only a summary is required here.[27] This generous offer was put before the town council in November 1871; the only condition was that a suitable room or gallery should be provided by the council, failing which the offer would be withdrawn and not repeated. The council swiftly accepted the offer, without reservation, and decided that the Public Libraries Act of 1855 should be adopted by the necessary procedure, namely a meeting of ratepayers with a two-thirds majority in favour, in order to be able to finance the building of a suitable room.

GEORGE POWELL

The necessary meeting was called in December of 1871, but the ratepayers favoured a library as well, and the Libraries Act was adopted, though only £75 could be raised under the Act, which would certainly not finance the building of both a library and a gallery. However, the town councillors then began to bicker. Should there be a special building? Shouldn't they wait for more gifts? The councillors were divided; the more generous faction favoured a new building behind the Town Hall (in which they were supported by George Powell), while the skinflints were willing only to rent temporary premises in the Market Hall. Matters were complicated by the proposed incorporation into the projected library of the collection of the Aberystwyth Literary Institute, nine hundred of whose books had been donated by George Powell on a previous occasion. When the owners of the

Market Hall demanded a rent of forty pounds a year, many councillors began to repent the alacrity with which they had accepted George Powell's offer of his art and museum collections. They began to query the value of the paintings. Who had valued them? In February 1872 Powell threatened to withdraw his offer unless a suitable and permanent building, to be approved by him, had been provided by August of the same year.

The council bowed to this threat, and decided to build. However, nothing was done immediately, and at the same time the Literary Institute's books were in pawn until that body's debts had been paid. In April the council determined to press on, but ratepayers' objections to the proposal began to mount, in particular, the unsuitable position of the proposed site behind the Town Hall. A large public meeting was held, to the indignation of some councillors; the ratepayers decided that they wanted a more favourable site, though no place was specified. A special council meeting was not called until late June, at which the councillors received an indignant address made on behalf of George Powell, expressing his astonishment at their dilatoriness, and his determination to withdraw his gift unless the building were under way by September.

However, the councillors, though still apparently favouring progress, were quite unable to achieve it. Meetings were late and discussion perfunctory, and the necessary authority from the government to raise the library rate had not been sought by the council's solicitor. When this was eventually done, it emerged in October that the Treasury was critical of the financial chaos in which the council laboured, and would not authorize the levying of a library rate. There was no building, no rate – and no gifts, for by the end of October George Powell had withdrawn his offer.

It is easy to blame the bumbledom of the council, its total inadequacy in face of an offer whose value many of the councillors had no means of assessing. Some councillors (and officers) were certainly incompetent to the point of idiocy, though others were generally supportive of the plan, and did their best on behalf of their potential patron. George Powell, however, can have had no realistic comprehension of the problem he had set the council, nor of the difficulties under which even an enlightened council would have had to labour. A £75 rate could hardly have sustained a museum, gallery and library, and the proposed gifts might well have suffered. Unfortunately, the paintings which George Powell proposed to give to the town seem never to have been listed, so it is difficult to know just how valuable an opportunity was lost.

However, Powell's affection for 'my dear but benighted town' was not snuffed out by the failure of the town gallery scheme. Instead, he left not only his library and music collection but also his works of art to the University College, where a museum had been founded and a curator appointed; Powell was the museum's first major benefactor.[28] Powell's will refers to his 'oil and water-colour paintings and crayon drawings, Roman Greek Egyptian and other antiquities . . . curiosities and objects of art ivory carvings bronzes Persian Faenza and Moorish ware statues brass repoussé work and Oriental embroidery'. The paintings and drawings (which of course did not include the portraits at Nanteos, which were heirlooms and not his to bequeath) numbered 150. Many were by Powell's acquaintances – Edward Burne-Jones and Dante Gabriel Rossetti. He commissioned works from his friends, Simeon Solomon and his sister Rebecca, Wilhelm Kumpel and Johann Baptiste Zwecker. He also bought two Turner watercolours, as well as works attributed to John Crome, John Constable and F.W.Watts. The sculptures in his collection, like the paintings, reflect an interest in the male nude figure. As Meyrick and Holland comment, 'Homoeroticism is undeniably one of the prime organising principles of Powell's collection of fine and decorative art.'

The rest of the collection is a magpie's nest of minor treasures – silver ornaments, rocks and minerals from Iceland, tiles from Anatolia and Persia, a Moroccan bowl, Limoges enamels, fossils, seahorses, Japanese netsukes and arrows, Persian needlework, a pair of Canadian snowshoes, and autograph signatures of Henry II and IV of France. The musical memorabilia include a cast of Mendelssohn's hand, and a coffee set which Powell incorrectly thought had belonged to Mozart. Almost all the collection came from his London house at 41, Mornington Crescent.

Powell lacked the financial resources to be a major collector or patron of the arts. Nevertheless, what he did with what he had is interesting enough. He gave financial aid to two musical centres (through Ouseley and Parry), to Icelandic culture, and to a number of artists. His collections are, in the words of Meyrick and Holland:

> [a] personal Theatre of Memory – they are representative of his personal enthusiasms, they had strong significance as precious souvenirs of friends and relics of heroes, as illustrations of his status as man of letters, a scholar, a benefactor, a patron to young genius and an equal among the great and the good – in his own words his collections were 'the reality of my dreams'.

George Powell's interest in promoting culture in Cardiganshire did not extend to local politics and socialising. His appearance in the list of High Sheriffs of Cardiganshire (for 1880-81) is surprising, and a letter to Swinburne reveals his violent dislike of local politics. He lists his ailments, including nervous headaches . . .

> . . . caused by worry about the damned Elections, into which nobody had a right to draw me, inasmuch as I am (very unexpectedly and to my *intense* disgust) High Sheriff of the county. A pretty High Sheriff, ma foi! Picture me to your mind's eye, next July, in the garb of a flunkey, with the addition of a cocked hat and sword, kootooing to the Judge and *sitting on the bench*! . . . My undersheriff does all the *work* luckily (except this) and I *pay*.

He sent Swinburne a hilarious account of the occasion:

> You will, I am sure, be glad to hear that my business at Cardigan, as high sheriff, went off splendidly. Never had such a "get-up" and "turn-out" been seen in the county. Without being in the least degree gaudy, everything was soberly splendid, as I used only two colours for my liveries, black and white or – as in the case of the trumpeters – black and silver. I used violet for the hammer-cloth and lining of carriage. I had only *two* accidents during the whole proceedings. The first was with my sword, and long white wand (a horrible instrument). The former fell at the Church gate, as I got out of the carriage,

out of its scabbard, with a hideous clatter, and the wand got between my legs, thus betraying me into a most undignified tumble, which even the prompt help of my footmen almost failed to redeem. However, I managed to preceed (sic) Mr Bowen, the pro-judge, into church, with appropriate majesty. My second misadventure was worse. On the next day, Saturday, I had the Grand Jury to lunch, most of whom were acquaintances, and kept them beyond after open court-time. Consequently Judge Thesiger (who had broken etiquette by taking my carriage without my leave on Saturday eve to spend Sunday in a neighbouring county – a fearful breach of good manners – and thus avoid the assize sermon) thought fit to lecture me on Monday morning about my "lack of respect."'

Powell related with detailed relish his public rebuke to the judge.

Powell's letters complain frequently of his various illnesses, including colic and diarrhoea, but without sufficient detail to suggest a medical explanation for his death at the age of 40 from what the *Cambrian News* described as 'a violent cramp', apparently unexpected, since he was due to take the chair at a concert in Aberystwyth on the evening of his death. A year before his demise he had sent Swinburne a charming account of a heavy snowfall at Nanteos, and the subsequent besieging of the house by starving birds, including a swan which would walk into any open door and wait on the hearth to be fed: 'I think of giving him a silver collar like Lohengrin's swans.' His last (undated, but definitely last) letter begs Swinburne to allow his friend the musician Ferdinand Praeger to publish his settings of Swinburne's songs free of copyright, and complains of a fearful cold caught driving in an open carriage near Nanteos with a party of cousins and guests.

Swinburne was genuinely upset by his friend's death, and in 1883 he published a small collection of poems, *A Century of Roundels*, including poems musing on the death of George Powell ('A Dead Friend' and 'Past Days') and another on the deaths of two friends, apparently Powell and Dante Gabriel Rosetti, who had also died in 1882. The poet looked back warmly on Etretat:

> Above the sea and sea-washed town we dwelt,
> We twain together, two brief summers, free
> From heed of hours as light as clouds that melt
> Above the sea.

He spoke of his 'friend of many a season', 'O gentle heart and true':

> Known and loved of few,
> But of these, though small their fold
> Loved how well were you.

With his death in 1882, George Powell's brief squiredom of Nanteos ended, and it was left to his cousin, William Beauclerk Powell, to attempt the sales and reforms necessary to save the estate. Such a dull enterprise would scarcely have appealed to George. Despite his involvment with Swinburne, which seems to have extended to at least some of the poet's wilder practices, and despite his venom towards his father, Powell seems to have been in some ways an attractive character. It remains unclear to what extent his fondness for depravity actually existed outside his own and his friends' imaginations. Friend of Icelandic independence and generous promoter of its literature, patron both of church music and the struggling Bohemians of London, he was a witty, cultivated and intelligent man. Much remains baffling: Why did he hate his father so intensely? What was the nature of his brief marriage? How did he feel about Nanteos once he had inherited it? Answers escape us. But if we may be generous towards this minor but remarkably interesting member of the Welsh squirearchy, then let it be in the hyperbole of his old friend Eirikur Magnusson:

> A nobler or more generous heart than his seldom beat in the bosom of man. His gifts of mind were great and beautiful. His musical talent was extraordinary. His poetical talent if it only had been assiduously cultivated would certainly have ranked high among his contemporaries. His love of art was wonderfully intense and his tastes very sound at least in his earlier years.

Swinburne's opinion was more measured, but no less kind; on hearing of Powell's death, he was shaken, and wrote to a friend:

I am really very much grieved as well as startled by the news of poor George Powell's death. I can hardly realize the idea that I shall never see him again with whom I have spent so many days and weeks together and exchanged so many signs of friendship in past years . . . The poor fellow was one of the most obliging and kind-hearted of men, and wonderfully bright-spirited under severe trial and trouble.

NOTES

[1] See D.L.Jones, 'George Powell – Swinburne's "Friend of Many a Season", *Anglo-Welsh Review* 44 (Spring 1971) 75-85; Richard Brinkley, 'George Powell of Nanteos: a further appreciation', *Ibid.* 48 (Winter 1972) 130-5. I am grateful to Mr Brinkley for a copy of his typescript catalogue to an exhibition of George Powell's books, music and MSS held in Aberystwyth in 1971, and for his many valuable comments on a draft of this chapter, particularly on the Powell bequests. My thanks also to Dr Caroline Palmer, who made valuable comments and suggestions.

[2] C.H.Nordby, *The Influence of Old Norse Literature upon English Literature* . . . New York, 1901.

[3] NLW MS 6734C, unnumbered. Dr Palmer points out to me that although W.T.R.Powell and his wife were buried in Llanbadarn church (as the Bishop's Transcripts show) there are no plaques or gravestones. George Powell willed a window memorial to his mother and his sister, while his father is commemorated in a window given by his nephew G.F.W.Powell, son of his brother Cornelius. This suggests a deliberate neglect of his father's memory by George Powell.

[4] Ibid.

[5] R.G.Thomas, 'George E.J.Powell, Eirikr Magnusson and Jon Sigurdsson', *Saga-Book of the Viking Society*, XIV (1953-7), 124-5. This, the NLW correspondence (most of which was deposited by the University College of Aberystwyth (as it then was), and the kind help and advice of Dr Andrew Wawn of the University of Leeds, are the sources of what follows.

[6] NLW Minor Deposit 1407A, unnumbered.

[7] NLW Minor Deposit 1399A.

[8] The last sentence is quite unexpected. Although Powell seems to have expressed no interest in Wales (he spent most of his life beyond Offa's Dyke), he made determined efforts to support the arts in Aberystwyth (see below), and gave his library and collectables to the newly-fledged University of Wales.

[9] NLW Minor Deposit 1408A, 46-7.

[10] H.M.Vaughan, *The South Wales Squires* (1988 edn., 103).

[11]Dr Caroline Palmer intends to publish elsewher the story of this extraordinary affair, which cost W.T.R. Powell £2,000 in damages.

[12] NLW Minor Deposit 1408A, 24-7.

[13] NLW Minor Deposit 1408A, 32. In fact, W.T.R. Powell did not stand again for Parliament in the 1865 election; he had become largely confined to a wheelchair since 1858.

[14] NLW Minor Deposit 1408A, 31.

[15] Cecil Y. Lang, *The Swinburne Letters* (Yale U.P., 1959-62), I, xl. Other quotations from Swinburne's letters are from this source.

[16] They are in the Brotherton Library at Leeds University, and I was kindly provided with copies by the Librarian and the keeper of special collections, for which I am most grateful.

[17] Philip Henderson, *Swinburne: the Portrait of a Poet* (London, 1974), p.144.

[18] Ibidem, pp.145-46.

[19] 'L'Anglais d'Etretat' in *Oeures Completes de Guy de Maupassant: Le Rosier de Madame Husson* (Paris, 1924).

[20] NLW Minor Deposit 1408A, 50.

[21] Quoted by Henderson, op.cit., 149. Solomon was arrested for soliciting males, and finished as a pavement artist, sleeping in doss-houses.

[22] D.L.Jones, 'George Powell – Swinburne's "Friend of Many a Season"' *Anglo-Welsh Review,* 44 (Spring, 1971), 78. It is a pity that this excellent article (pp. 75-85), has only a bibliographical note, with no detailed references.

[23] NLW Minor Deposit 1400A, unnumbered.

[24] NLW Minor Deposit 1403A, unnumbered.

[25] This collection must have included a letter from Byron to the editor of a journal, unnamed, which was exhibited in Nanteos mansion during the 1960s as 'a letter from Lord Byron to his publisher'. Ceredigion Library Local Collection, slide 4958.

[26] NLW Minor Deposit 1408A, 52. In an 1880 letter to Swinburne he refers to Goodwick as his favourite seaside abode.

[27] Norman Roberts, 'A Town and its Library', *Ceredigion* III, 2 (1957) 161-81. This is the main source of what follows. The article drew on local newspapers and the Powell correspondence in NLW.

[28] R.Meyrick & N.Holland, *To Instruct and Inspire: 125 years of the Art and Crafts Collection* (Aberystwyth, 1997), 3-6. What follows is an abstract of this valuable short chapter.

5.

A LANDED ESTATE
IN DECLINE
1800-1930

Richard Moore-Colyer

'In squandering wealth was his peculiar art
Nothing went unrewarded but desert.
Beggar'd by fools, whom still he found too late
He had his jest and they had his estate.'

John Dryden: *Absalom and Achitophel*

THOMAS POWELL of Nanteos died quite young in 1797. Although, as we have seen, he was a man whose vision exceeded his grasp, he was not without achievement; for example, he had been involved in the founding of the Welsh School in London. He left a widow, Eleanor (née Corbet), his nine-year-old heir William (b. 1788), a younger son, Richard, and two daughters, together with relatively modest contract debts of £12,000.[1] The broad, if infertile, acres to which William Powell was heir were widely dispersed throughout north Cardiganshire. While the bulk of the original Nanteos property was concentrated in the parish of Llanfihangel-y-Creuddyn between the Ystwyth and Rheidol rivers, with outlying farms in the mountainous country between Devil's Bridge and Ponterwyd, the family also held land bordering upon Cors Tregaron, part of the old Strata Florida Abbey estate in the uplands of Caron. Apart from six great mountain sheepwalks in the parish of Llanddewi Abergwesyn which represented the most easterly limit of Nanteos's 30,000 acres, and isolated holdings in Llanddewibrefi and Llangybi, the remainder of the estate was in Lampeter Rural parish to the south-east of Cribyn. A series of family settlements had ensured that a life tenant of the estate, while enjoying the right to draw income from, and raise mortgages upon them, was precluded from disposing of the above properties during the first three-quarters of the nineteenth century. On the other hand, inheritances and prudent purchases in the preceding century had led to the accumulation of a considerable amount of unsettled real estate, both agricultural and domestic, which successive life tenants were legally entitled to sell when adverse estate finances created a demand for ready cash.

Under the terms of his will, Thomas Powell had charged his wife and her co-trustees, John Hill (later Sir John Hill) and Thomas Morgan, with the maintenance of the estate

119

during William's minority. With a net annual income of £4,000 and fixed yearly outgoings of £2,000, Hill believed that the simple contract debts of the late life tenant could be readily discharged from income rather than having recourse to borrowing or further mortgaging of the already heavily encumbered estate. This was especially important since demands for the repayment of capital mortgage sums raised during Thomas Powell's lifetime were already being made upon the trustees. However, as Hill blandly observed in 1798, such demands would have to be 'passed over for a while' as no cash was currently available.

Before the death of her husband, Eleanor Powell had retired to London. Her departure was a mixed blessing so far as the fortunes of the estate after her husband's death were concerned. On the credit side, the vacant mansion could now be let, and after spending considerable sums upon repairs in 1798, the trustees managed to persuade one Samuel Pocock to rent both mansion and demesne for 300 guineas per annum. On the other hand, Mrs. Powell was rather more concerned with the furnishing of her London house and building up her position in polite society than paying off the estate debts. Her husband had provided her with a jointure of £800 per year in addition to an annual allowance of £600 for the maintenance of her younger son and two daughters. Due largely to Mrs. Powell's personal extravagance this proved to be quite insufficient and throughout 1800 she wrote persistently to her fellow trustees for an increase in her yearly allowance.

Mindful of his duties towards the estate, John Hill preached the virtues of economy to the widow, noting, somewhat primly, 'We must always keep in mind the circumstances of our Dear Wards, considering that the greater Oeconomists we are during their minorities, the more it will be for their advantage hereafter.' Hill was also adamant in his refusal to sanction the estate's paying £35 for young William to learn swordmanship; in his view a perfectly unnecessary extravagance. However, in 1800, notwithstanding the very small balance of cash in the estate account after Mrs. Powell's jointure, the children's allowances and general estate repairs had been paid, Hill and Thomas Morgan agreed to allow her an extra £180 a year to meet the costs of educating her elder daughter, Ellen Elizabeth Powell, and the two younger children. For the next ten years Mrs. Powell appears to have lived alternately in London and Dublin, accumulating the debts which were to plague her son William when he assumed responsibility for the Nanteos estate in 1809.

The year 1800 had witnessed William's embarking upon what was no doubt a miserable sojourn as a boarder at Westminster School, his expenses being defrayed from the estate account.[2] Of his scholastic attainments we know little, save that he survived the rigours of Westminster to attend Christ Church, Oxford, from which he graduated in 1807 at nineteen years of age. In common with many young men of his age and class without academic or ecclesiastical ambitions, Powell, upon graduating, immediately purchased a commission in a regiment of foot, for which the Nanteos agent drew £700 from the estate rental. While his military duties took him to Ireland and other parts of Britain, William Edward Powell's patrimony was managed by an ever-changing kaleidoscope of bailiffs, sub-agents and agents, orchestrated by a London solicitor, Robert Appleyard of Lincoln's Inn. During the heir's minority Appleyard, together with the estate trustees, had struggled manfully against the corruption of local agents, and the profligate expenditure of Mrs. Eleanor Powell to maintain sufficient income to discharge the late Thomas Powell's contract debts.

Despite their efforts, the new life-tenant was faced with a formidable debt burden of £20,377 when he came of age in 1809, £15,000 of which was the obligation to provide portions for his brother and two sisters. The possibility of discharging such a debt must have seemed distinctly remote to Powell whose gross estate income of £7,200 was effectively reduced to £3,770 by the time annual allowances had been met. His local agents, who were unreliable and unpopular with the tenants had, in the absence of any responsible resident member of the family, been systematically mulcting the estate.[3] Matters clearly required the close attention of Powell himself. In the spring of 1809, his grandfather Edward Corbet of Ynysmaengwyn implored him to return from Bath to oversee the collection of his rents, writing that, 'the fatal destiny and destructive measures now carried on require most active and instant preventatives.'[4] Corbet's concern was further expressed in a letter to Johnathon Marsden, lessee of the Cwmystwyth Mine, in which he urged Marsden to persuade Powell to look to his own mining interests and thus to avoid the financial loss consequent upon delegation to unscrupulous agents. 'He is,' wrote Corbet, 'of a kind and indolent, tho' very valuable disposition, chearful [*sic*], pleasant and winning in his manner and his Principles most honorable and replete with Integrity; but subject to every imposition . . .'

With the eternal optimism of youth, Powell chose to ignore the cajolings of his grandfather. Twenty-one years of age, married to a young wife and recently appointed High Sheriff of the County, he did not feel moved to burden his mind with the problems and responsibilities of estate management. Any suggestion of retrenchment being repugnant to him, he continued to pursue the pleasures of Bath and his Newmarket stud, leaving the management of Nanteos to Appleyard and his local solicitor, James Hughes of Glanrheidol. When the opportunity arose the young squire visited Cardiganshire where he involved himself in the activities of the local Agricultural Society and, much to the horror of his agent, who was constantly being pressurised by the estate's creditors, expended heavy sums on the improvement of the home farm. In 1809 large quantities of timber were sold to raise £6000 to stave off creditors.[5] Robert Appleyard was convinced that the estate was faced with imminent ruin unless Powell was prepared to take matters in hand, particularly with regard to the management of the servants who were taking every opportunity to exploit the absence of the life-tenant. Powell was advised, for example, to keep the key of the 'fine wine cellar' about his person and to employ an honest butler capable of resisting the temptation of dispensing good cheer to all and sundry.[6] When he audited the 1811 accounts, Appleyard was mortified to discover that household expenditure amounted to almost £900, much of which involved payments to servants for duties which had not been discharged: 'In short my good fellow you are involving yourself in every quarter and *selling your estate* to pay a set of servants and others who seem to be living upon you in all directions.'

William Powell, whose annual income after payments for estate repairs and allowances to annuitants and others now amounted to £2500, was spending in excess of £5000 a year. Robert Appleyard, who appreciated that this profligacy could only result in the ruin which most of the county were predicting, wrote to Powell in Ireland urging him to limit his expenditure to £1200-£1500 annually and thus to leave a surplus for the discharge of accumulated debts. After all, if the scale of the Nanteos household were restricted, and yearly expenditure pared to £1500, ' you can still afford a carriage and live handsomely.' Powell's lawyers, Hopkinson and Sons, from whom he had borrowed £4,500 early in 1811, were quite unequivocal: 'In order to arrange your matters it will be necessary only for you to fix on living on a certain part of your income and by no means to exceed it and to enable your Trustees to receive the other part to apply to the liquidation of your debts.' In May 1811, William Powell's general debts stood as follows:

Private creditors	£5,500	Sir Robert Vaughan	£6,000
Hopkinsons	£4,500	Goslings	£1,800
Morris of Carmarthen	£1,000	H. Hughes	£3,000
Bonds at Carmarthen	£2,000	Debts to grandfather	£3,000
	£13,000		£13,800
Aberystwyth Bank	£2,500		
		Total:	£29,300

The unenviable task of arranging for the settlement of these debts fell to Appleyard and Hughes who devised a scheme for the payment of the most pressing demands, those of the private creditors and of Sir Robert Vaughan of Hengwrt, Merionethshire, from whom Powell had purchased the Rheidol valley estate of Lovesgrove for £6,000. Sir Robert's purchase money was raised by the sale of unentailed outlying land in the Tregaron area, of farms in Llansantffraed and by further mortgage of the entailed

Nanteos estate. The purchase of Lovesgrove having been duly completed, the estate was immediately mortgaged for £4,000 which was apportioned among the Aberystwyth creditors. For the time being the other debts remained unpaid and the affairs of the estate remained in *status quo* for the next three years during which Powell was stationed in Ireland with his regiment. By 1813, he seems to have grown dimly aware of the necessity for retrenchment and he yielded to the insistence of his bankers (from whom he had borrowed a further £3,000 early in the year) that he dispose of his race horses at Tattersall's.

Meanwhile, the dowager Mrs. Powell's debts in London and Dublin had reached such a level as to provoke a prudent withdrawal to Boulogne in 1812. Here she lived with her children at a level substantially above her income. Powell himself believed that his mother was both squandering her allowance and neglecting his sister's education and thus he felt that it might be appropriate that as she was spending her money in a way by no means creditable, a proportion of her allowance be withheld and expended upon Anne Corbetta Powell's education. Sanctimonious letters from William Powell on the subject of economy must have struck a rather hollow note with his mother, who was only too aware of her son's own penchant for overspending. Indeed she seems to have taken little note of his remonstrations and continued to present heavy bills to Powell, which were eventually discharged from the estate account. Between 1809 and 1821 the estate paid off £5,419 of her debts; no doubt more had been incurred by her death in 1826.[7]

Although exiled to France, the old dowager maintained an active interest in the affairs of the family, especially respecting the marriage of her daughters Ellen and Anne Corbetta. When Ellen married Edward Tufton Phelp, Laura's brother and as poor as the rest of his family, Mrs. Powell was extremely angry at her daughter's alliance with a man whose estate was valued at only half the total sum of his family's debts. Moreover she asked her eldest son in 1811, 'Is it true that he *plays* [i.e. gambles] [and] belongs to several public hunts and clubs, which even in a man of fortune would be an insurmountable objection.' Anne Corbetta, who in 1817 was still living with her mother in

France, formed a liaison with a Mr. Ramsay who followed her across the Channel when she returned to England several years later. In the early stages the dowager had approved of this relationship, although by 1820, 'his fortune is so shrunk that it could never be considered an eligible match.' By this time also, Anne Corbetta's passion for Mr. Ramsay seems to have cooled in the face of the rather dubious charms of Roderick Richardes, who lived with his brother in Penglais mansion, Aberystwyth, where the young woman stayed upon returning to Cardiganshire. This resulted in a complete break with her mother who was appalled by the 'libertine characters' in Penglais and refused further to communicate with her daughter who had flown 'to the house of a Fool, Coward and Blackguard . . . extremely weak in his person and manner hideous.' After a severe beating by the Richardes brothers in 1820 the unfortunate Ramsay withdrew his suit, leaving the way clear for Roderick to lay siege to Anne Corbetta.

The Powells differed in their attitudes towards a possible match. William, the head of the family, seems to have taken little interest in the matter, while his brother Richard, who had himself developed, 'a foolish attachment' for Miss Richardes, was very much in favour of his sister's relationship with Roderick. The dowager Mrs. Powell, in trying to persuade William to introduce his sister to some young man of family and fortune, urged him not to give Richardes any encouragement before becoming properly informed of his circumstances. As a fickle man of unpleasant personal habits, he seemed hardly a suitable candidate for her daughter's hand: 'He lives now much beyond his income, besides he is reckoned extremely weak and his person and manner hideous.' 'Only consider,' she wrote to William, 'what Anne's feelings will be when she appears in the world with such a Man.'

No doubt to her eternal regret, Anne Corbetta agreed to marry the objectionable Richardes who soon showed his true colours. Mrs Powell wrote to William warning that a separation was in the offing:

> He makes such a dreadful iltempered husband... he calls her... dreadful horrid Names... and a short time since pulled

her nose and kicked her... even before they left Penglais he treated her so inhumanly and cruelly that it nearly cost her her life when she was confined of dear Alick.[8]

It seemed that by 1825 Anne Corbetta, who had come to Calais with her husband on one of his frequent flights from his creditors, could take no more, though it should be added that her sister expressed some sympathy with Richardes, feeling that Anne thwarted him too often. The following November, after Richardes had threatened to throw her out of their Calais residence, Anne returned to England with her six children and took up residence in Penglais. Here she remained for many years, living on an allowance of £30 per month from her estranged husband, who settled in Southampton upon his return from France in 1843. A year later, Richardes tried to persuade his wife to leave Aberystwyth so that he could let Penglais and the grounds of the mansion. This she refused to do, much to her husband's annoyance. To his solicitor, John Parry of Aberystwyth, he complained, 'Nothing good or useful, I am sure can be obtained by her remaining in and about that sink of iniquity and idleness, Aberystwyth, and the recent frightful and disgraceful act of her eldest son seems to make no impression whatsoever.' This son, Alexander Richardes, a persistent poacher who had incurred the wrath of both the Nanteos and Trawsgoed estate offices, had a child by his mistress in 1844, following which 'disgraceful act' his allowance of £60 a year was withdrawn. In the autumn of 1848 after more than a quarter of a century of marriage, Richardes and his wife were formally separated and the marriage was eventually annulled.[9]

While these various personal dramas were being enacted the Nanteos estate lurched from crisis to crisis. A generation of mismanagement by inept agents, corrupt bailiffs and indifferent tenants holding their farms at unrealistically low rents had produced the inevitable result of dilapidation and decay. Tenancy covenants had been neglected, farm buildings allowed to tumble to ruins, and hedges and walls permitted to fall into disrepair. Shortly before Adam Murray's 1814 valuation, which highlighted the decrepit condition of the estate, Powell was informed that James

Hughes had offered one of his friends a bottle of wine for every gate he could find on the property. Moreover, despite the large sums which had been spent upon it, the home farm was in a condition of dilapidation equal to that of the worst tenanted property on the estate. Such a situation merited drastic action, and by deed of March 1817, the year following his election as Member of Parliament for the county, Powell granted power of attorney to John Edwards and James Lyon of Bloomsbury and William Vaughan of Llantrisant to act jointly as his attorneys and to undertake the management of the estate and expedite the payment of outstanding debts.

The triumvirate acted immediately by dispensing with the services of Barber, the Nanteos bailiff, who had been systematically embezzling the estate over a long period of time. He had perpetrated, observed John Beynon, Powell's Tregaron agent, 'a more thorough system of theft and villainy (as) I have never heard related.' Barber was replaced by Adam Armstrong of Ty'n-y-rhyd who, in collaboration with Robert Appleyard, successfully persuaded Powell to abandon further expenditure on the home farm. 'There are very strong reasons for this,' wrote Appleyard in 1820, 'namely that he neither understands nor takes the least pleasure in farming; that it is a continual drain on his purse by misapplying the rents which ought to go to other purposes, and thirdly that he never knows nor has any correct means of judging what he gains or loses by it.'[10] This action met with the approval of resident landlords in the county who appreciated the folly of attempting to manage a home farm while living away from the estate. As Colonel Brooks of Neuadd Trefawr was informed by a correspondent: 'Powell judged very proper by selling by auction his North Devon cows, horses, sheep etc. to the tune of sixteen hundred pounds and let out his farm at a guinea per acre . . . to get rid of the expense of keeping a farm and not residing at home.' Abandonment of the farm was followed by the letting of the mansion and a substantial reduction in the population of the kennels and stables.

Beethoven once observed, with his characteristic lack of charity, that he looked upon his friends as instruments upon which he played as he pleased. In similar vein,

W.E. Powell of Nanteos seems to have regarded his agents in much the same way as most men would regard a pair of shoes; to be worn, used and finally rejected. Nanteos agents and bailiffs were regularly subject to salary reductions, summary dismissals and mischievous character assassination on the part of their subordinates. While there is ample evidence in the estate papers to suggest that certain agents and their assistants were less than honest, the combined effects of local intrigue and Powell's own capricious nature meant that the agency of Nanteos offered little in the way of long-term career prospects. Powell who, despite (or because of) his profligacy with money, was popular with his tenants, was frequently the victim of rumours and innuendos from disgruntled tenants, angered perhaps, at the insistence of the agent that rent arrears be paid, that encroachments be checked and tenancy agreements honoured. Thus one agent attributed his differences with Powell to local 'Malevolence and Rancour', while two dismissed bailiffs considered their misfortune to be due to local intrigue. 'I could forgive any trait of your conduct towards me.' wrote Adam Armstrong to Powell following his dismissal in 1820, 'save that of letting my character be blackened by people with a vested interest in breaking the confidence between us.'[11]

Midway through 1820 Powell decided to dismiss Robert Appleyard as his London lawyer as well as relieving Adam Armstrong of his duties. The year 1820 also witnessed the dissolution of the Edwards/Lyon/ Vaughan arrangement and the establishment of a management trust under the aegis of John Edwards of Bloomsbury and William George Cherry of Buckland in Herefordshire whose daughter was eventually to marry Powell's son in 1839. Cherry took his duties very seriously and constantly bombarded Powell with lengthy letters, usually advisory and from time to time censorious. Cherry was kept informed of the affairs of Nanteos by James Hughes, who had tenaciously clung to his position as local solicitor for the estate, and by George Warbrick who replaced the unfortunate Armstrong as bailiff.

By 1823 the financial affairs of the estate had once again reached a critical position. Total income from the Nanteos, Llanbrynmair, and Tregaron estates together with properties in Carmarthen amounted to £8,166, of which £2,928 was required to pay interest upon the mortgage debt of £58,550. £5,238 remained for the payment of jointures and allowances to the dowager Mrs. Powell and her children, the discharge of bond debts (currently in excess of £6,000) and the expenditure of William Powell himself. Following a dramatic encounter in November when sheriff's officers levied upon certain effects in Nanteos mansion in the name of a creditor and insisted, (much to the annoyance of the Nanteos tenant) in taking possession of the mansion until some of the creditor's demands had been met, Powell and his trustees decided that the time had come for drastic action. Inevitably, this involved the disposal of real estate. While Cherry and Edwards stalled for time by persuading the clamouring creditors in London and elsewhere that their demands would be met from land sales, Powell arranged for the sale of his unentailed property at Llanbrynmair in Montgomeryshire. The land was eventually purchased for £18,250 by Captain John Conroy, the ambitious Irishman who was ultimately to play such a major role in Court circles. Concerned that Powell might dispose of the sale money in an irresponsible manner, Cherry insisted that the whole proceeds be placed in the hands of the trustees to be appropriated to paying off both the Llanbrynmair mortgage of £6,000 and the bond creditors. Cherry was in a tough mood and warned Powell that without his 'unequivocal promise as man of Honor and a Gentleman', that this measure would be observed, he would personally institute a Chancery suit and advise the creditors.[12] This threat seems to have had the desired effect and the Llanbrynmair sales provided a temporary respite.

Over the next three years, Cherry and Edwards succeeded in raising sufficient loans and new mortgages to discharge the bulk of the arrears of interest on long-standing debts and by 1826 some £8,800 of contract and bond debts remained. Cherry argued that much of this could be paid if Powell were prepared to part with the Lovesgrove estate which of course, did not form part of the family settlement. While he agreed that it was a great pity to dispose of real estate, Powell would inevitably be forced to sell some of his unentailed property if he were to avoid law proceedings from his creditors. 'The question, in my mind, does not admit of a moment's hesitation – that is always provided you have any wish to get rid of your troubles (for really I sometimes fancy they act as a kind of stimulus or amusement to you). I once knew an old lady who was never so happy as when under the influence of a blister.' Although Cherry repeated his argument in July, Lovesgrove remained under Nanteos control until 1843 when it was purchased by John Evans for £7,500.

Since 1824, Powell's relationship with Cherry had become increasingly strained, and in the summer of 1826 he accused Cherry, for no apparent reason, of acting dishonestly in his capacity as a trustee. Refusing further communication with Cherry, he authorised one Victor Lozon of Barnstaple and the perennial James Hughes to attend to all matters between him and his trustees and to 'finally settle all and every outstanding account between me and my trustees, agents and stewards.' Having received a particularly hostile letter from Hughes, Cherry denied all accusations against him and invited Powell to have a *gentleman* (implying that such a term could not be applied to James Hughes of Glanrheidol) examine his accounts. The departure of Cherry was quickly followed by the resignation of George Warbrick, leaving the management of Nanteos for the next decade in the control of James Hughes, to whom part of the estate was mortgaged for £4,000. Throughout the late eighteen twenties and the thirties, Powell was constantly being reminded by his agent of the parlous finances of the estate and of the pressing need to exercise severe retrenchment. Having settled the account of William Roberts, the butcher who had come to him 'with tears in his eyes', on 1 June 1833, he counselled Powell: 'Therefore, dear Colonel, let me try and entreat you to turn these matters in your thoughts most seriously for it is very evident we are getting backwards and unless some change takes place you will be in the same unfortunate situation you were some years ago . . . In consequence of the difficulty I find in paying folks I have been obliged to stop all improvements on your estate.'

It is important to appreciate that although William Powell had never shown a great deal of enthusiasm for thrift and economy, his heavy expenditure in relation to his income was not entirely due to an excess of hedonism. He was, after all, no longer a plain country squire. As Member for the County, Lord Lieutenant and Custos Rotulorum he was expected to entertain lavishly both at Nanteos (which became his principal residence around 1830) and at his London home. Moreover, maintaining one's position and interest in the county necessitated heavy expenditure upon charitable causes, subscriptions to schools, churches, markets and any number of local building projects besides the crippling cost of appearing regularly in the hunting field.[13] The more important a man's position in county society, the more munificent were his charitable acts and

George White, Nanteos butler, in 1836, by W. Chapman.

the more expansive his style of life expected to be. Thus, having once achieved high social and political position a gentleman was frequently forced to encumber his estate with heavy mortgages in order to live in the style which society expected. Of course, a fine mansion furnished tastefully and expensively did a great deal to enhance his status, a fact which doubtless was in Powell's mind when he decided to refurbish the rather austere eighteenth-century edifice at Nanteos. Back in 1831 he had been considering certain alterations to the house, but had been dissuaded from so doing by his agent who wisely advised that the cost of constructing a portico could far exceed that set out in the estimate submitted by one Richard James. In 1845, however, when Hughes had despairingly abandoned any attempt to balance the estate accounts and no longer tried to restrain his employer's expenditure, Powell invited Edward Haycock, the Shrewsbury architect, to prepare plans both for a portico and a new wing for the mansion. During discussions, Powell agreed to provide rough stone, sand and oak timber from the estate and to undertake the transport of materials from Aberystwyth to Nanteos. These items apart, the final bill for the project, which was completed in 1847, totalled £2,880.

Within a few years of completing the Nanteos alterations, William Edward Powell was dead. After thirty-eight years as a Member of Parliament he expired quietly in 1854 and was laid to rest with his forefathers in the church of Llanbadarn Fawr. Under the terms of his will, dated 3 October 1852, his second wife, Harriet, was to enjoy the income granted her by his marriage settlement together with a further £500 a year which his executors were directed to raise. Moreover he willed that his wife be given the opportunity of selecting for her own use, any horses, carriages, household furniture and chattels from both Nanteos and the London house, any remaining chattels to be regarded as heirlooms. His outstanding debts and other legacies as set out in his will were to be discharged by the sale of unentailed property and the creation of further mortgages, while the Nanteos estate and all other settled lands devolved upon his son William Thomas Rowland Powell as tenant -in-tail.

W. T. R. Powell was born on 3 August 1815 and educated at Westminster. As a nineteen-year-old ensign in the 37th Regiment he served in Jamaica, where he seems to have sown his wild oats with considerable gusto. Like his father, Powell consistently lived beyond his means and despite the remonstrations of his commanding officer, he had, by 1834, accumulated debts of £530, besides having had a number of his bills dishonoured. Colonel Smart, commander of the 37th Regiment, while appreciating the young man's wish to 'cut a dash', explained to his father, 'The people here, [in Jamaica] amongst whom there are a great many Jews, always make a point of getting hold of any young man they see inclined to extravagance and your son unfortunately got into their clutches.' His debts having been paid by his father, young Powell retired from the regiment with the rank of captain and returned to Britain in

W.T.R. Powell suffered from partial paralysis of the legs. From his first "attack" in 1858, he was dependent on a wheelchair

N.L.W.

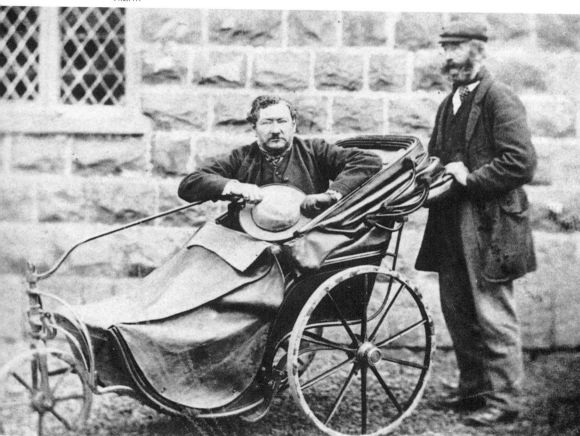

1839 when he married Rosa Edwina, daughter of W. G. Cherry, late trustee of the Nanteos estate. Of his activities over the next fifteen years we know little. However, upon the death of his father in 1854 he inherited the estate and was elected Member for the County five years later, a seat which he was to hold until 1865.[14] The fact that an inventory of the Nanteos stables for that year mentions '4 bath chairs for Colonel Powell' shows that he did not enjoy the best of health and may explain why he persuaded his cousin, William Edward Phelp, to come to Nanteos and assist with the management of the estate.

Upon Phelp, who enjoyed a life annuity of £250 for his duties, descended the virtually insuperable problem of maintaining estate income at a level sufficient to meet annuity charges and mortgage interest. By 1865, due largely to increased rentals, income totalled approximately £13,000 a year, from which £6,500 was annually to be deducted for mortgage, annuity and insurance charges. Given that normal estate expenditure was running at between £4,500 and £5,000 annually, little balance remained for the discharging of bond debts (£9,000 in 1866) or expenditure on estate improvements.[15] This meant that virtually every penny of the £10,841 expended upon estate improvement between 1862 and 1867 was raised by creating further debt. The inability of the estate to carry any further mortgages, in conjunction with the growing pressure from creditors precipitated the inevitable land sales and land to the value of £82,617 came under the hammer between 1868 and 1873.

One of the smaller drains on the estate was the provision of £300 a year for W.T.R. Powell's younger brother, Cornelius, who was a constant embarrassment.[16] In 1869, for example, he wrote to his brother from the Kenmore Arms Hotel in Killarney, where he had been arrested for being unable to pay his bill of £50. It was, however, a reflection of their late father's popularity in this part of Ireland when the Sheriff observed that he 'would never let the son of Colonel Powell go to jail as long as it was in his power'. The £50 was forwarded immediately.

Unlike his popular father, W. T. R. Powell did not enjoy the affection of his tenants. Neither he nor Phelp could

Election Poster, 1859
N.L.W.

TO THE
FREEHOLDERS
AND OTHER
ELECTORS
OF THE
COUNTY OF CARDIGAN.

GENTLEMEN,

The Right Honorable the Earl of Lisburne having declared his intention of retiring from Parliament, and as an immediate dissolution will place in your hands the important privilege of electing a Representative, I avail myself of the earliest opportunity that has been afforded me of offering myself as a Candidate for your suffrages and support. My Political opinions are known to most of you; at the same time I am not unmindful of the changes that have occurred and are taking place in our social and Political Institutions, I am, therefore, prepared to support any sound measure, having for its object an improvement in the Representation of the People, as well as other measures which may be necessary for the welfare of our Country. With regard to the question of Church Rates, I desire to see it speedily and finally settled, in a way that may be satisfactory to all classes and denominations of Christians.

It is unnecessary, I am sure, that I should in any way allude to the interest which I must ever have in the County of Cardigan, and to the connections which for so many years have existed between you and my family.

Should your Votes, therefore, place me in the proud position of being your Representative, I trust that I shall faithfully discharge the duties that will be imposed upon me, and be found deserving of the trust confided to my keeping.

I have the honor to be,
GENTLEMEN,
Your faithful and obedient Servant,

Nanteos,
April 12th, 1859.

W. T. R. POWELL.

speak or understand Welsh, relying almost entirely upon the services of a translator, one Davy Edwards, in their business affairs with the tenants. Both men had little understanding of their tenants and earned a great deal of odium in 1868 when they attempted to pressurise farmers on the estate to cast their votes for the Tory candidate at the notorious election of that year. Although no evictions followed when some farmers insisted upon voting for the Liberal man, E. M. Richards, the relationships between the estate office and the tenantry became permanently soured.

135

It is unlikely, therefore, that W. T. R. Powell's death in May 1878 was the occasion for a great deal of genuine mourning on the part of his tenants.

The thirty-six year old George Ernest John Powell, who had heartily detested his father, succeeded the old Colonel as life-tenant of Nanteos.[17] Perhaps the most cultivated and civilised of the Cardiganshire squires since Thomas Johnes of Hafod, George Powell had studied at Brasenose College, Oxford, and spent much of his time travelling abroad and pursuing his literary and dilettante activities. Poet, eccentric, scholar and friend of Swinburne and Longfellow, he was not a man for country pursuits. Although he frequently visited Cardiganshire with Swinburne in the 1860s he preferred to carouse in Aberystwyth with his friend rather than listen to mutterings of the old squire at Nanteos who was totally unsympathetic to his son's literary interests. Thus was he wont to refer to Nanteos as, 'my beautiful but unhappy home'. Such a man was hardly likely to relish the management of a heavily encumbered estate and the current trustees managed to persuade Sylvanus Lewis of Bronaeron, George's father's former private secretary, to assist with the running of the property. Four years later, however, nature took her revenge upon the many abuses to which George Powell had subjected his body and he died at the age of forty, having recently married a girl of obscure parentage from Goodwick in Pembrokeshire.[18] His remarkable story is set out in more detail in chapter 4.

George Powell's will of 5 July 1881 declared that in the event of his having no children the estate was to pass to his father's cousin, William Beauclerk Powell, son of Richard Owen Powell who had died in 1859.[19] Between them, W. B. Powell, his wife Anna and her brother Sylvanus Lewis managed the estate economically and efficiently, so earning the fulsome praise of the trustee's solicitor, Henry Cobb, who declared his pleasure in collaborating with the trio. By the late eighteen-eighties, the majority of the old annuitants were dead and a series of land sales had permitted the payment of all the bond debts and many of the mortgages, so that by 1887 the estate, although contracted in size, now carried a mortgage debt of only

£50,000. Indeed, matters had improved to such an extent that Powell decided to set about the improvement of the appallingly dilapidated houses and farms on the estate. Accordingly, he successfully applied to the trustees to sell off parts of the settled estate under the terms of the Settled Land Act of 1882 by which life tenants were empowered to dispose of entailed real estate and to use some of the capital released towards this objective. The results of his improvements may still be seen on many of the farms in the parishes of Llanbadarn and Llanfihangel-y-Creuddyn.

With the coming of age, in 1891, of his son, Edward Athelstan Lewis, Powell sought the advice of Frederick Procter of Lincoln's Inn regarding the future organisation of the estate and the most appropriate means of reducing the £50,000 mortgage, interest upon which absorbed £2,000 of income annually. Observing that Edward, 'has not the tastes which in the case of so many of his family who have gone before him have caused so much loss and trouble', Procter counselled Powell to join with his son in barring the entail in the family settlement, thus enabling settled lands to be sold and the mortgage debt to be reduced. Acting accordingly, the Powells secured the appropriate legal authorisation and sales of extensive parts of the settled estate began in 1882, when 1,547 acres were auctioned, together with properties in Aberystwyth.[20] Further sales in 1897-8 caused a reduction in the mortgage debt to £30,000 and in the size of the estate to a mere 4,336 acres.

Edward Athelstan Lewis Powell, who had retired from the Leicestershire Regiment with the rank of Captain in 1901, now became increasingly involved in the affairs of the estate. The imposition of Estate Duty in 1894, coupled with the fact that W. B. Powell was sixty-seven years of age in 1901, meant that sooner or later the estate would be called upon to contribute to the Exchequer coffers. To provide for this inevitable burden, a sinking fund was established into which surplus estate income was paid. This, it was hoped, would meet both death and succession duties upon the passing of W. B. Powell, and leave sufficient surplus for the payment of life insurance premiums against estate duty payments upon the death of

NANTEOS

Edward Powell. It soon became clear, however, that with the estate now only yielding a net income of £2,000 annually there would be relatively little surplus with which to feed the sinking fund. Thus in 1909 it was agreed to effect a major resettlement with the principle object of ensuring the continuation of the estate in the family, and, equally important, of minimising estate duty. Fortunately for all concerned, the resettlement was completed before the 1909 Finance Bill was enacted and the succession of the estate thereby ensured. Had this not been done, the Budget increases in estate and stamp duty would have cost an extra £4000. Having surrendered his life interest in the estate to his son under the resettlement, William Beauclerk Powell eventually died in 1911, and when his affairs were finally wound up some six years later, death duties amounted to slightly less than £6,000. Two instalments of the demand were met from the sinking fund, the balance being discharged by the sale of Trefedlin farm.

Like his brother-in-law, Sir Edward Webley-Parry-Pryse of Gogerddan, Edward Powell, although well into middle age, answered the call to arms when war broke out in 1914. Rejoining his old regiment, he saw active service in Mesopotamia, while his nineteen year old son William Edward fought in France. Several days before the Armistice the heir to the Nanteos estate was the target of a bullet, and as William Powell expired in the mud of Flanders, so perished his father's fond hope that the name

William Edward George Pryse Wynne Powell (1889-1918)
N.L.W.

of Powell would continue to be associated with Nanteos. Reviewing the long list of his various nephews and cousins, the disconsolate Edward Powell concluded that a suitable heir was not available. Consequently he secured a series of legal arrangements throughout the nineteen twenties permitting him to dispose of parts of the estate as and when he pleased, arranging, through his will, that his real and personal estate be sold upon his death to discharge remaining mortgages and provide an income for his wife during her lifetime. His death in 1930 brought about the final extinction of the male line of the Powells of Nanteos.

By way of a postscript, it should be made clear that few general conclusions about the overall condition of the landed estate in nineteenth century Cardiganshire may be drawn from the study of one estate in isolation. Nanteos, whose economic decline resulted largely from the lack of resolve of one life tenant to extricate the estate from its difficulties, is hardly typical of many of the

Lord Ystwyth at the unveiling of the memorial at Southgate, Aberystwyth, to W.E.G.P.W. Powell.
N.L.W.

smaller estates, whose owners, although financially hard-pressed, tended to live within their incomes and to accumulate relatively modest mortgage burdens. Indeed, had economic factors been the sole determinants of the decline of the gentry, many of these estates might well have passed largely intact through the trying years of the late nineteenth and early twentieth centuries. There were, however, other potent forces operating against the political, economic and social powers of the gentry. By the closing decades of the nineteenth century it was becoming clear that the occupation of large tracts of land no longer conferred political power and social prestige, and the newly-discovered political independence of the nonconformist tenantry, combined with the passing of the Ballot Act in 1872, left few county families in any doubt that their reign as the unquestioned political representatives of the people was drawing to its close. Out of Nonconformity grew local Liberalism, the seeds of which were to yield a harvest of parliamentary members and council seats, and was to break for ever the political hegemony of the gentry. The Local Government Act of 1888 removed the necessity for a property qualification on the part of a candidate for local office, and the routing of the gentry at the County Council elections of the following year and subsequently at the elections to the newly constituted Parish Councils, left a deep psychological scar. As a political institution the gentry was now a spent force. Reeling under the trauma of the inevitability of the breakdown of the old system, its members became increasingly uninterested in politics. Sir Pryse Pryse of Gogerddan spent more of his time overseas; at Nanteos pursuit of the fox took precedence over political interest, while at Trawsgoed, Lord Lisburne, traditional leader of the Tory party did not even consider it worthwhile to subscribe to the party Registration Fund. Rejected politically, embarrassed economically and continually subject to the rancour of Radical writers and politicians who questioned the whole institution of land ownership, increasing numbers of the gentry concluded that the time was ripe to rid themselves of their estates, which, for many of them, had become a burden rather than a pleasure.

The spectres of estate duty and other forms of taxation were of grave concern, especially as the income tax, succession duty, poor, county, highway, police and education rates fell heavily upon the landed interest, while the growing number of villa dwellers, whose incomes derived from non-landed sources, were virtually immune. Moreover, by the late nineteenth century, there were a growing number of alternative sources of investment, especially in the form of joint-stock companies, which yielded high returns on invested capital. As a result more and more landed gentlemen decided to avail themselves of the Settled Land Act, by which they were empowered to sell real estate, thereby freeing themselves of encumbrances and releasing cash for investment in commercial and industrial development. Thus was the scene set for the flood of land sales which characterised the early twentieth century.

NOTES

[1] This chapter originally appeared in substance in *Ceredigion* IX, 1 (1980), 58-77. The editor is grateful to Professor Moore-Colyer for permission to reprint the article, and assumes responsibility for changes made to avoid undue duplication with other chapters, though his assessments of characters have of course been retained. Prof. Moore-Colyer's sources can be traced by reference to the notes to his original article, using the more recently available Nanteos schedule in N.L.W. The valuable notes of substance have been retained or incorporated in the text. The appendix listing estate expenditure 1837-39 has been omitted, but some details are included in the text.

[2] Severe floggings were commonplace at Westminster. Robert Southey had been expelled from the school in 1792. Lawrence the future Governor-General of India and went to Westminster in 1811, said bitterly: 'I was flogged once every day of my life at school except one, and there I was flogged twice.'

[3] Especially the local solicitor, Hugh Hughes, who had been involved in a series of questionable actions regarding the lead mines on the Nanteos estate. He was eventually declared insane in 1809.

[4] Cynic, wit and eccentric, Corbet was 'a man of the world, and when he pleased a very polished gentleman.' An agricultural improver who studied medicine with a view to benefitting his tenants, he was well disposed towards all denominations, with the notable exception of the Methodists, whom he distrusted. (H.Thomas, *J.Merion. Hist. Rec. Soc.,* 4, 1962).

[5] N.L.W. N.L. 803.

[6] The Nanteos butler, White, was noted for his dedication to the bottle. When asked in verse by a London wit why his nose was so red, he replied:

'Nanteos ale both strong and stale,

Keeps my nose from looking pale.' (*Welsh Gazette*, 1 Feb, 1905).

[7] During her declining years Mrs. Powell was frequently arrested for debt by the French authorities, only avoiding prison by the intercession of friends. She died following a stroke on 7 September, 1826, her death being no doubt hastened by the doctor's insistence upon extracting 3 pounds of blood from the unfortunate woman within several hours of the attack.

[8] N.L.W. Nanteos L1125, 27 August 1825.

[9] N.L.W.Glanpaith 233. The deed of separation includes an inventory of Penglais mansion.

[10] The fact that Powell had spent large sums upon his home farm without taking 'the least pleasure' in it, suggests that he was merely following the current fashion of pursuing 'the spirit of improvement'. Expenditure on the home farm comprised 14% of total estate expenditure between 1815 and 1816.

[11] Mutual character assassination by estate employees was not peculiar to Nanteos. For other examples see R.J. [Moore-] Colyer, 'The

Hafod Estate under Thomas Johnes and the 4th Duke of Newcastle',
Welsh History Review 8, 1977, 257-84.

[12] Throughout the previous year Cherry had repeatedly castigated
Powell for devoting too much of his time to 'amusement' and too little
to his business affairs. He would doubtless have strongly disapproved of
Powell's purchase, for £273, of a new post chaise from Stubbs and
Hancock of London in the autumn of 1825.

[13] Thus in 1838-9 Powell subscribed £100 to the provision of public
lamps at Aberystwyth. . Only £57 went to other charities, out of a year's
expenditure of £10,138. Other expenditure in the same year included
£401 election expenses at Cardigan (despite being re-elected
unopposed) and 'cash lent Mr Morgan late tutor at Nanteos' £55.

[14] Powell was gazetted Lieutenant Colonel in the Cardiganshire
Militia in 1854 following his father's retirement (*Gentleman's
Magazine*, 1854, 518).

[15] These included the fitting out of a new billiard room at Nanteos.

[16] In 1838-39 Powell paid £390 for his commission in the Dragoon
Guards.

[17] For a more detailed study of George Powell, see above, chapter 4.

[18] This was Dinah Harries, who within a year of Powell's death was
remarried to a Ulysses T. Whildin of Illinois. This delighted the Nanteos
trustees' London solicitor, Henry Cobb, who was able to reduce Dinah's
annuity to £250 upon her remarriage.

[19] R.O.Powell had married Harriet Anne Wynne of Peniarth, by
whom he had three children, Athelstan Owen, William Beauclerk and
Elinor Laura Powell.

[20] The land realised £13,545, a figure which would have been
exceeded had the farm buildings been in a better state of repair. Some
indication of the poor condition of the farms and cottages on the estate
is provided by the frequency with which the Sanitary Authority invoked
the Public Health Act of 1875 and ordered the provision of adequate
ventilation in houses owned by Nanteos. James Hughes, sanitary
inspector for the Aberystwyth Rural District Council, often wrote to the
estate office concerning the conditions which many tenants were forced
to tolerate. In 1902 he noted that Gorsfach was in the same
unsatisfactory condition as at his previous visit, while 'the old cottages
where Walters lives [has] mud floors with big holes enough to bury a
dog in them'.

6.

NANTEOS:
EBB AND FLOW

J. Hext Lewes

NANTEOS

Nanteos in Winter (1991).

NANTEOS: EBB AND FLOW [1]

AFTER Mrs Margaret Powell became a widow in 1931, she lived on at Nanteos, doing her best to keep things together for her successor in various ways, such as letting the house each summer holidays to the head of a large family in Birmingham, who filled and enlivened the house. No rent was paid, but there was an informal agreement each year to carry out substantial and urgent repairs. In spite of financial stringency, she resisted to the utmost of her might any inroads on her property, particularly the compulsory purchase by the local council of all the land on which Penparcau is now built. Previously there had been only a few houses occupied around Southgate, then known as Piccadilly.

One of her main preoccupations was to choose an heir to take the place of her dead son. Many names were thought of, including my own. Having experienced the crippling effect of death duties on the estate, one of her principles was that her successor should be someone who would be able to deal with the death duties without further encumbrance on the estate, and who would be likely to cherish the place and try to keep it as intact as possible. I had the impression that had I been able to ante up the future death duties, then and there in 1936 the quest would have ended. But I could not, and family experience suggested that it might be a little perilous getting involved in financial dealings with a Pryse (she was of the Gogerddan family). My only connection was that Margaret Powell's mother was sister to my grandfather, and also that I was reasonably close in age to the real heir, killed in 1918.

Margaret Powell got steadily more deaf and isolated from the world as the years went by, but she was always a joy to visit. She used to go around on

Mrs Margaret Powell, holding her ear-trumpet.
N.L.W.

an old pony who understood her thoughts, and moved and stopped at her wish. She, though Anglican, regularly attended the chapel at Capel Seion, though she could not have heard a word of the service or sermon, despite her well-known ear-trumpet. During the second World War she gave shelter to a colony of French nuns who had been driven out of their own country by the Germans, and they were to stay at Nanteos until after the end of the war. They had a whole floor of the house. They were there from March 1941 until June 1945, when they returned to the Annonciade Convent at St Margaret's Bay, Dover.

The family solicitor in Aberystwyth, Mr Jessop, had on occasion apparently tried too much to influence affairs, and had been dismissed, the estate business being transferred to a less forceful personality. After the war still no-one knew whether the search for an heir had been concluded. The only Powell relation was a distant second or third cousin through the female line, whom the old lady did not greatly favour, but who in the end got the whole property unrestrained in any way.

On one occasion I had tried to give her some advice concerning action needed by the Development Bill. When I got home I wrote out what I had been trying to tell her in case I had not been able to make her hear. One never knew whether she had heard, or was saying 'Yes, yes, my dear' with a happy smile, just to disguise the fact that she had not. I added to the letter: 'Who your heir may be is, I believe, the best-kept secret in Cardiganshire, but would it not be a good thing now to let him or her start to take a part in the adminstration of the estate in order to preserve continuity?' Her only reply was: 'Thank you very much for your valuable advice which I will carefully consider.'

When Margaret Powell died in 1952, two or three years after the discussion just described, the lawyer knew of no will, and as far as he was concerned it was an intestacy, in which case the estate would be divided among the Gogerddan grandchildren, her own next of kin, namely Sir Loveden Pryse-Saunders, his sister Mrs. Briggs, and Mrs Loxdale of Castle Hill, Llanilar. A fortnight later, when Mrs. Loxdale and Maggie the maid were clearing up, Maggie found under the brown paper at the bottom of the stocking drawer a double sheet of lined foolscap, folded into four, with writing by Mrs. Powell herself and signatures, which looked like a will. The text of the will itself covered three and a quarter sides of the paper, and Margaret Powell's bold signature was just below the top fold which, however, cut the tops of the capital letters. Lower down there were the signatures of two of the French nuns who had been at Nanteos during the war – just the signatures themselves, without any attestation clause. Below that two unwitnessed codicils, one to let the nuns stay until the end of the war, and one naming two possible successors, named below. The nuns had been asked to sign on January 26, 1941.

The case went to the High Court for four days to prove whether there was a will, the contestants being on the one side the two persons named in the will, Betty Garnons Williams (later Mirylees) and myself, and on the other side, seeking an intestacy, were the Pryse cousins named above. The two nuns were brought to give evidence, dressed in magnificent medieval robes, and said that they had not witnessed a will. Mrs. Powell had brought them a blank sheet of paper, and they were certain that there was no visible writing, though it had been folded over at the top quarter. They had been asked to sign their names on it to allow them to stay at Nanteos until after the end of the war. There had been no mention of a will or of witnessing anything. They were quite certain that the top quarter of the sheet was folded back. They gave their evidence in French through an interpreter, whom they corrected from time to time if they did not agree with his interpretation.

A handwriting expert gave evidence that had the paper been folded before Mrs. Powell had signed, the surface would have been broken and the ink of the bold signature would have run in the crack, which it had not. The fold was therefore subsequent to the signing, so the signature must have been visible to the nuns when they signed, had they had a mind to see it. As the signature was presented by the person whose signature it was, this fulfilled the definition of 'signed in our presence'. There was no question that all three were present when the nuns signed, and the judgement was that there was no requirement for an attestation clause, nor even that the witnesses should know that they were witnessing anything, let alone a will. Their signatures were needed only to authenticate the piece of paper that they were on. So there was a will.

Eighteen months then elapsed before the case came up again, this time to decide if the will meant anything. The Pryse relations sought to prove a nonsense which would again produce an intestacy. The two persons named had an interest to prove it meant something. The essential parts of the will, after copying verbiage from old wills leaving her soul to Almighty God hoping he would have mercy on her sins and shortcomings were:

> I bequeath the whole of the Nanteos Estate etc. under the following conditions.
>
> My successor must be able to pay the death duties without selling anything belonging to Nanteos to help him or her do so, and no additional mortgage must be raised on the property to help him or her. He (or she) must not cut down or sell any standing timber on Llechwedd Dyrys, the Warren, the Cottage Dingle or the Flat Covert, and no ornamental timber at all. The silver with the Nanteos crest, the portraits and old Nanteos furniture are to be made heirlooms.
>
> With these restrictions I leave the whole of the Nanteos Property and everything which belonged to the Powell Family to Garnons-Williams (Betty), provided always that she makes a good, just and kind landlord, lives at Nanteos and keeps it up properly and does not have her parents to live there and does not have her grandparents there at all.
>
> Should she be unable to carry out my instructions I leave everything as stated under the same conditions to John Hext Lewes, Commander, R.N.

A sum of about £19,000 was required in death duties, and there was an overdraft at Lloyds Banks of £37,000 arising I think from the payment of death duties on the death of E.A.L.Powell in 1930. By mortgaging Llanllyr I could have raised the money for the death duties. It was thought that Mrs Betty Mirylees could not.

The court found that since payment of death duties on real estate could be spread over a period of seven years, to require them to be paid before entering into possession was an interference with the free enjoyment of the gift, and was of no effect. Most of the other clauses fell as being contrary to public policy or being too vague, and the only thing that remained was the name of Betty Garnons-Williams (Mrs Mirylees), who succeeded to the estate without any restrictions whatever, which was the one thing which the old lady wished to avoid.[2] After some years of residence the whole estate was sold, and the Mirylees family moved to Hay-on-Wye, taking the Nanteos cup with them.

*   *   *

Later Owners of Nanteos

Gerald Morgan

The Mirylees family regularly opened Nanteos to summer visitors during their occupation of the estate, which began in 1956. I have a lively memory of visiting the house in 1964. At that time there were far fewer country houses open to the public than now, and most of those that were open were the leviathans of England. Nanteos, by comparison, was small fry, with little of the fine furniture and none of the great paintings to be found at Petworth or Chatsworth. However, the very rarity of the experience, the delightful situation of the house and the atmosphere of family occupation all rendered the occasion memorable, not least the impact of the Pekinese dogs, which were not thoroughly housetrained. Particularly noteworthy was the silver plate, especially the two gravy-boats made of Cardiganshire silver. Equally memorable was the Nanteos cup, though it may have been that what we were shown was in fact a copy of the original.

When the Mirylees family left in 1967, they took the cup with them, and the splendid equine statue which stood over the stable entrance had been sold off. It is now in America. The 4,000 acres inherited in 1952 had dwindled to 2,600 by 1967, when this remainder was sold. Happily, the house had been given a grant for a new roof in 1958 which helped it survive the vicissitudes which were eventually to follow. The new owners, Mr & Mrs Geoffrey Bliss, kept the house open each summer, rented rooms in the attic to students and kept the place in repair. They sold the house in 1983, and after a brief occupancy the mansion passed into the hands of bankers, and inevitably looked to have fallen on evil days.

That the house avoided what seemed an inevitable fall into rack and ruin was due to Mr Gary Hesp. He bought the house, with 26 acres of land, in 1989, and set about restoring the place. A caretaker was installed, the house was dried out, some collapsing outhouses were propped up, others were repurchased, the ivy-wreathed dovecot was stripped of its heavy growth, work commenced on the gardens, furniture, kitchen copper and pictures reappeared, and slowly the house returned to life. Within a few years it was possible to open several rooms for bed-and-breakfast, and in 1995 a restaurant, christened Powells, was opened. One of the most attractive country houses in Wales had been rescued from decay, seemingly at the last minute, and restored to use. In 1999 Nanteos was sold to a Cardiff-based development company owned by Mr Timothy Gwyn-Jones whose staff are maintaining services to customers.

NOTES

[1] My thanks to Professor Richard Moore-Colyer, who supplied me with a copy of the original document given to him by Captain Hext-Lewes after he had written it in 1979.

[2] Capt. Hext-Lewes's text has an appendix of figures for the valuation of the estate at Mrs Powell's death. The total land value was £96,136, with a further £6,125 for furniture and silver, and £3,300 for other effects. Almost all the farms were let on tenant-repairing agreements for well under £1 an acre.

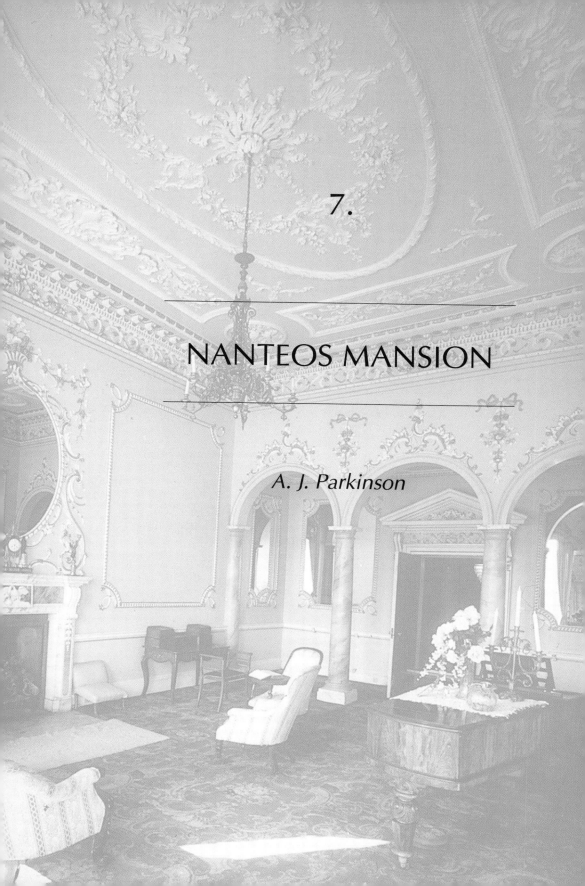

7.

NANTEOS MANSION

A. J. Parkinson

NANTEOS

Nanteos in 1888 (by courtesy of the Earl of Lisburne).

NANTEOS MANSION

Introduction

THE development of the architecture of the great house in England and Wales from the Middle Ages to the later eighteenth century may be summed up as a series of steps towards formality and elegance. In the later Middle Ages the houses of the greater magnates consisted of a number of connected but discrete units centred on the great hall; this was a combination of a communal living area and a public space for judicial and ceremonial purposes. In Wales one of the best examples is the fourteenth-century Bishop's Palace at St Davids, with its immense first floor hall.[1] The mediaeval hall had very pronounced axial symmetry, but this was entirely internal and there was rarely any attempt to unify or formalise the design of the exterior.

By the end of the sixteenth century there was a considerable change, for a number of reasons. One of the most significant was the social factor of an increased desire for privacy, which led to a greater separation of private and public apartments. Another was the influence of the Renaissance, which introduced new design parameters based on classical ideas, originating from Italy but filtered through France and the Netherlands. External symmetry became fashionable, and decoration included exotic classical motifs; examples are Plas-mawr, Conwy (Caerns.) of 1576-80,[2] and the new porch at Old Beaupre (Glam.) of 1580.[3] At the highest social level there were a group of 'prodigy' houses, of immense size and often based on abstract designs, such as Wollaton Hall, Notts;[4] a relatively small example is Plas Teg, Hope, of 1610.[5] Such designs originated in court circles, and both Plas-mawr and Plas Teg were built by prominent Welsh courtiers.

In the early seventeenth century there was a period which, although brief, was in the long run very significant: a completely new style of architecture was introduced to London and the court. Inigo Jones and John Webb built a series of houses for Charles I and his associates in an impeccable Italianate style based closely on the ideas of the sixteenth-century architect and writer Andrea Palladio (1508-80). Among them were the Banqueting House in Whitehall[6] and the Queen's House, Greenwich, which was completed in 1635.[7] However, this very formal style made little impact beyond the Metropolis, and after the Civil War there was a reaction against it. In its place there developed the Baroque classicism of Sir Christopher Wren, Nicholas Hawksmoor and Sir John Vanbrugh.[8] This was a style in which rich surface decoration combined with bold profiles, using classical motifs and principles in a somewhat adapted form. In north-east Wales architects such as Richard Trubshaw (1689-1745)[9] built houses in this style, one of the best being Pickhill Hall (Flints.) of c.1720.[10] The style reached as far as west Wales, an example being the seventeenth-century house at Trawsgoed, sketched in 1684 but completely rebuilt around the beginning of the nineteenth century.[11] By the end of the seventeenth century there had also emerged a quieter version of this style popularly known as 'Queen Anne style', in which the classicism was often little more than a matter of rhythm and detail. An early example was Coleshill (c.1662);[12] on a similar scale was the first phase of Erddig (Denbs.), which was built in the 1680s.[13] This style retained its popularity among the minor gentry for much of the eighteenth century.

However, towards the beginning of the eighteenth century there was a second architectural revolution, which may be attributed to the efforts of three men – two architects and their patron. The patron was Richard Boyle, 3rd Earl of Burlington (1694-1753), who put forward the idea that Great Britain should have a national architectural style: the

W.R.Coultart's 1841 elevation for twin wings at Nanteos. Only the east wing was built.

N.L.W.

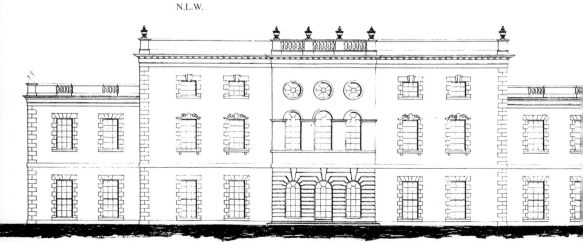

architects were Colen Campbell (1673-1729) and Giacomo Leoni (c.1686-1746), who published a series of books from 1715 onwards which made available to the discerning nobility – and later, in cheaper editions, to practising builders – illustrations of what they considered to be the best of British building of the previous hundred years. Most of these were in the style of Andrea Palladio as interpreted by Inigo Jones and his followers, and for the next half-century or more a high proportion of major new buildings followed the canon of style laid down in Campbell's *Vitruvius Britannicus* or Leoni's and later Isaac Ware's editions of Palladio's own *Four Books of Architecture*.[14]

Palladianism, as the style came to be called, had very strict rules both in its original Italian form and in its seventeenth century English derivative. However, it was also capable of considerable adaptation of scale, since many of the really big Palladian houses (such as Castle Howard) were in fact a grouping of units, balanced and linked with each other but fundamentally complete by themselves. This allowed several sorts of development to take place. Firstly, there were the new grand palaces, with wings and courtyards. Secondly, there were the updated older houses which were given a new Palladian facade, such as Leeswood Hall (Flints).[15] Thirdly, there was the new class of small villas, on an altogether more modest scale but still employing Palladian ideas. A late example is Llanerchaeron (Cards.) of 1794, by Nash.[16] But as time wore on it is noticeable that many of the later designs became blander than the prototypes, since they derived not from ideas taken from three-dimensional buildings but from the slightly understated drawings of those buildings published in *Vitruvius Britannicus* and elsewhere.

The Architects of Nanteos

Nanteos is one of the few great houses of Cardiganshire to have survived without undergoing the major rebuilding in the Victorian period which so altered houses like Trawsgoed or Gogerddan. Unfortunately documentation relating to the house itself is rather patchy. There are a number of plans and specifications for new work in the

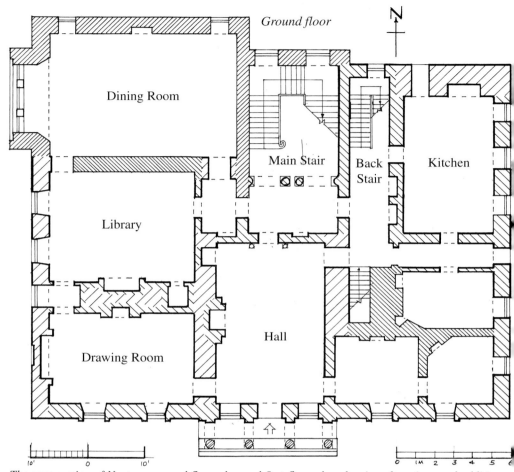

The core section of Nanteos, ground floor plan and first floor plan showing alterations and additions to its construction. The rear butler's pantry and east wing are not described.

(Crown Copyright: the Royal Commission on the Ancient and Historical Monuments of Wales)

I – c. 1700

II – 1739-59

III – 1815-40

IV – 1848-50

Nanteos archive, plus accounts for the payment of architects and builders; but the plans are more valuable for showing work already completed than the intended new work, since most of them seem to show proposals which were never acted upon.[17]

The architect of the eighteenth century house is unknown; however two architects are recorded as having worked on the building in the nineteenth century, William Coultart and Edward Haycock. William Ritson Coultart (b.1796) is a rather shadowy figure.[18] He was in practice in Lancaster in 1828-9, then in Leamington Spa in the 1830s. He may not have been very successful: he left at the time that the main bank in Leamington closed, causing a

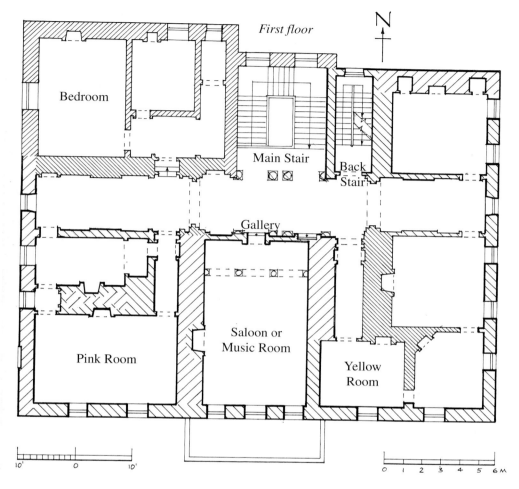

First floor

N

Bedroom

Main Stair

Back Stair

Gallery

Pink Room

Saloon or Music Room

Yellow Room

10'   0   10'

0   1   2   3   4   5   6 M

number of bankruptcies, and even those buildings attributed to him may not have been to his designs. He arrived in Aberystwyth by 1836, and by 1840 was living in North Parade, Aberystwyth. His first recorded job was to survey Ysbyty Cynfyn church, although he was not architect for the restoration.[19] He was in charge of the rebuilding of Llanafan church in 1836-40.[20] He designed the Bronglais workhouse of 1839-41, in a style which was 'a mixture of Old English, Elizabethan and the simple gothic of earlier ages.' The effect is somewhat collegiate.[21] His most successful piece of work was the new County Hall, a very elegant piece of classical architecture 'in the Grecian style'.[22] The 1841 contract having been awarded, there was little progress after the laying of the foundation stone in 1844 because of problems over finance, since there was a disagreement over whether it was to be the Town or County Hall. Eventually it was completed in 1851.[23] Unfortunately it was badly damaged by fire in 1967 and the front has been rebuilt.

Coultart had other commissions in and around the town as well. In 1836 he valued all rateable property in the town for the Town Commissioners (who then queried his bill).[24] In 1846 he designed the new Penparcau Schools, in 'Old English style' with ornamental gables;[25] this was altered in the 1890s. Finally in 1847-8 he was supervising extensive (but undocumented) work at Hafod Uchdryd, Upper Llanfihangel-y-Creuddyn, for Henry de Hoghton.[26]

Coultart lived with his wife and children in Aberystwyth for some years, but by 1851 he had disappeared from the local record. He was evidently retained as the estate architect for Nanteos by 1841 (indeed, the Nanteos connection may have secured him the commission for the County Hall), and a number of drawings survive for proposals to alter the house. He produced a design dated 1841 for providing two wings for the house, but only the east wing was built.[27] By 1846, however, estate records list payments to Edward Haycock of Shrewsbury. Haycock (1790-1870) was a third-generation architect and builder who had a major practice in Shrewsbury. As well as being County Surveyor for Shropshire (1834-66) and a notable character in the social and political life of Shrewsbury, he undertook a number of projects in Wales[28]. His favoured style seems to have been Greek revival, and his design for Clytha Court (Monmouthshire) shows his ability; he may also have designed Glynllifon (Caerns.), which is in the same style.

Most of Haycock's work in west Wales was less noteworthy. He designed Gothic churches at Machynlleth (1827), Barmouth (1830), Aberaeron (1835), Carmarthen (St David's, 1835-6), Llan-non (Carms., 1841), and Llanwddyn (Mont, c.1844). In 1830 he designed the second St Michael's Church, Aberystwyth, of which only part of the vestry survives. His work at Nanteos includes the portico, which was designed in 1845-7 among other alterations, some of which suggest that he had at his disposal designs from his father and grandfather which he was able to adapt to the preferences of his patron.[29]

The Architecture of Nanteos

We will begin with a look at the house in its present state, and a discussion of parallels and some of the stylistic origins of the details. Since the essence of English Palladianism was its external appearance, we will begin with the outside. The materials of the house are typical of great houses of this period. The walls are of a local stone, of uncertain precise origin, laid in lime mortar and originally concealed by lime render or stucco which may have been grooved to imitate ashlar. The roofs are of north Wales slate, hidden behind low parapets. The decorative stonework of the windows and the portico is of a fine-grained sandstone from Grinshill in the West Midlands. It would have been imported by sea, and brought to the site by wagon.[30]

The main elevation of 1739 (which was originally designed without the central portico) is very formal and symmetrical, but also rather staid and unexciting. It seems to draw elements from several earlier houses of note, but possibly from published drawings rather than from actual observation. The most striking similarity is with Castle

Elevations and ground-floor plans of Castle Howard and Nanteos.

CASTLE HOWARD

NANTEOS

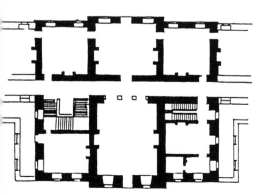

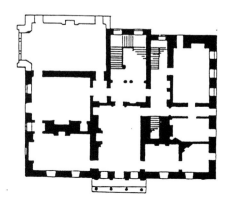

Howard (Yorks.), designed by Sir John Vanbrugh around 1700 and published in *Vitruvius Britannicus* in 1715.[31] Both the height and the length are similar, as in the division into three bays. However, the vertical division into three storeys is more like another house illustrated in *Vitruvius Britannicus*, Amesbury Abbey.[32] The central bay of the house has circular openings, a detail used by Vanbrugh and architects before him, as at The Vine, Sevenoaks, of c.1718, but at Nanteos it is not certain if they were ever meant to be functional, since they are barely above the ceiling of the Saloon.[33] They are at present blind, but the Coultart designs in the Nanteos papers show them glazed.[34] The windows of the side-bays and of the side elevation have elaborate scrolled pediments. This is an oddly archaic detail, more appropriate for a house of 1700 than of 1739; its significance will be discussed below. Finally, there is a lack of articulation on the main facade – usually effected by pilasters or a portico – which suggests that the architect was not altogether at home in the Palladian style. It compares poorly with (for example) Ynysymaengwyn, Tywyn (Mer.), built in 1758, or Taliaris, Llandeilo (Carms.), which was refronted in the 1780s. So perhaps the design was by a local builder or even by Thomas Powell himself, working from published drawings such as those in *Vitruvius Britannicus*.

The plan also shows similarities with those of other Palladian houses, but with peculiarities which may be the result of incorporating parts of an earlier building. The plan of that original house is a matter of guesswork, although a few reused details may give some hints. There are also some lengths of thick wall, which suggest that the kitchen fireplace and a couple of internal walls may be early. An unexpected change in level of the cellar floor which coincides with a change of wall-thickness above may mean that the present south facade 'squares up' the irregular plan of the earlier house.

The resulting basic envelope is somewhat similar to Castle Howard[35] and to Wilbury House (Wilts);[36] in each one a central hall leads to a second space projecting slightly from the rear wall. At Nanteos this contains a stair, unlike Castle Howard but similar to Amesbury (Wilts.);[37] this makes it also broadly similar to a house-plan very

Nanteos: main staircase. 1997.   (Crown Copyright: the Royal Commission on the Ancient and Historical Monuments of Wales)

popular among the minor gentry of south-west Wales in which the stair stands in a rear turret. An example is Dyffryn Llynod, Llandysul (Cards.) of 1785.[38] This stair ought to have been the dominant feature of the centre of the house, and indeed on plan it appears so, with a pair of columns in front not unlike those at Ynysymaengwyn, Towyn (Mer.).[39] But in practice this effect is ruined, because there is a wall in the way. Nor is it likely that this wall is a later addition, since both the hall and the stair-hall are independently symmetrical; and while there is a central axis leading through the hall to the stairs, the whole of the stair-hall is offset to one side.

The stair itself is quite elegant, and leads up to a rather more successful landing. The details of the staircase are mid-eighteenth century, perhaps towards the 1757 date on the leadwork rather than the beginning of construction. The moulded and ramped handrail, spiral newel and slender grouped balusters compare with examples from York, such as nos. 7 & 9 New Street of 1746,[40] or Salisbury, such as no. 32 High Street of 1773.[41] The stair windows, however, are probably by Haycock, who was paid the balance of a bill for repairing both staircases. There are also payments to a 'Mr Evans of Salop' for painted glass in 1837; he was probably one of the partners of the firm of Betton & Evans of Shrewsbury, who produced a great deal of stained and painted glass.[42]

The rest of the plan of the ground floor shows considerable irregularity in the layout and size of rooms. This is probably because the 'pattern book' houses illustrated in *Vitruvius Britannicus* and elsewhere tended to have basements for service rooms, whereas at Nanteos the kitchens and other service rooms were located on the ground floor. The plan now consists of three sections – a central circulation area, living rooms to the west and service rooms to the east, each more or less separate. The first floor also has three units – the gallery and stairs for circulation, the saloon for entertaining, and the bedrooms. The model may again be Castle Howard, which has a circulation corridor. The second floor also has a gallery, and there used to be a complete third floor of attic rooms, removed when the pitched roofs were replaced by a flat lead roof in the 1950s. There are no strong reasons for thinking that the main plan is not of the mid-eighteenth century, but many of the details in the rooms are clearly later than that.[42a]

The earliest details are the back stair and the kitchen fireplace. The back stair may have been repositioned, but seems to be complete; its detailing is late seventeenth or early eighteenth century. The kitchen fireplace may also be late seventeenth century, with a wide stone arch and perhaps originally a smaller arch alongside for an oven. Several of the bedrooms in the first and second floors have panelling of a style probably of the 1740s, with raised fields to the panels. The main stair, perhaps of the 1750s, has already been mentioned. Later details include the vaulted vestibule between the Dining Room and the Library, which is Regency in character, panelling in some of the bedrooms of perhaps a similar date, the splendid

NANTEOS MANSION

'Ironbridge' fireplace which cannot be earlier than 1780, and an early Gothic revival cupboard in the service passage. Finally there is the Dining Room, with doorways and plasterwork of 1848 designed by Haycock, and woodwork in the Drawing Room and some of the bedrooms of probably a similar date.

This leaves the problem of the hall, the long first-floor gallery and the Saloon or Music Room. Simply stated, the problem is this – is the decoration of these three parts of the house of the mid-eighteenth century or not? The hall has a mixture of details. The fireplace is based on designs by William Kent from the 1720s, but it does not have the integral overmantel which he usually included. The side doorways are of a design which was already in use in the 1740s but became most popular in the 1770s. The

Nanteos: Gallery and stairwell 1997.

(Crown Copyright: the Royal Commission on the Ancient and Historical Monuments of Wales)

exception, the doorway to the stair-hall, has the broken pediment which was popular in the early eighteenth century, but with very coarse detailing which recurs elsewhere. The plaster mouldings on the ceiling look nineteenth century in style; finally the huge moulded plaster panels with added moulded plaster motifs do not look authentically of the eighteenth century.

The same heavy details recur in the gallery, with the same panels and door-frames, but this time combined with detailing similar to that on the portico. Since this was added by Haycock in 1848, it seems likely that he was also responsible for the decoration of the gallery and of the hall.

The Saloon poses more of a problem. It has evidently undergone alterations at various times; the floor had to be replaced in 1799 after an attack of dry rot.[43] The level of the ceiling may have been altered, since there appears to be another ceiling above the level of the present one, which would make the Saloon into a diminutive version of the 'double cube' which became popular after the building of Wilton House.[44] The plaster decoration is in French Rococo style, which was popular for a short period in the mid-eighteenth century, c.1750-1770, and is characterised by free-flowing asymmetric curlicues. It was associated primarily with the architect Isaac Ware and Chesterfield House, which he decorated (it is said reluctantly) for Lord Chesterfield in 1749. A Welsh house with this style of decoration was Llanwern, Monmouthshire (1760).[45] Within twenty years it had gone out of fashion and was replaced by the very formal Classical plasterwork decoration which is associated with the brothers Adam. A local example was at Ynysymaengwyn, Tywyn (Mer.), where the decorations were of c.1790.[46]

The decoration of the saloon at Nanteos is indeed rococo in style, but less flamboyant than Ware's designs, and there are several reasons to doubt its authenticity. Firstly, the moulding is somewhat clumsy and heavy. Secondly, the fireplace (although not unlike eighteenth century examples) is actually incorrectly designed: the console brackets should support the whole entablature, not just the mantel-shelf. Finally, the mirrors set into the panels are very large for the 1750s. So, although this style of decoration would have been in fashion at the end of the main building phase, say 1755, it seems more probable that it was put in later. It is most unlikely to have been part of the repairs of 1799 (which were in any case a matter of necessary work only), and the most probable period was during the overhauls of the late 1840s by Haycock, who might have had access to designs or pattern-books from his father and grandfather to guide him.

There is still the question of how much of the earlier house survived into the 1730s. The answer may rest with the windows on the front and on the west side elevation. At first sight they seem almost identical, but a closer look shows that there are differences in the details. Those on the side have simple jambs and moulded sills: those on the front have quoins, bracketed sills and dropped keystones. The main facade is dated 1739, but the pediments with scrolls should be at least a generation earlier; they were used, for example, at Drayton House, Northants, of c.

1700.[47] Perhaps, therefore, they were reused from the older building. However the sills and jambs of the windows of the west elevation (excepting the 1840s version above the Dining Room) seem to be of early eighteenth century style as well as the scroll-pediment heads; this suggests that the west elevation is part of the earlier building. As noted previously, the plan of that early house is beyond recovery, although thick interior walls may give clues to its extent. However, there are sufficient window-heads reused in the south facade in an up-to-date 1739 manner for another two bays of a grand facade.

Ancillary Buildings

Nanteos: Stable entrance 1948. Note the statuary which has since been removed
(Crown Copyright: the Royal Commission on the Ancient and Historical Monuments of Wales)

Two ancillary buildings may also be mentioned, the lodge and the stables. The lodge is Italianate in style; the estate records include specifications and bills which suggest that it was built in 1857 to the design of Richard Kyrke Penson, though his design does not survive. Penson (1815-86) was

Nanteos: Stable frontage 1993 (Crown Copyright: the Royal Commission on the Ancient and Historical Monuments of Wales)

County Surveyor for Cardiganshire and Carmarthenshire from 1857, and a prolific builder of churches, vicarages and schools, usually in Gothic style. He may have been influenced by an unexecuted design for the lodge by Haycock, which was also Italianate but simpler. There is a similarity between the lodge and the billiard room which might indicate that they are by the same architect.

The stables are rather a mystery. The architect is unknown, although there is a persistent legend that they were designed by Samuel Pepys Cockerell, architect of Middleton Hall (Carms.). The complex was certainly complete by 1845, and payment for repair of the cupola may indicate that it was built well before 1839, before either Coultart or Haycock is known to have visited Aberystwyth.[48] If it were by either man, Coultart is the more likely, since the classical detailing on the entrance screen differs from that of the portico of the house. The design is fairly simple, a standard symmetrical stable yard with coach-houses and stables around a courtyard. The fourth side – possibly an addition – consists of a screen-wall with a central entrance in the form of a Roman triumphal arch (formerly with statues of a horse and two eagles on top) and 'appliqué' pedimented pavilions with dummy windows not unlike those added by Joseph Bonomi to Sir John Soane's Piercefield, Monmouthshire after 1785.[49]

As well as his elevations of the mansion in 1814 (see note 43), John Nash produced plans and elevations of a number of proposed 'picturesque' buildings for the estate in 1814. These are referred to in Chapter 8.

Summary

Finally the development of the house can be put into the family context. The pre-1739 house was of uncertain size and plan, but it seems to have been of three storeys and with fine details of about 1700: it was therefore built either for Cornelius le Brun, or more likely for William and Avarina Powell. After William's death, major rebuilding began in 1739 for his son Thomas, perhaps helped by his wife Mary's dowry. The source of the design was probably *Vitruvius Britannicus*, and the actual plans may have been produced by a local builder, or by Thomas himself. The work was finished by Thomas's brother William (who dated the rainwater heads in 1757), perhaps in competition with his in-laws at Ynysymaengwyn. After a lull of some fifty years, internal alterations began again, leading up to the addition of the east wing by Coultart in 1841 and the portico and dining-room by Haycock in 1848, all for Col. William Powell. By this time it is possible that only the main front was still rendered and painted ochre, with the dark stone of the other walls being exposed.[50] Haycock was probably also responsible for the internal plasterwork. With the addition of the billiard room in the 1860s and the completion of the stables, the complex was complete.

DETAILED DESCRIPTION

Nanteos stands in a much-reduced parkland, with pastures to the front, a lake, and mature woodlands to the west. The best view of the main facade is from the road to the south; the approach to the house, however, winds through woodlands so that the house appears all at once, with no vista to acclimatise the unsuspecting visitor to its size.

Exterior

The west elevation is of coursed rubble with facetted ashlar quoins and string course. The chimneys are of rubble and brick, with arched panels. The eaves have a projecting dentil cornice below a solid parapet, with urns on the corners. There is an added square bay to the Dining Room (by Haycock, 1845-7) in sandstone.[51] The lead downpipes have moulded hoppers inscribed 17 WP 57 (i.e. 1757 for Rev. William Powell). The ground floor has full-height 18-pane sashes with flat rubble heads and ashlar keystones; the sills appear to have been lowered. The first floor has 15-pane sashes in ashlar surrounds with scrolled broken pediments and moulded sills, similar to those at Drayton House, of c.1700.[52] The top floor has 6-pane fixed-light windows in similar surrounds.

The south facade is of coursed squared rubble with an ashlar plinth, and a string-course and cornice like that of the west elevation. The central bay is of deeply facetted sandstone ashlar below the portico and ashlared rendering above, topped by a balustraded parapet with urns. Under the portico are two windows flanking the doorway, all with semicircular heads and radiating fanlights. Above the portico are three semicircular arched windows with a linking hood, above them three blind oculi. The portico is an addition of 1848 by Haycock, with tall Tuscan columns and a Greek Doric frieze and cornice below the flat roof.[53] The outer bays have tall 20-pane sashes to the ground floor, with projecting quoined jambs, flat voussoir heads and a dropped keystone. The first floor windows (15-pane sashes) have similar quoins, broken scroll pediments with dropped keystones, and bracketed sills. The top floor windows have similar qoins, dropped keystones in slab lintels and plain sills. The datestone (of 1739) on the corner is almost completed eroded and illegible.

The added bay to the East is of 1841, by Coultart, with details copying the earlier block.[54] The Billiard Room of 1862-7, possibly by Penson, has three conjoined semicircular headed windows with Bath stone dressings.[55] The rear elevations are of exposed rubble masonry, with shallow segmental rubble voussoir arches over the openings.

Cellars

There are tall ceilings to the main cellar with rough beams and joists. Some may be reused sections of scarfed crucks. The main south wall of the central cellar (set back from the outer wall of the house) has two eighteenth-century two-light wooden windows with square mullions rebated for glass, and thin stanchions. The floors are cobbled with pebbles, containing original drains running towards the centre. The rear cellar has a higher floor-level and pebble cobbling. Under the portico the present front wall has sash windows with thin glazing bars. There are brick arches over the junctions between the cellars; at the change of floor-level there is a breach through a 3' thick wall. The wine cellars have brick bins of 1848, put in by Haycock.[56]

Ground floor

The entrance hall has square-headed architraves to the doorways (similar to Ynysymaengwyn, 1758). The walls have large plaster panels, some shouldered; that over the fireplace has moulded swags, and a band of Greek key fretwork. The fireplace, of a composition imitation marble, has a moulded mantel-shelf and grotesques. It is in the style of William Kent (1720s), but is later in date. The doorway to the inner hall has fluted columns, a Greek

Nanteos: the Dining Room 1967.

Nanteos: the Library 1967

Doric frieze similar to that of the portico, and a broken pediment, of early eighteenth century style. The trabeate ceiling has a plain dentil cornice, with flat ribbons and floral motifs on the soffits of the beams.

The Drawing Room has elaborate doorways with multiple mouldings and circlets in the shoulders, possibly Regency. A niche with early nineteenth-century fan-shaped panelling of Adam style, having guilloche moulding (like that of the south-east room in the first floor) conceals a blocked window. The marble fireplace has a cast-iron grate. The ceiling has a cornice of interlinked rings, and mouldings as those of the panelling.

The lobby between the Drawing Room and the Library has an elegant little Regency four-rib vault with a central quatrefoil. There is an old brick arch over the window; by tradition it was through this window that the Nanteos Cup was passed when loaned.

The Library is nineteenth century in date, with panelled window-reveals, an elaborate plaster ceiling and a marble fireplace. The moulded doorways are of Regency style with multiple mouldings.

The Dining Room (by Haycock, 1845-7) has a trabeate ceiling with classical mouldings. The fireplace is of black marble. The doorways are very elaborate, with scrolled heads to the doorcases. Beyond is the Butler's Pantry. The specifications of 1845 list a 'handsome marble chimney piece with slab' worth £25, and 'plain marble chimney piece' worth £8 for the bedroom above.[57] The external walls were to be hammer-dressed with freestone quoins, and a plinth, coping and cornice as already existing. The 'bow' window was to be of freestone over brick. The bedroom windows above were to have moulded architraves and a 'carved scroll on top of the lower one.' The floor was of dowelled oak boards, the ceiling had a 'bold plaster cornice with two enrichments and roses or paterae at the intersections on the lower face of the beams.'

The passage to the Kitchen has a Picturesque-style neo-Gothic cupboard, similar to woodwork at Rhyd-y-gors, Carmarthen, of early nineteenth-century date.[58] The Kitchen has a huge stone arched fireplace, with a possible second stone arch to the side for an oven (later cut by a doorway); this may be a fragment of the pre-1739 building. The south-east service rooms have been modernised for a caretaker's flat.

Staircases

The main stair has a moulded ramped handrail, thin turned balusters (three to a tread) and a spiral newel with four balusters in the 'eye'. It is probably of the mid eighteenth century, and comparable with 25 Bootham, York, of 1766,[59] or 45 Castle Street, Salisbury, of 1750.[60] At the base of the stair are two very clumsy columns and two half-columns behind a screen wall; they have capitals, but no linking architrave. There are tall shouldered panels and smaller panels below the dado-rail, all with ogee moulding. The top landing has a colonnade with egg-and-dart mouldings to the cornice below dentils alternating with rosettes. The trabeate ceiling has egg-and-dart mouldings, and floral trails on the soffits of the beams. The stair-windows have painted glass, some of it heraldic, possibly by 'Mr Evans of Salop', 1837.[61]

The back stair has a square grip and turned balusters of later seventeenth century style, as at 68 Micklegate, York, of the mid seventeenth century,[62] and Eltham Lodge, Woolwich, of 1663-5.[63] Both stairs were repaired in about 1848.[64]

First floor

The long first-floor gallery has a deep classical ceiling cornice similar to, and probably contemporary with, that of the entrance hall by Haycock. On the walls are large plaster panels with broken pediments. The doorways have square headed or semicircular-headed architraves, of eighteenth-century pattern but coarser in execution.

The entry from the landing into the Saloon (or Music Room) leads into a shallow anteroom behind an arcaded screen with four plaster (scagliola) pillars. Above the arcade are asymmetrical swags with garlands between. The doorway has a pedimented doorcase with scroll volutes and a dentil cornice with scrollwork on the entablature. The panels on the walls contain mirrors. The ceiling has an egg-and-dart cornice, with formal motifs in panels.

The Saloon has a marble fireplace with a central panel of the fable of the Fox & the Stork between volutes and swags. Above it is an oval mirror with vine swags emerging from a basket. To either side are plaster panels with ribbon bows in the corners. There is a huge mirror in a panel opposite. The tall windows with semicircular heads have later mirrors between them; the shutters are nineteenth century in date. The ceiling has a band of scrollwork below a dentil cornice with fretwork ornament. A central oval panel has a central leafy 'rose' and is surrounded by a naturalistic floral garland. The outer panels, rather smaller, are surrounded by fronds of seaweed. In the corners are four circlets with trophies: a vine-scroll, jug and cup (north-west), arrows and flaming torch (north-east), a lute, flute and oboe (south-west), and a pen, paintbrush, palette and notebook (south-east). This ceiling is below an earlier ceiling level visible in the floor above. The plasterwork is French rococo in inspiration. It is not unlike Chesterfield House of 1750-70,[65] but is generally heavier, with larger panels; the combination with doorcases of early eighteenth century type suggests that the whole room is actually neo-rococo, by Haycock. Letters of 1798-9 refer to repairs to the sycamore floor of the Saloon, which was suffering from dry rot.[66]

The Pink Room (a secondary suite of rooms) has a plain marble fireplace, a moulded ceiling cornice and nineteenth-century doorcase.

The north-east room has a plain fireplace (possibly secondary), and early eighteenth century panelling with raised fields and ovolo-moulded styles. The east room has a shouldered marble fireplace, possibly eighteenth century, and the adjacent closet has eighteenth century panelling. The south-east room has elegant nineteenth-century guilloche decoration to the fireplace and below the window. The south (yellow) room has nineteenth-century detailing – wave-moulding below the window and a plain dentil ceiling cornice. The access corridor has a nineteenth-century dentil cornice and panelled walls.

The access corridor to the south-west (pink) room has a similar dentil cornice. The shouldered fireplace is of marble and painted plaster, with garlands and classical moulding. The cast-iron grate represents the Iron Bridge, and has the inscription A VIEW OF THE IRON BRIDGE OVER THE SEVERN. This appears to be a third variant of a fireplace type produced by the Coalbrookdale Company and by their great rivals the Carron Iron Foundry after 1782.[67] The panel over the fireplace has a broken pediment, and formerly contained a painted panel. The ceiling has rococo plaster swags with busts in the centres of the sides and a central rose. The doors have raised fielded panels with ogee moulded styles.

The west room has nineteenth-century panelling with ogee-moulded styles. The marble fireplace has a cast iron grate. There is a deep recess, formerly for a bed, with pilasters and capitals. The plain ceiling has a moulded cornice.

Second floor

The south rooms retain early eighteenth century panelling and dado rails, with raised fields to the panels and ovolo mouldings to the styles and the dado rails. The windows, shutters and doors have nineteenth-century mouldings.

The room over the Kitchen may have been the nursery or the housekeeper's room. It has a cast-iron fireplace with twisted columns, flanked by arched alcoves; one window has painted glass. The top-floor landing has built-in linen cupboards with panelling with nineteenth-century mouldings.

Attics

The roof was replaced in the 1950s, having formerly been three pitched spans. Fragments of the old trusses remain, with pegged sprockets for the valley gutters. The south parapet has a brick inner face. There is the line of an old floor-level between the truss-feet. A photograph shows that the trusses had pegged collars and long yokes, with flat leaded ridges.

Stableyard

The Stables were built in the 1820s or 1830s (the cupola was repaired in 1839) with an added screen wall, perhaps by Coultart. The site slopes steeply across the facade. In the centre is a 'triumphal' arch breaking forward with a semicircular arch flanked by two Tuscan columns in grey ashlar under a Greek Doric frieze and cornice. At either end is a 'pavilion' with four flat pilasters with bases and capitals under a Greek Doric frieze, and a triangular pediment; between the pilasters are three blind windows.

The stable yard is symmetrical. On either side is a four-bay coach-house with grooms' quarters above. The walls are of coursed rubble masonry with a sill-band, the hipped slated roofs have deep bracketed eaves. There are tall semicircular headed doorways with dummy tympana, and sash windows above. To either side and across the end are single-storey stables; the walls are of roughly squared coursed rubble with low-pitched roofs and parapets. The doors and windows have shallow segmental arched heads, the windows are mullioned and transomed with small fixed lights. The roofs are on king-post trusses. There are cobble floors, with brick-paved drains having slate covers. The stables originally held four horses each (total 24), later (1890s?) altered to loose-boxes. The original stalls have octagonal dividing posts and boarded valances over.

Close to the house and next to the Stableyard is a square structure, possibly a Laundry, or Dairy, probably of early nineteenth century date. The walls are of rubble masonry; the slate roof has very deep eaves overhanging a verandah on cast-iron columns. There is a very large chimney and tall windows (some blocked) with flat voussoir arches.

Lodge

The Lodge is of an Italianate design by D.Kyrke Penson of 1857, with white rendered walls, and bracketed hoods and sills to the windows. The first floor has linked pairs of semi-circular headed windows (cf the Billiard Room). The Tower has a pyramidal roof. The specifications survive.[68]

Nanteos: the Lodge. Engraving by W.D. Lewis.

(Crown Copyright: the Royal Commission on the Ancient and Historical Monuments of Wales)

Notes

[1] P.Smith, *Houses of the Welsh Countryside* (London, 1975), fig.1, pl.1-2.

[2] Ibid, figs 135-6: Royal Commission on the Ancient Monuments of Wales [hereafter R.C.A.H.M.W.], *Inventory of..Caernarvonshire* I (London, 1956), pl.72-4.

[3] R.C.A.H.M.W., *Glamorgan* IV (ii) (London, 1981), pl.2.

[4] N. Lloyd, *History of the English House* (repr. London 1975), fig. 123-4.

[5] P.Smith, op.cit., pl.72.

[6] N.Lloyd, op.cit., fig.162.

[7] Ibid., figs.163-5.

[8] G.Beard & A.Kersting, *The Work of John Vanbrugh* (London 1986), *passim.*

[9] H.Colvin, A Biographical Dictionary of British Architects, 1600-1840 (London 1978), 841-2.

[10] E.Hubbard, *The Buildings of Wales: Clwyd* (London & Cardiff 1986), 251.

[11] T.Dineley, *The Official Progress..of the..Duke of Beaufort .. 1684* (London 1888), 246.

[12] N.Lloyd, op.cit., fig 171-2.

[13] P. Smith, op.cit., fig. 152a.

[14] Royal Commission on Historical Monuments [hereafter R.C.H.M.E.], *Wilton House and English Palladianism* (London, 1988), 1-23.

[15] E. Hubbard, op.cit., 381.

[16] P.Smith, op.cit., fig.188.

[17] In the National Library of Wales.

[18] H.Colvin, op.cit., p.236; for further information, and references 19-26 below, I am indebted to Mr Thomas Lloyd.

[19] Incorporated Church Building Society [hereafter ICBS], file 1756 (Lambeth Palace Library).

[20] ICBS file 1971; the church was later restored by Butterfield in 1862-7.

[21] *Carmarthen Journal* 2.4.1841

[22] Hunt & Co., *Directory* (1849), *sub* Aberystwyth.

[23] The *Pembrokehire Herald* of 13.6.1851 relates that it was 'nearly finished'

[24] *The Welshman*, 13.1.1837

[25] *Carmarthen Journal*, 6.2.1846.

[26] *The Welshman*, 2.7.1847.

[27] N.L.W., Nanteos Dep. I/20, 21, 24.

[28] H.Colvin, op.cit., 405-7.

[29] N.L.W., Nanteos I/23; specification in Box 5.

[30] A letter of May 1847 about 'new building' mentions the haulier John Morris: N.L.W. Nanteos Box 5.

[31] G.Beard & A.Kersting, op.cit., fig.12.

[32] R.C.H.M.E., fig. 132.

[33] G.Beard & A.Kersting, op.cit., fig. 94.

[34] N.L.W., Nanteos I/24.

[35] G.Beard & A.Kersting, op.cit. , fig.17.

[36] R.C.H.M.E., op.cit., fig. 179.

[37] R.C.H.M.E. op.cit., fig. 132.

[38] Plan in National Monuments Record for Wales.

[39] P.Smith, op.cit., fig.153-4.

[40] R.C.H.M.E., *City of York* V (London 1981), pl.192.

[41] R.C.H.M.E., *City of Salisbury* I, (London 1980), pl.88.

[42] Letter of 1956, in National Monuments Record for Wales.

[42a] The proposed elevations of 1814 by John Nash (R. Suggett, *John Nash – Architect-Pensaer*, RCAHM 1955, figs. 48-9) and the corresponding plan (copy in NMRW) indicate that the basic plan and elevations were already complete by then.

[43] N.L.W., Nanteos Dep. L/175.

[44] R.C.H.M.E., *Wilton House . . .*, 52ff.

[45] T. Lloyd, *The Lost Houses of Wales* (London 1986), 103.

[46] P. Smith, 'Ynysymaengwyn, Merioneth', *Archaeologia Cambrensis* 109 (1960), 178.

[47] J.A.Gotch, *The Growth of the English House* (London 1909), fig. 163).

[48] N.L.W., Nanteos Dep., Account Book for 1839. Since the old stable is known to have been pulled down in 1827, the rebuilding may have been much earlier than 1839.

[49] T. Lloyd, op.cit., 99.

[50] 'Col.Powell proposes to colour [the middle bay of the main elevation] dark like the Stone of the other parts instead of its present Ochre Colour but leaving the Stone round the window ocre [sic] as they are now' – Nanteos Box 1/22 of c.1832.

[51] N.L.W., Nanteos Dep. Box 5, specification of 11.10.1845.

[52] See note 47.

[53] N.L.W., Nanteos Box 5: specification of 22.12.1847. Several earlier designs for the portico survive in N.L.W.: an undated sketch of c.1832, a measured elevation by David Moore of c.1839 showing unequal spaces between the columns, and three drawings by Coultart of c.1840.

[54] N.L.W., Nanteos I/20.

[55] R.J.Colyer, 'Nanteos: A Landed Estate in Decline 1800-1930', *Ceredigion* IX (1980), 69, 74 n.38.

[56] N.L.W., Nanteos Box 5. It may be suggested, especially in view of the Meyrick print (S.R. Meyrick, *The History of Cardiganshire* (1808) p.405, that prior to the creation of the portico, the cellar windows gave onto a small sunken area which lit these windows; it must have been crossed by a very short bridge to the door, thus giving a basement effect (Editor).

[57] N.L.W., Nanteos Box 5.

[58] T. Lloyd, op.cit., 65.

[59] R.C.H.M.E., *City of York* IV (London 1975), fig 8e.

[60] See note 41.

[61] N.L.W., Nanteos Account Book, 1837 (ref. in litt, National Monuments Record for Wales).

[62] R.C.H.M.E., *City of York* III (London 1972), fig.17a.

[63] R.C.H.M.E., *London* V, (London 1930), pl.27.

[64] N.L.W., Nanteos Box 5 – payment to Haycock for 'repairing both staircases'.

[65] N. Lloyd, op.cit., fig.718.

[66] N.L.W., Nanteos L/175, 185.

[67] S.B.Smith, 'The Iron Bridge Fireplace', *Design History Society Newsletter* 1(8 April 1983), 25-31.

[68] N.L.W., Nanteos I/101.

8.

SOARING AMBITIONS IN THE NANTEOS DEMESNE

Caroline Palmer

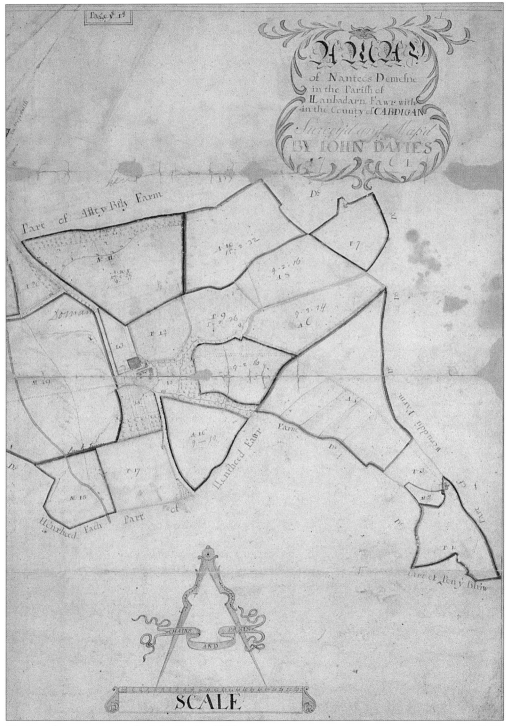

Nanteos demesne: survey by John Davies 1764.

N.L.W.

The Eighteenth Century Demesne[1]

THE first cartographic evidence of the form of the Nanteos demesne derives from the handsomely executed estate maps of 1764 which were drawn by John Davies for the Rev. Dr William Powell.[2] By this time the Powells had acquired considerable power, influence and land. The maps, most of which survive, each detail an individual tenanted farm, infuriatingly depicted with no respect for the later convention of north at the top of the page. Pieced together, they reveal that the Powells and the Joneses had amassed ownership of all the contiguous farms around their demesne, extending from Penglanowen in the west to Rhoserchan, Ty'n-y-cwm and Gilfach-goch in the east, bounded to the south by Cwmygaseg, Cwmheulog and Pencraig and to the north by the Devils Bridge road. Outside this core area a greater mosaic of land-holdings existed, but substantial areas also lay in the lower Rheidol valley. Field boundaries are extremely conservative features of the landscape and it is possible, with very little error, to redraw these land parcels of 1764 on the twentieth century map. The outline of the Nanteos demesne itself is a clear testament to the amalgamation, some sixty years earlier, of two modest demesnes, Llechwedd Dyrys on the south side of the valley and Nanteos on the north. The marriage contracted between William Powell of Llechwedd Dyrys and Avarina le Brun in 1690 led to the abandonment of Llechwedd Dyrys, which was surveyed as 'site of house and garden' in 1764.

This alliance brought together the wealth and legal expertise from one family, and land and mining expertise from the other. William Powell and Avarina le Brun's sons, Thomas and William Powell, and grandson Thomas contributed to the further acquisition of contiguous lands. The family seat of Nanteos pre-dated the present house and was presumably demolished and/or incorporated into the later structure. It is likely, though, that aspects of the environs of the house, such as the position of the orchard and the kitchen garden were already established.

Thomas Powell and his wife Mary Frederick (daughter of Thomas Frederick, Lord Mayor of London), raised the profile of Nanteos with the construction of a Palladian-style mansion, commenced in 1739. In 1752 Thomas Powell died childless, aged 53, of an apoplectic fit, and the property passed to his brother the Rev. Dr William Powell who had been living and raising a family at nearby Rhoserchan. The Rev. Dr William Powell lived until 1780 when he died 'suddenly in his chair, without a groan, universally respected and regretted age 75.'[3] This chapter commences with a description of the demesne in the mid-eighteenth century, drawing on the John Davies survey and other documents, and may thus include features created by either Thomas Powell or his brother William.

During this period the roads, both on the estate and in the adjoining countryside were different from today; the turnpikes later to lead towards Devils Bridge and Trawsgoed had yet to be built. Several roads traversed what had become the demesne, one running west-east passed along in front of the mansion, turned north-east around the side of the house and continued eastward to Rhoserchan. From this road three routes crossed the valley to the south, one road ascending diagonally up the slope under Llechwedd Dyrys, a second crossing the valley just west of the mansion, and a third branching southward from the end of Garden Covert and crossing the tenanted lands of Henrhyd Fach. All three routes gave access to Gors and to New Cross.

The enclosed garden features at Nanteos in 1764 were confined to a two-acre pleasure ground situated to the west of the house, and to the east a kitchen garden, and orchard, together three acres in extent. Such a pleasure garden might be expected to have had a formal geometric layout, and to have featured trimmed bushes such as rosemary and box, and scented shrubs such as mock orange. The cartographic evidence shows little but a pattern of paths in the as yet unwalled kitchen garden, and a single path running round the rear margin of the pleasure ground. The lie of the land in the pleasure ground, now densely grown with trees and shrubs, could indicate terracing, whilst the abundance of naturalised double snowdrops, giving an almost unbroken cover in spring, indicates the antiquity of this part of the garden. Animals would have been excluded from the pleasure ground, and of course from the kitchen garden. Both these features may well have pre-dated the new palladian mansion which Thomas Powell erected on the site.

Garden design complementary to the new house is likely to have been influenced by the romantic, classical designs beloved of William Kent or the uncluttered landscape style of 'Capability' Brown or his follower, William Emes. Landscape ideals sought to incorporate the estate as a whole into the garden. The highly influential Miller's Gardeners' Dictionary emphasises the importance of a lawn – 'a great plain in a park' – which, for a large park, should be 30-40 acres in extent and situated to the south-east of the house front.[4] The orientation of the mansion is thus close to ideal, and the Davies map of 1764 shows a handsome 32 acre lawn, Waun Dan-y-Cwrt, through which Nant Paith and its tributaries took a sinuous path. The southern margin of the lawn was bounded by the road to Llechwedd Dyrys, and the

18th Century bridge in the lawn at the foot of Cottage Dingle. Early 19th Century plantings of beech clumps on the slope beyond.

The ruined façade of the 18th Century Eyecatcher Dog Kennel.

eastern margin by a sunken fence or ha-ha. Several small arched stone bridges were probably built about this time, one giving access from the house to the parkland, another crossing the stream at the foot of Cottage Dingle, and a third at the south end of the ha-ha. The former two survive today, and would in any case have been necessary if, as appears likely, the stone for Nanteos was quarried from the disused quarry in Cottage Dingle.

These bridges also allowed access from the house to a classical eye-catcher Dog Kennel which was built on Cae Syfi (strawberry or raspberry field), one of the fields belonging to the tenanted farm of Cwm Hwylog. While this feature does not appear on the map of 1764, it is marked, and utilised as a major landmark in the turnpike trust route proposals of 1788,[5] so it may safely be judged to have already been in existence for some time. The masonry facade was 46 feet long and its two ends survive, standing some 15 feet tall. It was built of local stone with mud mortar, and appears to have been stuccoed with lime mortar over the surface. At the outer margins were blind Venetian windows, each a tall arched recess flanked by shorter rectangular recesses on a common sill. The centre of the facade is now totally destroyed, but may have included a doorway. There is no indication that masonry extended round the sides of the rectangular dog enclosure which was concealed behind it. The situation was carefully selected for both practical and scenic reasons: it was close to the then road and had a natural water supply, it is also the lowest position on the slope which gives a framed view out of the landlocked valley to Pendinas and a triangle of sea. It would have made a focal point for walking out from the mansion.

Even more extravagantly romantic was the construction on Powell land in the Rheidol valley of Plas-crug castle. Much debate has attached itself to this building, which was demolished in 1967 to make way for the county primary school. Ralph Griffiths has explored the inconclusive evidence for the site having featured in the medieval conflicts between Owain Glyn Dŵr and the occupants of Aberystwyth Castle.[6] However, prior to its demolition the composite building which it had become was assessed by the Royal Commission on Ancient and Historical Monuments, and judged to consist in part, of an eighteenth-century folly, and deemed in consequence of no great historic interest. A picture by Gastineau (1832) and works by subsequent artists and photographers show a farm building attached at one side to a tower with gothic windows and at the other to a piece of more ambiguous masonry. A wall, against which a lean-to thatched building has been constructed, extended to the rear. A plan watermarked 1870 shows the intention to add a further room to the stable, house and tower of which it then consisted.[7] However, inspection of the John Davies map of 1764 shows the site to have been occupied by a four-towered structure, square in plan and two chains (132 feet) in exterior dimension.[8] Linking walls are drawn with a thickness which implies that the four rooms of the towers could have been linked by passages and enclosed a square inner yard. The triangular five acre site was surrounded by water, the Rheidol on the south, a mill leat enclosing the margin of Morfa Mawr to the east and north, and the Morfa Mawr waste to the west.

NANTEOS

The castle stood on a naturally rocky eminence, and, rearing above the unbroken marshland, would have been a commanding and romantic eye-catcher. In the light of the parallels drawn in Chapter 7, between Nanteos and Vanbrugh's Castle Howard, it is interesting to note how much this structure must have resembled some of the eleven towers on the castellated estate wall at Castle Howard. Its function remains uncertain: it could have been a picnic spot or banqueting house, conveniently placed outside Aberystwyth, and on the route to Llanbadarn church. However it appears that access was never by more than by a footbridge across the mill-leat, and one which was considered a wretched structure by the traveller Thomas Martyn in 1801 when he visited the

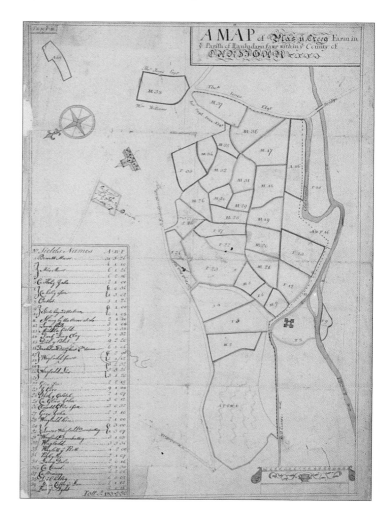

Plascrug, mapped by John Davies in 1764. Note the four-squared plan of the Plascrug building, and the early representation of Llanbadarn church (upper left).

N.L.W.

nothing of these things, I will however introduce my sketch as some small Apology for my weakness, at the same time it will be a lesson to me in future.

Watercolour of Plascrug Castle by Thomas Martyn, who toured to Aberystwyth in 1801. His "Apology for my weakness" alludes to his disappointment at learning, from the publican, that this ancient ruin he had visited was in fact a recently built folly.

already dilapidated building.[9] An alternative possibility is that this was, like the Dog Kennel, a functional folly, concealing salmon coops, similar to a salmon coop castle folly built in the Vanbrugh style at Netherby in Cumbria[10]. Such a live-fish storage system would at least provide a logical explanation for the persistent legend reported by Dr Mavor[11] in 1798 and by Malkin in 1804 that a tunnel runs through or from Plascrug.[12] Such a tunnel would undoubtedly have flooded, useless for human use as an escape route, but very desirable to ensure a flow of aerated water to the fish.

Other buildings on the demesne were of a more simply functional design, such as the group of houses and smithy adjoining the road near the present lodge. It is not clear whether any lodge existed at this time, though a small building close to the road could have served this function. A greater sense of style is indicated by the stable block, a D-shaped structure shown east of the mansion on the map of 1764. A detailed, but undated plan of this building shows an elegant design, incorporating five coach houses, nine stable stalls, six loose boxes and a small dog kennel.[13] The architect is unknown, but the quality of design and the style of the script suggest that it may have been executed by the unknown architect of the mansion itself.

Few trees are likely to survive from the 18th century, but the disposition of woodland is, like field boundaries, remarkably conservative. Woods once established are extremely time-consuming to grub out and will naturally renew themselves. The estate plans of 1764 indicate woodland corresponding with today's Llechwedd Dyrys (Rookery) Wood and clothing the valley of Cottage Dingle. Woodland also extended behind the mansion, up Sawmill Dingle. Isolated clumps existed adjoining what is now the lake, and at Target Covert and Garden Covert. Of scenic significance are the individual trees surveyed on the sloping field Cae Dan-yr-Allt, south of the old road to Gors. Ancient oaks survive in these positions, and the larger ones are reaching the end of their natural span. One oak (girth 550 cms) which was ring-counted when it blew over, was shown to have approximately 200 annual rings, dating it at about 1772.[14]

The Opportunities created by the Turnpike Act of 1770

On the death of Dr William Powell in 1780 the estate passed to his son Thomas. While little is known of his affairs on the wider stage, there is good evidence that he was much exercised with the local turnpike trust, on which he followed his father as a trustee, and with the opportunities it proffered to trustee landowners to improve the amenities of their own estates. In 1788-89 the trustees agreed that the road past Nanteos should be re-routed, particularly in view of the ease with which wagons became stuck on the Llechwedd Dyrys slope. Work was carried out in 1789;[15] the new road to New Cross cut across the south margin of Llechwedd Dyrys wood and probably obliterated the site of the former house, or isolated it on the south side of the new road. As a consequence of its completion Powell was able to close off the old road and rearrange the boundaries of the park to take advantage of the greater privacy obtained. A rough plan of the demesne was sketched in 1793 which shows that Thomas Powell had added to it part of Cae Dan-yr-allt, south of the old road, and a part of Cwmheulog Farm, including the dog kennel site to the lawn in front of the house, and enclosed the area

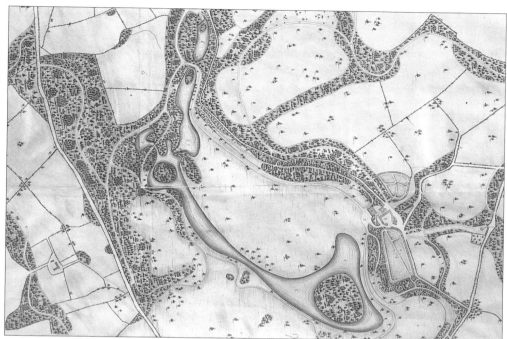

Lavish rococo swirls characterise John Davenport's ambitious 1791 design for the Nanteos Demesne. [Detail viewed from the East. The long lake was never created. The road at left is the present B4340 Aberystwyth-Pont-rhydfendigaid road.]

N.L.W.

on the south and east margins in rails.[16] Lawn between the house and the river extended to 33 acres, and new parkland, 'between the river and the rails', a further 25 acres. The road running past the front of Nanteos seems to have been replaced by a footpath running the length of the park but not leaving the estate, and Nant Paith has been canalised in front of the house to create the impression of unbroken parkland. The vehicular approach to Nanteos now swerves up hill behind the pleasure ground and gives access to the stable area and to the road which descends from Moriah.

There is little doubt, though, that Thomas Powell was seriously considering much more radical improvements and aggrandisement of his estate. In 1791 the architect and landscape gardener John Davenport of Burlton Grove, Wem (Shropshire), produced an extremely lavish landscape plan for the demesne, indeed the most elaborate plan to have survived from his career.[17] John Davenport's design was in the picturesque style, and prescribed a remarkable range of garden buildings, a greenhouse, gothic temple, rotunda, ruins, tower, gothic seats, cottage and castle. The plan involved incorporating the six adjoining tenanted

193

farms into the demesne, and creating a sinuous marginal coach drive skirting the periphery of the enlarged demesne and visiting the various picturesque follies on the route. Additionally he proposed a new Eastern approach down Cottage Dingle, and paired, gated lodges at both this and the western approach. In all it would have required the creation of 12 miles of new carriage drive, and a water feature consisting of a chain of three lakes linked by cascades along the valley bottom. Farms and field boundaries would be eliminated and a fringe of woodland planted around the margin of the demesne. The kitchen garden and both the approaches to the mansion would be screened by shrubberies and a second flower garden placed to the north-west of the house. If executed this plan would have been extraordinarily expensive, far more so than at Hafod where only footpaths and simple bridges were constructed to open up the landscape. In contemplating a carriage circuit of the much extended demesne he would have been emulating some of the grandest of eighteenth century English landscaped gardens. Also in 1791 Davenport was vigorously protesting at his dismissal, by Warren Hastings, Governor General of India, from a similarly elaborate landscape project involving lake and garden buildings at Hastings' Daylesford House in Gloucestershire[18]. It seems that at Nanteos his plan never left the drawing board, for the 1793 sketch plan of the estate does not appear influenced by these proposals and at about this time inventories of the household effects were taken prior to an agreement for Thomas Robson to take agency of the estate, live in the house and accommodate auditors and friends of the Powells. Thomas and Eleanor Powell and their growing family removed to London in 1795. The details of the agreement specify the use of vegetables for Thomas Robson but retain pigeons and rabbits to the Powells. Probably therefore there was already a warren on Warren Hill (the first occurrence of the name is on the Davenport plan) and a pigeoncote, though not the one which survives today. Thomas Powell died not long afterwards, in 1797, leaving an eleven-year-old heir, William Edward Powell and three other infant children.

No improvements were made to the estate during

William Edward Powell's minority, and Davenport's great linen plan for Nanteos languished among the estate manuscripts, but it may none the less have served as an influence upon W.E.Powell when, twenty years later he was making his own mark upon the estate. That it was commissioned at all seems a somewhat lavish gesture, but some doubt hangs over whether it was ever paid for.[19] An explanation for this flight of fancy may lie in family ties. Eleanor Powell's maternal aunt was married to John Hill of Prees, brother of the second baronet of Hawkstone Hall, Shropshire, and later to become third baronet himself. There was considerable contact between the families, John Hill being a trusted family friend. Hawkstone is a prime example of a picturesque landscape, adorned with every manner of castle, tower, tunnel and grotto and was embellished in its heyday with lyric poems inscribed or hung at key locations around the walks. While William Emes is known to have built the lake which forms a sham river in the landscape, the designer of the walks and follies is undocumented, and it has been suggested that the picturesque landscape at Hawkstone was inspired by successive Hills themselves.[20] However, indentures dated 1790 and 1792, relating to a debt of £7000, link the four names John Davenport, John Edison, William Emes and Thomas Johnes of Hafod.[21] This acquaintance might also have brought Davenport to Wales. Following Thomas Powell's removal to London and premature death, Eleanor Powell remained in London, Robson was displaced to a more modest property, and the mansion was let to Samuel Pocock for three hundred guineas per year.

William Edward Powell gains control of his estates

As is shown in chapter 2/3 above, when the young William Edward Powell came of age in 1809 he lost no time in marrying Laura Phelp, while living well above his income, and leaving the affairs of the estates to the care of his London solicitor Robert Appleyard and James Hughes of Glanrheidol, so that there followed a period of maladministration and enormous expense. In 1812 Hopkinson's, Powell's lawyers, insisted that he 'find some respectable professional man in your own neighbourhood who would take the management, under your direction, of all your property.'[22] John Edwards of Bloomsbury Square thus became an important influence upon the young W.E.Powell and obviously devoted considerable time and attention to personally rescuing the estate from neglect and embezzlement. His correspondence contains many very specific suggestions for improving the estate.[23] John Edwards' own family home, Rheola in the Vale of Neath, was being remodelled and enlarged in the style of a large picturesque cottage by Edwards' cousin, the up-and-coming Welsh architect John Nash. It was doubtless through John Edwards' influence that Nash and his assistant George Repton came to produce, in their turn, lavish plans for remodelling Nanteos mansion and grounds. Edwards was eager that Powell should also enhance his status by purchasing Aberystwyth Castle, from its then owner Thomas Johnes of Hafod.[24]

John Edwards's letters were sent to W.E. Powell at a variety of addresses as he moved about the country with his regiment. They propose a sequence of management and design alterations to the estate. In them he clearly seeks to improve the image of the estate. In 1813, in a letter proposing alterations to the drive in front of the house he wrote 'By thus extending the drive I think you will

West elevation of Nanteos. Watercolour attribuated to John Nash's assistant George S.Repton c.1812.
(R.C.A.H.M./N.L.W.)

improve it and make it more suitable to the size of the house.' In 1814, addressing improvements to the gardens and pleasure grounds, he recommended raking, liming and stocking hard with sheep to restore the quality of the grass around the mansion, and ploughing, planting oats and then reseeding the lawn opposite the kitchen garden. His letters also contain proposals for a flower garden, and discussion of the proper location for a greenhouse. Mr Barber the resident agent was about to commence the kitchen-garden wall, and there was debate about the best location for a greenhouse. Laura Powell apparently wished to have it 'placed in the shrubbery further from the house' – perhaps as Davenport had suggested – while the aesthetic sense of Edwards dictated that the greenhouse would look too small and squat in relation to the mansion when viewed from the road (the new Aberystwyth – New Cross turnpike). Spanning a couple of years, and in some cases accompanied by working sketches, Edwards's letters represent progress reports and recommendations, all of which seem to have been implemented. His sketch plan shows that in 1813 there was already a greenhouse up against the bank to the west of the mansion, and a plantation occupying the corner to the east and screening the stables from view.[25] His plans to extend the apron of the drive in front of the house incorporates an iron fence adjoining the drive and an iron gate on the road at the immediate approach to the house. An adjacent gate would give access to a shrubbery on the site of the former pleasure ground, and another would 'lead out of the drive to the lawn next the garden.' These measures would effectively banish animals from grazing right up to the door.

The eventual location of the new greenhouse is unclear, but Edwards favoured placing it in the kitchen garden, 'against the wall which crosses the garden to divide the kitchen garden from the future flower garden beyond.' He also proposed a 'peach house and grapes' at a cost of £300-£400.[26] The correspondence shows Edwards was keen to progress his proposals and in a letter to Powell in April 1814 he wrote 'I should be glad to know whether Mrs Powell liked my plan for making a flower garden by the old wall, for if she did Mr Barber should have instructions about it.'[27]

The Nash-Repton plans for Nanteos are unsigned but are on paper watermarked 1811 or 1812, and so were doubtless commissioned by Edwards and Powell at this time; they have been described by Richard Suggett.[28] Beautifully executed water-colours show two elevations of the mansion, embellished with two triple-bay porticoes and a new service wing screened by a one-storey conservatory sixty feet by twenty feet, attached to the east side of the facade.[29] A setting of lawns, trees and island beds in 'gardenesque' style is indicated. Also in water-colour, and accompanied by ground plans are proposals for four charming picturesque estate buildings: a lodge for the western entrance from the Aberystwyth road, a lodge for the rear approach from Moriah on the Devils Bridge road, a circular dairy over a subterranean ice house 'to be built in the plantation near the garden' and a keeper's cottage (to be appended to an existing kennel, probably the one situated east of the house). Nash's office regularly produced such 'fair drawings' of estate buildings for clients, his charges being 3 guineas apiece, and a further 3 guineas for working drawings, though this second fee was waived if the designs were executed and a commission charged.[30] Similar lodges were built and survive today at Blaise Castle and at Attingham Park, Shrewsbury, and a similar ornamental

The Nash design for a lodge at the entrance to Nanteos from the Aberystwyth road. This lodge was probably built. Watercolour attribuated to George S. Repton c.1812

(R.C.A.H.M./N.L.W.)

dairy was built at Blaise Castle in 1804. Had they been built at Nanteos it would have been in the very height of fashion for the times. Full workmen's drawings and details were also produced for a two-bedroomed gardener's house,[31] with exterior styling very similar to designs for cottages at Blaise Hamlet.[32] It is remarkable compared with the Blaise Hamlet cottages for its generous size, having not just one, but four good downstairs rooms, and two bedrooms over. This house was designed to straddle the existing garden wall, its principal elevation featuring a single handsome window and inset seat aligned with 'the grass walk'. The garden wall would conceal the full breadth of the house, the rear elevation of which was three rooms wide and faced 'the nursery ground'. This can only mean this house was destined for the end wall of the main walled garden, facing back towards the stables – the very same wall against which Edwards, in 1814, proposed a greenhouse.

If any of the Nash proposals left the drawing board, there are no surviving traces on the ground to prove it. However it is probable that the lodge on the western entrance from the Aberystwyth road was built. Pencilled queries on the back of this drawing address specific details of materials to be used for roof and for verandah columns,[33] and a building in this position was surveyed in 1819, and was subsequently demolished to make way for the present Italianate lodge on the site. It is significant that the outline of the garden surrounding the present lodge follows the curved contour specified on the Nash-Repton plan[34].

The remodelling of the mansion did not take place. It has been commented that for certain landowners, Humphrey Repton's 'Red Book' of proposed landscape improvements may have been a sufficient status symbol, without the necessity of the further expense of actually implementing them. Perhaps Nash and George Repton were being similarly used, for it seems inconceivable that the estate could have afforded such a massive building programme at this time. The plans included detailed architectural drawings of three alternative proposals for remodelling the ground floor of the mansion, where the

The Nash design for a dairy and Icehouse. Watercolour and plan, attribuated to George S. Repton.

N.L.W.

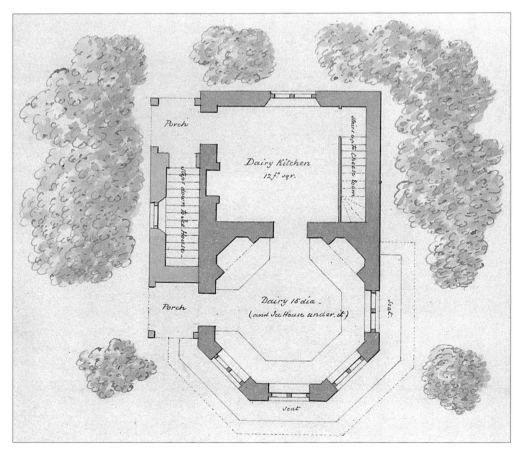

attached new servants quarters would be screened by a conservatory.[35] This, an elegant 7-arched arcade, was to house a longitudinal bed of flowers on the ground, with paths on either side of it, and a rear staging for potted plants. It would have led through the length of the conservatory from the dining room into the garden.

Notwithstanding his financial straits, the first ten years of Powell's majority saw steady alteration and improvement to the appearance of the demesne, primarily under the influence of John Edwards, but perhaps drawing on the concepts contained in two expensive pipe-dreams, the Davenport plan and the Nash designs. Pursuing a fashionable life in London, Powell and Edwards mixed socially with Nash, and will have been sensible of Regency style. A summary of the developments which actually took shape is provided by the meticulously drawn estate survey by William Crawford Jr., a land surveyor of Edinburgh, which was completed in 1819 and consists of a bound volume of ninety accurately surveyed and hand-coloured maps of all Nanteos holdings in Cardiganshire and Breconshire.[36] Its function was doubtless to allow a valuation on the basis of which further funds could be raised through loans and mortgages.

The Crawford map of the demesne defines a much larger outline than does the Davies map of 1764. The farms of Rhoserchan, Henrhyd Fawr and Henrhyd Fach have been incorporated into the demesne, as has the northern portion of Cwmhwylog lands. This extends the northern and eastern margins beyond the area designed by Davenport, but field boundaries and land use have not been emparked in this outer penumbra. Davenport's many follies have not been built, with the possible exception of his Cottage Ornée; destined for the margin of Llechwedd Dyrys wood, it seems instead to have been built beside the picturesque stream which descends the wooded Cottage Dingle. Davenport's influence may also be detected in the four acre lake, situated below Warren Hill, and in the two much smaller slivers of lake held back by weirs on the Nant Paith, one in front of the mansion, and the other adjoining the lodge. Davenport's lavish water features were designed without any evidence of detailed survey, and may have proved impossible to execute.

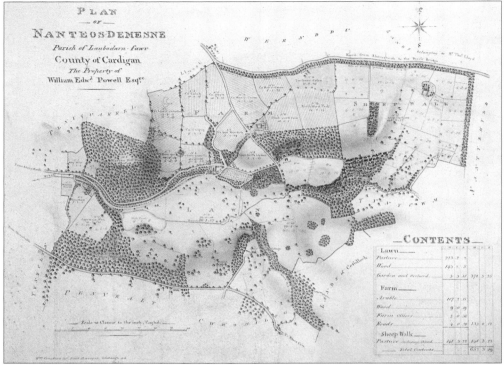

Nanteos Demesne, from the estate survey by William Crawford Jr., of Edinburgh 1819.

N.L.W

Other features which first appear on the Crawford survey owe more to the style of Nash and of George Repton's father Humphry. The road which formerly crossed Henrhyd Fach from Nanteos to Gors has been reduced to a track, and four rounded clumps of beech trees have been planted on the slope east of Cottage Dingle. A further clump on a high mound at Pant y Carne may have been planted at the same time to form a feature on the Nanteos horizon. These clumps make a handsome 'Reptonian' contribution to the landscape today. The lodge marked at the western entrance from the Aberystwyth road is at the confluence of the upper and lower drives and may well be the one proposed by Nash and Repton. The kitchen garden appears to have been walled only on the north and east sides with screening shrubberies to the south and west, and a wall-encircled flower garden, ornamentally planted, beyond it. The survey indicates the implementation of many of Edwards' recommendations but show no trace of the proposed gardener's house. The tulip tree on the margin of the flower garden, a vast bole of 483 cm girth with suckering regrowth, is very possibly a living survivor of this phase of Nanteos' history, and the cedar of Lebanon outside the kitchen garden wall (girth 630 cms) may be of similar age. Several other buildings make their appearance on the Crawford map: a pigeoncote (or, just possibly, Nash's circular dairy/ice house) to the east of the stables, a servants' wing adjoining the north east corner of the house, a courtyard building of farm offices at the Home Farm and a U-shaped dog kennel adjoining Building covert. It is to this dog kennel that Nash's picturesque keeper's cottage would have been attached.

By 1823 Powell was a widower, and in serious debt. The enforced sale of his Montgomeryshire lands ameliorated the position,[37] and having rejected the passionate opposition of his brother-in-law and trustee William Cherry, he embarked upon the demolition of the old Georgian stables, and their replacement with a handsome neo-classical building believed to be by Haycock.[38] In 1827 the agent, Pughe wrote 'The old stable will be pulled down in a few days and the garden wall begun'[39], and in 1829 he reported the postponement of an order of fruit

A detail of Crawford's survey of the demesne shows the mansion, outbuildings, kennels, offices, kitchen garden and flower garden in a parkland setting.

N.L.W

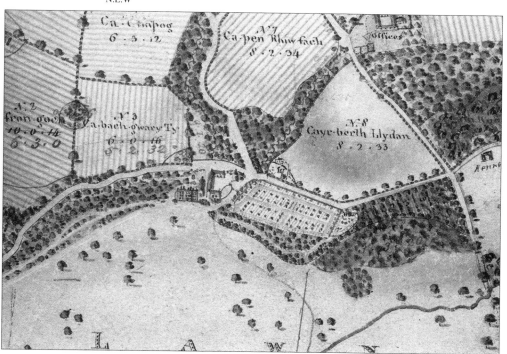

trees. It is probable that reclaimed stone from the old stables was used to build the west and south walls of the kitchen garden. By 1828 the estate was also being managed for game, and Powell's brother-in-law Cecil Phelp reported that he could show 40-50 brace of pheasants, and numerous hares any day.[40]

William Rice, mason, and several men were employed in building work on the estate and his working account book of 1831-1833 shows that in addition to running repairs on the mansion and estate buildings, two new projects were undertaken.[41] An ice-house was commenced on 17 August 1831 and took 82 man-days, costing £10-5-0 to complete. A greenhouse was commenced on 25 October 1831 and took 130 man-days, at a cost of £17-10-7, to build. The location of these structures is not clear, but the ice-house could have been to the Nash design (which had been proposed to be built 'in the plantation near the garden at Nanteos').[42] The greenhouse may have been east of the stables, or in the further flower garden or nursery; structures are indicated in both of these locations in agent Thomas Griffith's sketch survey of c. 1831.[43]

A plant order survives from 1832, which was supplied by John Miller of Bristol.[44] Trees and shrubs include 2 copper beeches, 25 common laurel, 10 Portugal laurel, 3 mespilus, 2 evergreen oaks, 4 white lilacs, 15 laburnum and 1 *Ribes sanguineum*. Some of these were almost certainly destined for the shrubberies outside the walled garden. A surviving copper beech, laurels, Portuguese laurels and an evergreen oak probably derive from this order. The ginkgos, one of which is a particularly fine specimen, the largest in Ceredigion, may also date from around this time.[45] Three Weymouth pines also occur in the order; two were planted symmetrically below Llechwedd Dyrys wood and one survives today. Flowers purchased include double sweet briar, evergreen sweet briar, *Lobelia cardinalis*, Blush moss rose, Pelargonum 'Mount Vesuvius', Crown Imperial, three cultivars of narcissi, double jonquils, four sorts of crocuses, hyacinths, *Paeonia fragrans*, and three dahlias 'to replace'. Such a plant list indicates a serious interest in ornamental gardening, both in named cultivar varieties, and in new imports from China and the New World.

SOARING AMBITIONS

The walk through the former 18th century pleasure ground now extended, as Davenport had proposed, to the lake, and had also been planted as a shrubbery. Vegetation today is of cherry laurel, Portuguese laurel, yew, box and hornbeam and may include plants derived from the order of 1832. The path passes among large trees, oriental plane, sweet chestnut, small-leafed lime, hybrid lime, silver fir and Douglas fir. This last, *Pseudotsuga menziesii*, at 36m tall and 345cm girth is the tallest in Ceredigion. The species, introduced to Britain in 1827, is one of the botanical discoveries from the western USA for which botanist David Douglas was celebrated.

The progress in estate improvement in the 1830s was steady, and is indicated in Thomas Griffiths' estate survey of c.1831 and in a sketch map executed by him c.1835.[46]

The dovecote behind the mansion, photographed 4 June 1948.

(Crown Copyright: the Royal Commission on the Ancient and Historical Monuments of Wales)

The latter shows the stables are completed and there is a circular structure, probably the present dovecote, behind the mansion. The upper drive to the stables had been diverted further up hill to join the lane descending from the Devils Bridge road. Problems had apparently been encountered with the waterworks, and the small upper and lower pools have disappeared. It is likely that the Nant Paith stream rapidly filled them and the original large lake with silt, for the stream is depicted in the Crawford survey entering at the top end and leaving at the bottom. By 1835 the Paith had been diverted through a cut which runs along the south side of the lake and rejoins the lake overflow via a cascade, downstream. An island had also appeared.

A substantial bout of improvement to the mansion itself seems to have followed on William Edward Powell's second marriage, in 1841 to Harriet Bell Ackers, widow of George Ackers of Moreton Hall, Cheshire. The previous year the architect William Ritson Coultart[47] of Aberystwyth had been urgently summoned to Nanteos following a fire in the servants' hall,[48] and by August 1841 the new servants' wing, a 70' long building at the rear of the house had been completed.[49] In the autumn of that year Coultart drew plans to close off the road approaching from behind the house with a large coal cellar, wood store and ash pit to create a yard to be accessed from the east.[50] He also submitted plans not totally compatible with the foregoing to put wings on both sides of the front of the house,[51] and for a subterranean icehouse to be constructed within a 40' x 30' thatched enclosure.[52] This suggests that the new buildings would overlap the pre-existing icehouse built in 1831-2. A modest version of the extension, one two-storey wing to the east was eventually built,[53] and the new road and yard shape adjusted to accommodate it. The new icehouse was presumably also built, for in January 1843 W.E. Powell instructed that the icehouse should be filled with ice.[54] Its location is no longer apparent.

The years 1842-1844 also provide insight into the productivity of the walled kitchen garden, through the gardeners' books of John Phillips and John Evans, which itemised excess produce sold from Nanteos gardens.[55] Doubtless some choice fruit and vegetables were never in surplus, being grown solely for the Nanteos table. Certainly grapes and peaches, though proposed by John Edwards in 1813,[56] never appear, and only two melons were sold during the three years of records. Costing two shillings each, equal to a female gardener's weekly wage at the time, they would have been out of the reach of most purchasers. The surplus sales provide a picture of a productive annual round of sea-kale, broccoli, leeks, carrots, asparagus and rhubarb, followed in June, July and August by beans, peas, potatoes, cauliflower, lettuce and artichoke. Soft fruit surpluses were of strawberries, gooseberries, cherries, raspberries and blackcurrants, followed by a large quantity and variety of apples, pears and damsons. Spanning the months from August to October these fruit generated the greatest part of the garden income. Cucumbers and melons, which would have been grown on hot beds of horse-dung under glass frames, were sold sparingly from April to August, excess cabbage seedlings for growing on in other gardens were sold in May and in August, and onions in October to December.

In 1846 part of the mansion was subjected to a substantial refit by Edward Haycock, with rear extensions comprising butler's pantry, bedrooms and workrooms, a triple bay on the dining room, and a rearrangement of the attic storey.[57] Plans for a portico had been under consideration for some years, possibly as early as 1832, and designs were drawn by David Moore, Coultart and other hands.[58] It was eventually built in 1847 by Haycock, who also drew plans for a lodge with elegant arched portico,[59] and in 1848 a second, less elaborate design, which was priced, on 12/12/1848 at £380 by Aberystwyth builder John Lumley.[60] A memorandum of 8 May 1851 records an agreement with William Rees, Carrier 'to carry stone, lime and sand to the new lodge about to be erected at Nanteos.'[61] If it was built, it was replaced only six years later by W.T.R. Powell, and it seems more likely that this plan was shelved. William Edward Powell's life ended in 1854, completing 45 years of squiredom which had developed the demesne from a somewhat dilapidated park with extensive lawn, scattered oaks and an eye-catcher folly, to a mature landscape with lake, walks, shrubberies, walled garden, greenhouses and exotic plantings.

William Thomas Rowland Powell

William Thomas Rowland Powell inherited the estate in 1854 at the age of 39 and was squire of Nanteos for twenty-four years. His known contributions to the landscape are modest: he appended the billiard room to W.R. Coultart's wing and probably built the new Keeper's cottage, now known as Pen-y-bont, south of the road at Llechwedd Dyrys. Plans for a building similar to the present cottage were drawn by Roderick Williams,[62] Aberystwyth builder, in 1864.[63] In 1857 the italianate lodge on the Aberystwyth approach was built. The design is remarkably similar to that for an extension wing to Castell Malgwyn which was drawn up by Willam Burn of Edinburgh in 1867.[64] No architect's drawings survive, but the building specifications by R. Kyrke Penson laid down that the whole of the materials from the existing lodge become the property of the contractor, but may be used in the new building with the permission of the Architect.[65] The grates, if possible, were to be re-used. Perhaps the Nash lodge was being thus cleared away. There are also drawings for a handsome pair of iron gates, which until recently closed the drive at the lodge.[66]

Labourers' account books show that in 1862-3 the estate employed four workers in the garden, the men being paid 8/6d per week and the women 5/-.[67] Plant orders show roses and verbenas ordered from Hale Farm, Tottenham,[68] for three outdoor beds, and gladioli from Newton Nursery, Chester.[69] A much larger bill, for £153.17.3d came from James Veitch, the Royal Exotic Nursery, King's Road, Chelsea and incorporating £9.2.3d for 1864.[70] Prolonged non-payment of bills was a frequent vice of the Powells, so this could be the accumulated debt of ten years' gardening. It is likely that Veitch would have supplied the Wellingtonias, *Sequoiadendron giganteum* which were planted on the old pleasure ground and in Penglanowen wood. Introduced to Britain around 1853, they are unlikely to derive from W.E. Powell's time. Veitch may also have supplied the greenhouses and frames which by 1886 were surveyed in the walled garden.[71]

W.T.R. Powell was, by 1866, confined to a wheelchair

and occupied quite a lot of his time in sketching in pen and ink. Most of his sketches date from 1868-1874 and many show scenes of Cardiganshire, of hunting, and of Nanteos. His work, though not always taken from life, provides a valuable pictorial record of Nanteos in the mid-nineteenth century. Four pictures are of particular historic interest. One, dated 1873 shows the view from the mansion.[72] Tantalisingly, the eye-catcher Dog Kennel is but crudely indicated and partly obscured by the mounded clump of trees behind it. The artist is much more interested in the scattered distribution of trees in the park, and particularly in a natural archway formed out of two adjoining parkland oaks. Another sketch, of 1867, 'The Warm Corner, Garden Covert, shows W.T.R. Powell in his wheelchair blazing away at a score of pheasants while a hare hops to safety under the guns.[73] The picture is valuable in its detailed depiction of gates, woods and the new dog kennel beyond the sportsmen, though it could be less than perfectly accurate since it was drawn from memory in Brussels. This habit may explain the confusing detail in a view of the lodge, dated 1873, which unaccountably has the tower attached to the wrong corner of the property, but in other details corresponds excellently with the lodge today.[74] Conifers in Penglanowen wood and Building Covert break through the deciduous cover. These are likely to be Wellingtonias and Douglas firs, planted in the mid 19th century, some of which survive today. Most evocative of all is the depiction of an otter hunt, in the Nanteos lake, with Col. Pryse of Gogerddan's otterhounds on 12 August 1872.[75] Two wheel-chaired figures gesticulate from the bank, men scurry around the lake shore, dogs swim in the lake, and two men in a small boat are approaching the island. However much we may, from a late 20th century perspective, deplore otter hunting, this was a red-letter day, and is recorded in lyric detail in the published diary of Captain Newton Wynne Apperley:

> I never did enjoy an otter hunt in my life equal to this; the cry of the hounds in the willow bed was quite heavenly, nothing could surpass it; and to see all the eager and bloodthirsty sportsmen on the banks of the lake, craving for blood; also Colonel Powell and General Samon, both in

Otter hunting in Cardiganshire. Sketch by W.T.R. Powell 1866.
N.L.W.

their invalid chairs, with three men to each chair, holding umbrellas over themselves and holloaing like the devil. In the excitement, the men in charge of the two invalids loosed hold of their chairs, which proceeded to run down the drive, amid the curses of the occupants, whose language at this time was more profane than sporting.[76]

W.T.R. Powell stocked the pheasantry adjoining the old rear drive to Nanteos, in 1871 buying 500 pheasants from George Basil of Wood Pheasantries, Hemel Hempstead.[77] He also made large purchases of agricultural supplies, various species of grass seed, clover, trefoil, swede and mangel for the Nanteos farm, implying an active interest in agricultural improvement. The itemised order to Arthur Dickson & Sons Chester in 1869 names finest rib grass, superfine trefoil, English alsike, trufair grass, Scotch perennial rye grass, Ruck's meadow grass, Devon evergreen grass, timothy, annual rye grass, Pacey's perennial rye grass, Haban rye grass, mixed clovers – clearly a concerted effort at pasture improvement, and a reminder that the Victorian innovators were already making substantial alterations to the native grass ecology of Wales.[78] Defiance purple-top swede, red mangel and Col. North's improved yellow globe mangel were also bought and grown for winter fodder.

There is an intriguing correspondence of 1874 between W.T.R. Powell and H.A. Hickman at Powis Castle, in which Powell proposes to send them a stag from Nanteos. Hickman sounds less than keen, enquiring as to the breed and state of health of the animal and emphasising that transport costs of £5 – £6 must be met by Col. Powell.[79] The stag was nonetheless transported, for a further letter written from Powis Castle, a year later alludes to the efforts to shoot the stag and send the venison to Nanteos.[80] There is no evidence that deer were ever kept at Nanteos, and the former deerparks at Trawsgoed and Lodge Park were long disused.

During W.T.R. Powell's years as squire, much of the administration of the estate was in the hands of his first cousin and agent Captain William Edward Phelp, who lived at Sunny Hill, Tregaron and received remuneration of £250 per annum. Compared with the extravagant enthusiasms of the three previous squires, the partnership between squire and agent was stable and resulted in few ostentatious changes to the estate. The evidence of the sporting estate has faded in the ensuing century, but the memory of a hunting man's affections live on in the twenty-two dogs' gravestones in the shrubbery, now

The hunt assembles at Nanteos.
N.L.W.

The new dog kennels, built and altered in the 19th Century, are now a dwelling known as Nanteos Cottage .

situated around the mulberry tree. Most were members of the Nanteos harriers, hare-coursing hounds, and one, a large hound of the retriever type called Nelson, is also immortalised, running with four harriers, in a pen-and-ink sketch by W.T.R. Powell dated 1842.[81] One of the oldest stones commemorates 'Poor Jack the Coon and Jenny his wife', an unlikely appellation to apply to a dog. Since the stones were removed in the 1960s from their original positions scattered about the shrubbery, disinterment does not offer an opportunity to resolve this mystery.

In 1878, W.T.R. Powell died, aged 63. His contributions to the landscape of Nanteos were concerned with timber, farm improvement, sport, and billiards. He may not have been quite as ignorantly boorish as others, particularly his heir, suggested. The evidence of the sketch books shows that he travelled widely in France and southern Europe, and cultivated a quirky sense of humour. He was succeeded as squire for just four years by his aesthete son George.

George Powell and his successors

Estate management during George Powell's four years of largely absentee squiredom was carried out by his father's secretary Sylvanus Lewis of Bronavon. On his death in 1882, Nanteos passed to William Beauclerk Powell (son of William Edward Powell's younger brother, Richard) whose wife, Anna Maria, was Sylvanus' sister. The Ordnance survey 1st Edition of 1886 probably provides a summary of the estate as W.B. Powell inherited it. In addition to the lodge and billiard room, the property had acquired the verandah'd laundry/dairy building which leans against the southern wall of the stable block, and a free standing game larder in the yard adjoining the back door. The kennel by Building Covert had been modified and rebuilt since 1819, and comprised three separate buildings framing a fenced yard, as was depicted by W.T.R. Powell.[82] A sawmill had been built in Sawmill Dingle behind the kitchen garden, and a dam behind the Farm Offices served a piped aqueduct to a fountain in the middle of the walled kitchen garden and to the house. The old farm and former agent's residence at Ty'n-y-rhyd near the lodge had been demolished, and new houses at Rhydyfirian and Glan-paith had been built. Also, a second pond, which features large in Newton Wynne Apperley's accounts of otter hunting, had been created by damming Nant Paith south of Nant-yr-hydd. Some additional woodland had been planted, creating Black Covert and extending Coed Penglanowen. Purely ornamental features, such as the Cottage Ornée had disappeared, and the old eyecatcher Dog Kennel was disused and derelict. Plas-crug castle, at Llanbadarn Fawr had long ago degenerated to a depressed farmhouse.

The frugal and efficient management of the estate by W.B. Powell and Sylvanus Lewis brought forth complimentary letters from their London solicitor, (surely a first in Nanteos history),[83] while land sales contracted the estate to just 4,336 acres and reduced debts. That the grounds were opened to the public is evidenced by printed cards entitling the bearer to pass through Nanteos Lodge gates.[84] It is more difficult to identify many significant changes in the landscape during this period. The kitchen garden was kept up, and a new quarter span vinery by W. Parnham was purchased in 1893.[85] The walled garden, before entering terminal decline in the twentieth century, contained a melon house, a vinery and a greenhouse, both the latter heated by hot pipes from a boiler. Within the walled flower garden to the east was an orchid house, also heated by its own boiler.

W.B. Powell lived until 1911, and Nanteos then passed to his son Edward Athelstan Lewis Powell, who was married to Margaret Pryse, daughter of Sir Pryse Pryse of Gogerddan. The early twentieth century was not a good period in the fortunes of country houses in general, and Nanteos is no exception. There was a little additional planting of specimen trees, chiefly firs, along Nant Paith opposite the mansion and a westerly extension of Llechwedd Dyrys wood as far as Tan-y-coed bridge. The decline of Nanteos is apparent in the absence of any entry for it in the Gardeners' Chronicle *Horticultural Directory and Year Book* of 1917.[86] Just eleven Cardiganshire estates are listed, including Crosswood, Hafod and Gogerddan, with details of their owners and head gardeners. In 1918, the heir, William Edward George Pryse Wynne Powell was killed, some say by his own men, and with the subsequent deaths of his father in 1930, and his mother in 1952, two hundred years of Powell occupancy came to an end.

For the estate, the inter-war years compounded the dereliction and neglect. New vigour was brought to the walled garden in the early 1930s, when Reg Newman, an experienced nurseryman whose father had grown carnations for Lord Rothschild, leased it as a commercial vegetable garden.[87] His workforce swelled by Land Army girls in the second World War; he also cultivated the park in front of the mansion for cabbage, cauliflower, sprouts, lettuce and potatoes.[88] Since those days the whole has reverted to grass, and most garden structures within the walled gardens were cleared away in the 1960s and 1970s. A bungalow now stands on the site of the orchid house in the second garden.

While the losses to the estate in the last hundred years include the disappearance of the statuary on the stable block (a horse and two eagles),[89] and the sale of most of the land, the landscape setting of the mansion has largely escaped alteration. In 1969 the lake, empty for more than twenty years, was repaired and refilled by the then owner, Geoffrey Bliss.[90] Only one farm building and a distant radio mast impinge on the outlook from the rococo music room on the first floor. The beech clumps on Henrhyd Fach have grown to fine proportions and they and the old oaks on the slopes are subject to tree preservation orders. With the ongoing restoration of the house it is still possible, with little suspension of belief, to imagine oneself in a Georgian or Regency landscape.

NOTES

[1] The material in this chapter is largely derived from an unpublished report, *Nanteos – a survey*, by Caroline Palmer and Ros Laidlaw (1995), on behalf of the then owner, Mr Gary Hesp.

[2] N.L.W. Nanteos [Maps] 308, 311, 317, 318, 319, 321, 325, 326, 333, 343, 355 *et al.*

[3] *The Gentleman's Magazine* 1780, 591.

[4] Miller, Philip, *Miller's Gardeners Dictionary*, 8th Ed., London (1768)

[5] Proposed new road from Pencwmhwylog by Llechwedd Dyrys and Wengrug, 1788, N.L.W. Nanteos 301.

[6] R.A. Griffiths 'The three castles at Aberystwyth.' *Archaeologia Cambrensis* (1977) cxxvi 74-87, reprinted in idem *Conquerors and Conquered in Medieval Wales* (Sutton/St Martins, 1994), 322-36.

[7] N.L.W. Nanteos 84.

[8] N.L.W. Nanteos [ma] 329.

[9] N.L.W. MS 1340C. (Thomas Martyn manuscript journal, 1801).

[10] Jones, Barbara, *Follies and Grottoes*, 2nd Ed, Constable , London (1974)

[11] Mavor, William Fordyce, *The British Tourists' or Travellers' Pocket Companion through England, Wales, Scotland and Ireland* (1798)

[12] Malkin, Benjamin Heath, *The Scenery, Antiquities and Biography of South Wales* (1804).

[13] N.L.W. Nanteos 124.

[14] A.O.Chater, Recorder for Ceredigion, Botanical Society of the British Isles, pers. comm.

[15] N.L.W. Minute Book (A1) of the Cardiganshire Board of Turnpike Trustees.

[16] Nanteos Demesne 1793, N.L.W. Nanteos 304.

[17] Plan of intended improvements at Nanteos, the Seat of Thomas Powell Esq., in the County of Cardigan by John Davenport, 1791, N.L.W. Nanteos [map] 76.

[18] Colvin, Howard, A Biographical Dictionary of British Architects 1600-1840 3rd Ed. (1995)

[19] Amongst the Nanteos papers is a plaintive request from Arthur N. Davenport of Orange Grove dated May 1811 for payment of another instalment on a long overdue interim bill for £100. Credit of two years had already been given on this sum and Davenport further enquires 'when it will be convenient to discharge the balance.' N.L.W. N.L. 674

[20] Walding Associates: *Hawkstone – A short history and guide*, Hawkstone Park Leisure (1993).

[21] R.C.A.H.M.W. Additional Info File Hafod N/CD/87/73/E, document supplied by Tom Lloyd, N.L.W. MS Derry Ormond 88.

[22] N.L.W. N.L.764.

[23] N.L.W. N.L. 689-712.

[24] Nash would also have been familiar to Powell as the architect of Llanerchaeron mansion, built in the early 1790s for William Lewis. William Lewis' wife was Corbetta Williama Powell, W.E. Powell's aunt.

[25] N.L.W. N.L.694.

[26] N.L.W. N.L. 702.

[27] N.L.W. N.L. 703.

[28] Suggett R. *John Nash, Architect in Wales* (Aberystwyth, 1995).

[29] N.L.W. Nanteos 130, 131.

[30] Temple, N., *George Repton's Pavilion Notebook. A Catalogue RaisonnÈ*. Scolar Press 1993

[31] N.L.W. Nanteos 136.

[32] Temple, N., *op. cit.* especially PNB 61, 63, (Rose Cottage), PNB 65 (Double Cottage).

[33] Suggett, R, *op.cit.*

[34] Suggett, R., *op. cit.*, fig 50c

[35] N.L.W. Nanteos 127.

[36] N.L.W. [Maps] Vol. 45.

[37] N.L.W. N.L. 563.

[38] Colvin H. *op.cit.*

[39] N.L.W. N.L.1149

[40] N.L.W. N.L. 1042.

[41] N.L.W. Nanteos A12.

[42] N.L.W. Nanteos [map] 126.

[43] N.L.W. [Maps], Vol. 14..

[44] The order was placed with John Miller, nurseryman, of Bristol. N.L.W. N.L. 1008.

[45] A.O.Chater, pers. comm.

[46] See note 29, and the Nanteos Demesne and Farm map of c.1835, N.L.W. Nanteos 304B.

[47] Recent authors, Colvin *op.cit.* and Joyner, P. *Artists in Wales c.1740-c1851*, N.L.W. 1997, spell 'Coulthart' with an 'h'. Inspection of his signature on plans, on letters (N.L.W. Nanteos 101), and of his name in the baptismal records of his children confirms that the spelling 'Coultart' is in fact correct.

[48] Powell to Coultart 17/12/1840 in N.L.W. Nanteos 101.

[49] N.L.W. Nanteos 105.

[50] N.L.W. Nanteos 27.

[51] N.L.W. Nanteos 20, Nanteos 21.

[52] N.L.W. Nanteos 89.

[53] Engraving: *Nanteos, the seat of W.E.Powell Esq. M.P.* (1852). Stonnard and Dixon N.L.W. Picture collection 139.

[54] Letter of 26/1/1843, in N.L.W. Nanteos MSS box 20.

[55] Gardeners' books, N.L.W. Nanteos A18, A19.

[56] N.L.W. Nanteos L 702.

[57] N.L.W. Nanteos 104.

[58] N.L.W. Nanteos 22/2, 23, 25, 26

[59] Haycock plans for lodge, 1847, N.L.W. Nanteos 111.

[60] Haycock plans for lodge 1848, N.L.W. Nanteos 113.

[61] N.L.W. Nanteos A20.

[62] Roderick Williams designed and built the gateway at Llidiardau in 1876. N.L.W. Llidiardau 30, 31.

[63] N.L.W. Nanteos 123.

[64] N.L.W. Cilgerran 1-4.

[65] N.L.W. Nanteos 101.

[66] N.L.W. Nanteos 110.

[67] N.L.W. A27.

[68] N.L.W. N.L. 1704.

[69] N.L.W. N.L. 2670.

[70] N.L.W. N.L. 1718.

[71] O.S. 1st Edition 6", Cards sheet IX.

[72] N.L.W. Vol. 47, 3.

[73] N.L.W. Vol. 45,144.

[74] N.L.W. Vol. 47, 5.

[75] N.L.W. Vol. 46, 119.

[76] Apperley, Newton Wynne, *A Hunting Diary*, (London1926).

[77] N.L.W. N.L.1765.

[78] N.L.W. N.L..1599.

[79] N.L.W. N.L..2682.

[80] N.L.W. N.L..1636.

[81] N.L.W. Maps, Vol. 46, 102.

[82] N.L.W. Maps, Vol. 45, 144.

[83] Chapter 5.

[84] N.L.W. N.L. 3880.

[85] N.L.W. Nanteos 74.

[86] *Gardeners' Chronicle Horticultural Directory and Yearbook for 1917* (London).

[87] He had formerly been head gardener at Bronwydd and Falcondale.

[88] Arthur Newman, pers.comm.

[89] *Nanteos*, Visitor guide, prefaced by Geoffrey and Rose Bliss (Aberystwyth, n.d.).

[90] *Western Mail* (Northern Ed.). *16 June 1969*

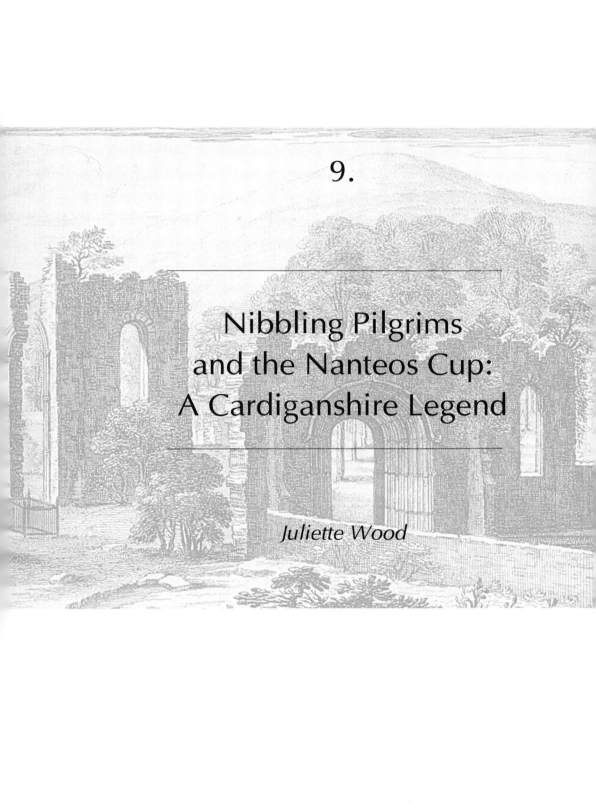

9.

Nibbling Pilgrims
and the Nanteos Cup:
A Cardiganshire Legend

Juliette Wood

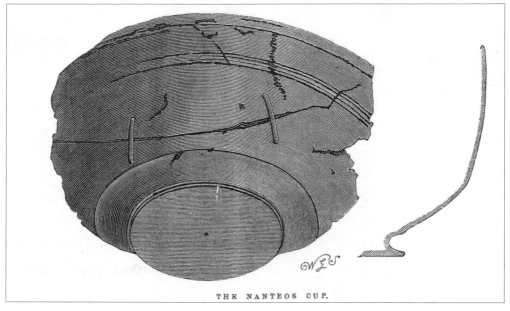

THE NANTEOS CUP.

The oldest sketch of the Nanteos cup, from Archaeologia Cambrensis, 1888.

N.L.W

THE NANTEOS CUP

THE Nanteos cup is a small wooden medieval mazer bowl, for many years in the possession of the Powell family and kept at Nanteos. The cup has been known since its first exhibition in the nineteenth century. It has a reputation for healing, particularly diseases involving bleeding. It could be borrowed and some small pledge left until the borrower had recovered and the cup returned. Some users would leave notes testifying to their cures. At some point in the twentieth century it became associated with the Holy Grail Legend and visitors began coming to Nanteos, not just seeking cures, but to see a supposedly sacred relic.

The story of the Holy Grail in Britain is linked to the legend of Joseph of Arimathea, and reflects an anachronistic belief in the importance of the Holy Grail in earlier periods.[1] According to the legend, St Joseph took the cup from which Christ drank at the Last Supper and later used it to catch the Redeemer's blood as he hung from the Cross. When Joseph supposedly came to Britain, he settled at Glastonbury, so the story goes, which became a focus for pilgrim activity until the dissolution of the monasteries at the beginning of the sixteenth century, when the cup was secretly taken to Strata Florida Abbey in Cardiganshire and eventually came into the hands of the Powells. It was removed from Nanteos in 1967 when the house was sold, and it is still in the possession of the Mirylees family, who had inherited the estate on the death of the widow of the last of the Powell family. My initial interest in the object was in the survival, and indeed not inconsiderable fame, of what seemed to be a pre-Reformation relic in a Protestant context. What emerged through examination of the records and interviews with informants was that, while the Nanteos cup was known for healing for over one hundred years, the Holy Grail aspect of the legend was comparatively recent, dating only to the beginning of the twentieth century. In addition both the Powell family and the object itself were the focus for traditions which revealed much about the interplay between local people and a dominant gentry family over several generations.

The legend attached to the wooden cup kept at Nanteos tells us that at the moment Henry VII's minions descended on Glastonbury Abbey (according to one account under the leadership of the King's minister, Thomas Cromwell himself), seven monks escaped carrying the precious relic. After a difficult journey across the mountains, they came to Strata Florida Abbey. Here they were supposedly taken under the wing of the Stedman family who owned the land and abbey. As each monk died, he passed on the cup. The last surviving monk gave it into the keeping of the Powells[2] or the Stedmans[3] 'until the Church should claim its own'. After the two families intermarried, the custody of the cup passed into the hands of the Powells. The object has been displayed at Lampeter, Aberystwyth and even in the United States. As the custodians of the object, the Powell family allowed sick men and women to drink from it in the hope of miraculous cures. The Mirylees owners still make water from the cup available to those who request it.

The story of the monks' flight is a dramatic one and accords well with the popular idea of Henry VIII despoiling the monasteries as recorded in the antiquarian work of scholars such as John Stow.[4] Some versions even add a dig at one of his most infamous ministers, Thomas Cromwell. Further historical validation is apparently

The Nanteos cup with notes of attestation as it was displayed at Nanteos.
(Crown Copyright: the Royal Commission on the Ancient and Historical Monuments of Wales)

provided by a reference in Dugdale's chronicle to six or seven Strata Florida monks receiving pensions and continuing to live in the monastery.[5] The general tone of the legend and some of the details have been influenced by antiquarian writings. The Tudor historian John Stow epitomised contemporary chronicles into a popular and influential history of religious changes during the reign of Henry VIII. Stow updated his own account several times, and it was further updated after his death. His work contains references to despoiled monasteries, fleeing monks and the fate of famous relics, and his tone contains more than a hint of nostalgia for the past, an ideal background for the creation of a legend about a mysterious object.

The seven monks with their hair-raising escape are entirely appropriate as legendary survivors of a disaster that supposedly disrupted the calm of monastic life. The drama of their survival is further underscored by the belief that each monk hands on responsibility for the sacred cup to a companion until the last monk gives the relic into the keeping of a secular protector. Indeed the story accords almost too well with dramatic expectation. Survivors of disasters are a powerful traditional theme. Noah and his family survived the Flood, the Jewish Remnant escaped Babylon and returned to the Holy Land; the poet Aneirin survived the desolation of the battle at Catraeth; Arthur, though wounded, is waiting in Avalon for the appropriate time to return. The 'epic of defeat' as it has been called derives its impact from the expectation of renewal as well as the pathos and tragedy of loss.[6] Looked at from this perspective, the story says more about a view of the past than about actual events. Dugdale's monks were actually the last members of the Strata Florida community rather than refugees from Glastonbury, and the Stedman family cannot be placed at Strata Florida before the 1570s. However, traditions connected to the Dissolution were already being attracted to ruined or partially deserted abbeys by the end of Henry VIII's reign, as the works of antiquarians such as John Stow abundantly illustrate. The story of Joseph of Arimathea is apocryphal, but further legends were attached to his name during the Middle Ages.[7]

Another version of the Nanteos cup tale suggests that the object was always at Strata Florida. Here historical possibility and speculation intermingle. The practice of retiring to an abbey and even taking vows was not an uncommon one and several important medieval figures spent their last days at Strata Florida.[8] However, some historians have seen this as evidence for the importance of the Abbey as a pilgrimage centre. Such highly romantic accounts suggest that the monks exploited the lucrative pilgrim market by acquiring a *phiol* (sic) known as the *Cwpan Nanteos* which attracted thousands of pilgrims to the Abbey, or that they built a road to carry the sick to Strata Florida and constructed Bedd Taliesin as a shelter for pilgrims.[9] Even the greatest historians have fallen victim to the multiplication of groundless testimonials to the Nanteos cup. Indeed T. Jones Pierce elaborated on the theme without the slightest substantiation: 'to make a visit to Strata Florida more attractive to the pilgrim . . . the monastery acquired its own sacred relic, a kind of mazer bowl – the *phiol sanctaidd Ystrad Fflur* – which according to tradition was displayed to pilgrims as . . . the Holy Grail.[10] Even Sir Glanmor Williams was partly seduced: 'there is not a word [i.e. in the *Valor Eccesiasticus*] of Strata Florida's own famous mazer bowl, a relic which attracted tremendous veneration in later centuries which it was known as the cup of Nanteos.' Sir Glanmor's footnote shows that he relied on T. Jones Pierce as his authority.[11] There are no records of such pilgrims, but one hopefully romantic account makes the interesting observation that the Nanteos cup has its primary 'sphere of influence' in Cardiganshire.[12] Traditions about its curative powers do cluster in the Cardiganshire/ Carmarthenshire area, but the reasons, as will become clear, have more to do with social and economic structures in the nineteenth and twentieth centuries than with medieval pilgrimages.

The first documented appearance of the object is as late as 1878, when George Powell allowed it to be exhibited at St David's College Lampeter at a meeting of the Cambrian Archaeological Society. Indeed the Nanteos cup is listed along with another wooden bowl 'supposed to possess curative powers' owned by Thomas Thomas at Lampeter.[13] This was the occasion of its first written academic description, a mixture of tradition and highly speculative archaeological 'fact' which has continued to characterise its appearance. Indeed archaeological and local journals have played a considerable role in creating the legend of the Nanteos cup. According to one description, its reputation as a healing cup was already well established 'over a wide district of Carmarthenshire and Cardiganshire'.[14] Sick people would drink from the cup and even borrow it after leaving a pledge. This account is the first to mention the testimonials of cures, some dozen of which survive with the cup at present. According to the 1888 account the number of cures is large but not quantified. This report mentions another curative object, a piece of slate from Builth which 'equally with the Nanteos cup' was believed to cure hydrophobia. There is significantly no mention of the Grail, rather a suggestion that the object is made from wood of the True Cross. The first drawing signed WGS (i.e. Worthington Smith) was published with the 1888 report (see p. 220). It shows an incomplete object with ragged edges and without a metal rim, and there are clearly two metal staples holding it together.[15]

Even at its first authenticated description, the cup does not seem to have been complete, and the poor condition of the object was ascribed to pilgrims biting off pieces as relics. Indeed nearly everyone who has written or spoken about the cup mentions the supposed practice of nibbling the edges to obtain souvenirs. When the bowl was exhibited in 1977, the archaeologist Douglas Hague, of the Royal Commission on Ancient Monuments in Wales made a detailed study of it.[16] He pointed out that the protective metal lip was missing and it bore no evidence of a central metal boss, both of which are features of other mazer bowls. It is likely that the cup was found in an already poor condition. The pilgrims who allegedly caused the damage are therefore part of the developing legend, but they are an important part. To those who believe, the condition provides further credibility as to age and authenticity. For the more sceptical, the suggestion that the pilgrims took pieces for souvenirs is perhaps the single apparently non-speculative element which allows the legend to be told with a degree of belief.

The Powell family correspondence contains a number of letters concerning the cup which illustrate Mrs. Powell's careful and tactful dealing in regards to it.[17] References describing the object as the Holy Grail abound from the late 1930's to the mid 1940's. Mrs Powell encouraged the belief, although as two of the letters indicate, she was reluctant for correspondents to make specific claims in print. One of the earliest and most elaborate descriptions of the legend by Ethelwyn Amery entitled *Sought and Found* published in 1905, while obviously referring to Mrs Powell and Nanteos, leaves such details as names and places vague. Similarly two descriptions published in the *Cardigan Antiquarian Transactions* in 1937 refer to the *Cwpan Nanteos* as a healing cup, but not as the Grail. One of these descriptions contains an interesting Nanteos 'miracle'. The writer George Eyre Evans recalled that when a meeting of the Antiquarian Society was held at Strata Florida, Mrs Powell gave permission for the cup to be put on a table placed where the high altar of the Abbey had been. Evans claimed that the heavy rain suddenly stopped and a shaft of sunlight illuminated the cup just at the moment it was placed on the table, and the bad weather returned as soon as the object was put away.[18] Mrs Powell's solicitor wrote to her in 1937 worried about how newspaper interest might affect her parlous financial state. Although the newspaper clipping is no longer attached, it evidently claimed that the object escaped the rapacity of Henry VIII because a monk was out visiting the sick when the King's men came to the Abbey, adding yet another variant detail about how it was saved. Mrs Powell took the line, and stated this quite clearly to at least one other correspondent, that the cup was not owned by the family, but in its custody, which is why it never appeared in any will or inventory property list.

One letter mentions another object associated with the Holy Grail, an 'Antioch Cup'.[19] However, the correspondent assures Mrs Powell that the one at Nanteos is the real 'National Treasure'. Following a radio broadcast in Canada,

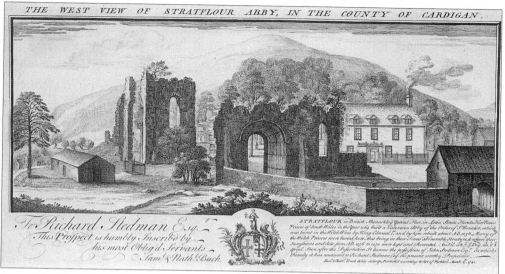

THE WEST VIEW OF STRATFLOUR ABBY, IN THE COUNTY OF CARDIGAN.

Strata Florida abbey and house, home of Richard Stedman.

N.L.W

another correspondent sent a crucifix to be touched to the Cup; while an Oxford correspondent keen to publish on the subject agreed to honour Mrs Powell's caution about saying too much too specifically in print. Interest in relics of the Passion was wide-spread during the 1930's, partly due to a general interest in both alternative religion and partly out of scholarly interest in finding links between Christian sacraments and pagan rituals. Perhaps the most poignant letter is from the then vicar of Lampeter in 1938 asking that a mother and her epileptic son be allowed to visit Nanteos. The letter does not express belief in the cup's efficacy so much as the feeling that the mother would derive comfort from the action.

The longest and most colourful correspondence occurred between Mrs. Powell and the Rev. Lionel Smithett Lewis, Vicar of Glastonbury in 1938-1940. About a dozen of his letters survive among the Powell family letters in the National Library of Wales.[20] Smithett Lewis was an unabashed enthusiast and quite convinced that this was the Holy Grail. At one point he brought in a Palestinian scholar, probably Sir Charles Marston, to authenticate it. He was shocked by the state of the cup, appalled that the pilgrims who came looking for cures had so little respect for it and urged the lady never to lend it out again. Lewis's colourful but woefully inexact writings on

Glastonbury tried to establish it as the foundation of 'A National Church' in Britain which preceded that at Rome.[21] His knowledge of existing material is extensive if not exact, and he recommends to Mrs Powell A.E. Waite's *Hidden Church of the Holy Grail*,[22] which propounded a complex theory about the meaning of the Grail in connection with early Celtic Christianity and a secret wisdom tradition. Waite himself visited Nanteos a few years before he died.[23] Lewis contributes his own mite to this saga by suggesting that the monks escaped at the behest of Abbot Whiting, the last Abbot of Glastonbury and notes that the church at Ozleworth near Wootton had a little cupboard which housed the Grail when the monks were visiting the sick and could not get back to Glastonbury before dark. Eventually he requested the return of the object to Glastonbury where he assured Mrs. Powell it would be housed in a splendid and secure reliquary. His request was evidently denied, whereupon the correspondence ceases. There is no mention of this episode in Smithett Lewis's book on Joseph of Arimathea, perhaps because Mrs Powell was disinclined to allow specific reference to the Nanteos cup as the Holy Grail in print. Nevertheless, the substance of the correspondence appears in several popular articles.[24]

Printed accounts hint at the existence of 'traditional sources'. Print is an important stabilising factor in twentieth-century legends and is a means of disseminating them more widely. This particular legend contains features typical of modern narratives which describe the survival of some ancient object into the present. Among the important motifs in this kind of legend is a series of dramatic and sometimes miraculous events which explain the appearance of the object in an unexpected place. The conclusion of Joseph's legendary journey at Glastonbury provides a reason for the existence of the Holy Grail in Britain. Although Strata Florida was a daughter house of Whitland Abbey not Glastonbury, the attribution of a medieval monastic background helps to validate the sacredness of the object. The dissolution provides a cataclysmic context which disrupts the stability of the medieval world and threatens the existence of the sacred object. Another series of events provides circumstances for a dramatic rescue and preservation in secret by those who recognise the object's true worth. Finally the object reappears, carrying with it, and transmitting to those who accept its reality, some of the beneficial qualities of the past.

I myself first heard about the Nanteos cup when I was a student at Aberystwyth. Although the Mirylees family had left, and Nanteos was being used as a combination craft centre and youth hostel, a postcard with a photograph of the cup was still on sale in Aberystwyth shops. Casual reference in print and from friends and informants over the years suggested that the wooden bowl in possession of the Powell family might fit into the small but interesting group of pre-Reformation relics which became integrated into later cultural contexts. However, it soon became obvious that traditions of medieval pilgrimage and links between Glastonbury and Strata Florida were late and impossible to substantiate. In written and even more clearly in verbal descriptions of the Nanteos cup, two sets of social relationships surface again and again. The first one concerns the relationship of the Powell family to its neighbours, namely a gentry family and its social inferiors. That a dynamic tension should exist between country house and the inhabitants of the surrounding area who fall within its sphere of influence is not surprising. The second (and less expected aspect of Nanteos folklore) however, suggests a strong local identity centred on mid-Cardiganshire. Three country houses dominated this area, Nanteos, Trawsgoed and Gogerddan. The houses stood within a few miles of one another and their families dominated the economic, social and political life of the area from the end of the seventeenth century to the beginning of the twentieth. In contrast, the smaller landowners, the merchants and craftsmen of the towns and the *gwerin* were a predominantly Welsh-speaking community. On the whole, the Powells were well-liked. Nevertheless, folklore surrounding the Nanteos cup, with all its variations and contradictions, can be seen as part of a negotiation of position between groups and as a contribution to the local identity of the region. This strongly suggests that the Nanteos cup is less a relic of early Christianity than a later icon of social identity and power sharing. The belief that it was saved from the depredations of the Dissolution can be seen as a symbol of continuity for the old order. So too the role of both Stedmans and Powells as protectors not despoilers of the monks and their treasure makes them appropriate custodians of the object. Several accounts stress the relatively restricted area in which the cup was known and venerated. Although the context is the religious meaning of the object, these observations serve to reinforce the cultural and social links inherent in the developing legend. A striking feature of the oral accounts, whether they express belief or disbelief in its authenticity, is the close link maintained between the object, the behaviour of the Powell family, and the local area.

There is no early evidence for the existence of the cup. William of Malmesbury does not list the Holy Grail among the relics of Glastonbury,[25] nor does Samuel Rush Meyrick mention it among the antiquities of Cardiganshire in his early nineteenth-century description.[26] Nor is it mentioned among the Stedmans' possessions in any of their wills or inventories. There is a tantalising inventory reference in 1617 to 'wooden vessels', but alas such bowls were commonplace household objects and these are valued at a mere 20s.[27] The origins of the Stedman family are obscure, but they were originally associated with Staffordshire. A charming tradition claims that Richard Stedman was a Crusader, son of the duke of Arabia and friend to Richard the Lionheart, banished to Wales.[28] More recent traditions claim that the cup is lathe-turned, made of olive wood and dates to first-century Syria. The murky period of the Crusades in which warrior figures devoted to unclear objectives died violently or survived mysteriously is an ideal setting for the transfer of relics to Europe. Nearly all the relics of the Passion, the Shroud of Turin, the True Cross, the Crown of Thorns were believed to be in the hands of Crusaders at some point. Richard the Lionheart was believed to have deposited a piece of the True Cross in the Tower treasury.[29] In this context the reference to the Stedmans as Crusaders is a dramatic cliché, especially since they cannot be placed at Strata Florida until the late sixteenth century. So too the reputation of Richard the Lionheart increased with the popularity of nineteenth-century historical novels, although there is a Tudor reference that he presented Excalibur to Tancred of Sicily.[30] County historians were keen to give their local worthies the right pedigree and the most oblique traditions could produce elaborate family histories. There is however no evidence to link the Stedmans, much less the Powells, with Strata Florida at the time of the dissolution.

The cup remained available to be used for cures and observed by visitors to Nanteos until 1968 when it was taken away and has been kept safely in a bank in Hereford. Many Cardiganshire residents recall seeing the cup at Nanteos together with testimonials to its efficacy. The cup was displayed in a glass or wood case and some visitors remember that the object was handed round. Many informants remember visiting Nanteos as part of their school outings in the 1960's. One earlier report described the healing cup as a 'small shred of crumbling wood enshrined in a glass case' used as a drinking vessel in Strata Florida where cures were effected by taking food and medicine from it.[31] It was indeed in a wooden box when it was brought back by the Mirylees family to Aberystwyth in 1992. There are only a dozen or so testimonials kept with the cup at the present time. Possibly the alleged number of cures is due to exaggerated memory, or to material having been lost. The cup itself was kept in a cupboard in the library at Nanteos, and one informant recalled that when Mrs. Powell opened the cupboard numerous documents fell off the shelves onto the floor; these were from grateful visitors who had been cured. Another suggested that whenever someone came seeking cures from the cup, Mrs Powell would leave them alone with the object.[32] A copy was made, according to the present owners, by a local craftsman, because the original was in such poor condition, and it was the copy that visitors were allowed to handle, although the original cup was made available to those seeking cures. The copy has its own traditions. One correspondent wrote that the real cup had been sold to a rich American because the family was short of cash and the copy replaced it to save face in the community.[33] In the late 1980's many university students still knew about the cup, its reputation and the chequered fortunes of the house since it had first been sold in 1968. Several students had been told that there were monks' graves under the cellar at Nanteos and that a secret passage ran from there to Aberystwyth Castle. Similar traditions have been repeated in recent newspapers articles both in Britain and in the Welsh-American newspaper *Y Drych*.[34] On a tour of Nanteos in 1992, we passed through a short narrow corridor leading to the Library where the cup used to be kept. Someone pointed out a large window as the one used by local farmers to return the cup without having to enter the main door. Nanteos folklore is still very much alive.

About a dozen slips of paper all in the same hand about four inches by three inches are at present held with the cup in its wooden box. They record the name of the borrowers and their illnesses, the dates of lending and return, what was left in pledge and the outcome. The earliest records the cup being lent on 1 Sept. 1857 to Ebenezer Vaughan for the use of his wife. He left £1 and when the cup was returned on Oct. 1857, the slip was marked 'cured'. On 27 Oct. 1858 'Wm Roulendt, Tregaron' borrowed it for his sister 'ret'd 2 Jan 1858'. From 23 Jan 18?2 to 27 Feb., it was 'lent to John Herbert for his mother-in-law.' On 26 Jan 1860 'Richrd Jones (labourer) Llangowsa' (sic) borrowed it for his wife 'bleeding stopped 7 March 1860.' The most recent slip indicates that on 13 Aug. 1862 Wm. Jones of Llanbadarn left a silver watch. These correspond with the dates in Douglas Hague's report on the cup, and he is one of the few to give any precise information.

There may have been more testimonials of course. An article in *The Church Times* in 1906 mentions two. A harpist scoffed at the cup in 1888, but repented and on 4 May 1888 noted 'Mind completely at ease'. In 1901 the cup was lent for the use of Evan Perry's wife of Penham (?) Blaenpennal.[35] Interestingly the most dramatic cures seem to have occurred to people from outside the Cardiganshire area. A priest from Herefordshire who was apparently cured of rheumatism became convinced that the cup was indeed the Grail, and preached several sermons about how it might have come from Glastonbury to Aberystwyth. None of the local informants mentioned this or could recall the incident when asked directly. It was recounted in some detail in the two popular articles already referred to above, one of which appeared in the Sunday Express and one in a so-far unidentified American magazine in the 1960's.[36] When the cup was exhibited in the National Library in 1977, several experts, among them Douglas Hague, examined it and produced an exact and careful description and drawing.[37] The consensus was that the cup could be dated sometime between the end of the fourteenth century and the sixteenth century, is made of wych-elm, not olive wood, and is consistent in shape with a common form of medieval domestic vessel known as a mazer bowl.

The legend is a complex one. Accounts of its supposed history vary as does the degree of belief or disbelief among informants. However the enthusiasm to respond on either side of the argument suggests that the cup was, and will continue to be, a focus for local interest. Varying and sometimes self-contradictory traditions suggest that the Nanteos cup is the Holy Grail kept (during the Middle Ages or in the aftermath of the Crusades) either at Glastonbury or Strata Florida. A correspondent from Pembrokeshire remarks on the fact that a sick child was taken from Narberth all the way to Nanteos seeking a cure and describes the cup as 'the most cherished treasure of the abbey of Strata Florida'.[38] Some accounts claim that it is a curing cup, perhaps made from the True Cross, but not the Holy Grail.[39] These accounts are often supported by ancillary traditions about pilgrims, crusaders, and the events of the dissolution. Once the idea of curing becomes established, one finds a number of secondary traditions about pledges, testimonials, cures and pilgrims taking pieces as personal relics. The fortunes of the object in the twentieth century are linked to those of the Powell family and in this context another set of traditions relate to copies being made, whether it was deposited for safe-keeping in a bank and which bank.[40] Other locations and objects become drawn to the legend. For example a large red earthenware crock found in a cottage in Ysbytty Ystwyth is said to come from the Abbey and was intended to hold the cup.[41]

Looked at from this perspective, the traditions about the Nanteos cup are too late to be authentic. There is no mention prior to the 1850s, and no mention of possible connections to the Grail until 1905. The most likely explanation is that a wooden bowl was found at Strata Florida no earlier than the eighteenth and probably as late as the nineteenth century as indicated in Chapter 1, when the Powells took over the Strata Florida site following the death of Richard Stedman. The fact that Meyrick does not mention it in his lengthy description of Strata Florida supports the later nineteenth-century date for the object and its attendant legend.[42] The Holy Grail theme is even later linked to the widespread interest in such relics and into the numerous theories on the meaning of the Grail which were put forward at the beginning of this century. Speculations about the relationship between Christianity and mysticism propounded by writers such as Arthur Machen, A.E. Waite and Jesse Weston were popular, as was Lionel Smithett Lewis's desire to link the Grail with a 'national' British Church. At least two other 'Grails', the so-called Antioch Cup,[43] and a glass bowl associated with Chalice Well in Glastonbury,[44] were attracting some attention, and it is no doubt against this kind of background that we should evaluate traditions associated with the Nanteos cup legend.

Guide books to Aberystwyth provide an indicator of the level of interest. The 1816 Aberystwyth Guide includes a description of Strata Florida with references to Leyland and Dugdale and lists W.E.Powell Esq. of Nanteos among the subscribers, but there is no mention of a cup.[45] Nor is it mentioned in an 1885 guide which does however gives directions to the house.[46] By 1923 however, Nanteos is said to possess 'the Tregaron Healing Cup, which resembles the Holy Grail' and the same information is repeated in 1924.[47] By 1934 the town guide confidently informs visitors that Nanteos 'preserved the precious medieval relic called the Cup of Healing, the surviving portion of a wooden bowl, a large part of which has been taken by believers in its magical properties'.[48] Medieval pilgrimage to Strata Florida to venerate the cup is taken as fact, with Ysbytty Ystwyth and Penrhydfendigaid respectively being described as a hospice and way-stop for pilgrims. When the mansion was opened to visitors the guide book described the cup

> . . . Little more than a fragment of blackening wood, this is reputed to be the Cup used by Christ at the Last Supper . . . In 1538 came the Dissolution of the monasteries and the community at Glastonbury fled to Strata Florida . . . The Cup then passed into the hands of the ancestors of the Powells of Nanteos . . . for 200 years the Cup has been here, and the story of its healing power has become known all over the world. The present owner herself has received requests for water from every continent. At one time over-zealous pilgrims bit pieces out of the cup as relics, that is why it is so sadly diminished . . .[49]

The Holy Grail is, however, only one aspect of the Nanteos cluster of legends. Other traditions, many of which are characteristic of country house folklore generally, are associated with the mansion. Ghosts, furniture with curious histories, blacked-out windows, secret passages, endless anecdotes about family fortunes and family eccentrics are not infrequently associated with such houses and their occupants. The 1960's guide to the

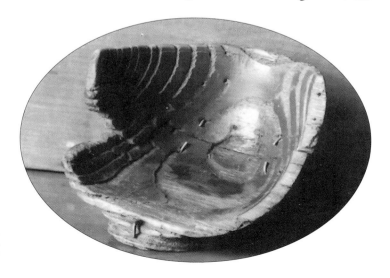

Another view of the Nanteos cup.

(Crown Copyright: the Royal Commission on the Ancient and Historical Monuments of Wales)

house gives an indication how the Nanteos cup fits into a more general background of this type of folklore. It mentions a blackened window from which someone saw a fatal accident, a white lady who foretells death, a heart-shaped table presented to Admiral Nelson by his mistress and a photograph of Richard Wagner. This last was claimed to be a souvenir of his supposed visit to the house to see the cup and to write his opera *Parsifal* which tradition says that the object inspired.[50] Mundane explanations can be offered for many of these elements, although they in turn can be traditional. For example, a blacked-out window as a way of avoiding the window tax or Wagner's picture as a souvenir of a visit to honour the composer. George Powell, the owner who first exhibited the Nanteos cup, was a great admirer of Wagner. Guidebooks such as these help create a feeling that visiting a country house should be a special experience and legendary material is an important element in this process.

The pattern of traditions associated with the cup suggests a manufactured legend. There is no convincing evidence to link it with the Holy Land, Crusades or Glastonbury. In so far as folk legends are concerned with the nature of belief rather than with the accuracy of legend details, the existence of such traditions reveals a great deal about the process of legend formation. The folklorist Richard Dorson coined the term 'fakelore' for synthetic and manufactured traditions and in many ways the legend of the Nanteos cup fits his criteria very well. However, using such a term obscures the wide range of attitudes manifested by the various sources for this legend. Some informants do sincerely believe that the object is special and take great care to explain its existence, using a mixture of romanticised past and folk memory which characterises the transmission of such legends. Lionel Smithett Lewis's aspiration for a national British church, as described in the books on Glastonbury which he wrote in the 1950s, was echoed by one member of an audience at a talk who announced that this object (i.e. the Nanteos cup) had been the rightful possession of the Welsh for thousands of years and should be returned to public display in Wales.

Printed accounts, especially ones which appear in

newspapers, are at least sympathetic to the mystery surrounding the object.[51] Most oral accounts however, are surprisingly sceptical, and are likely to be linked to the history of the Powell family and their role in Cardiganshire society. Of particular interest are George Powell, often referred to as 'gentle' George Powell, aesthete and friend of Swinburne, who exhibited the mazer bowl for the first time, and Mrs Powell, who fostered its reputation as the Grail.[52] Oddly, although the cup has a reputation for healing, comparatively few cases of its use in this context can be authenticated.[53] Even sceptical informants, however, recount that its poor condition is due to people biting off bits during use. The nibbling pilgrims may be just as fictional as the links with the Grail, but it is evidently an element which even sceptical informants find acceptable and is one of the most constant features of the reports. Descriptions of the Nanteos cup appeared in archaeological journals at the late nineteenth and early twentieth centuries.[54] Since the earliest authenticated cures date only to the middle of the nineteenth century, this suggests that its reputation as a curative object also dates from about that time. The descriptions in these journals undoubtedly introduced what was a very local belief to a wider audience and provided a means for stabilising and transmitting the details of the legend.

The lack of a clear context for the Nanteos cup invites elaborate and speculative explanations, and in this aspect it is by no means unique. The same issues of *Archaeologia Cambrensis* which describe the Lampeter exhibition in which the cup first appeared also mention the Caernarfon Talisman, supposedly a Gnostic object, and a bronze vessel found in the Goginan mines which might be a Roman lacrimatory.[55] An excavation in 1847 of a megalithic site known as the Cheesewring in Cornwall produced an ancient vessel and a local legend about a cup which cannot be emptied[56]. These descriptions are not so much a way of describing the historical reality of such objects as a means of attributing cultural importance to them. Many treasure trove legends contain similar legendary incidents.[57] In these circumstances a mysterious history is often created to account for an object's appearance. A well-known example is the Shroud of Turin which, like the Grail, is a relic of the Passion. Several features were taken as indicators of antiquity and these supposedly concrete and factual details support the more mysterious aspects of the shroud such as the reversed image, and the contentious history of its ownership in which the Templars figure prominently.[58] Similarly the supposition that the Nanteos cup is made of olive wood is taken as positive indication of genuineness,[59] although as we have seen, expert opinion suggests that it is made of wych-elm and is typical of medieval mazer bowls, not first-century Palestinian objects.

Mysterious ownership is also a feature of these legends. The Crusades and the Templars provide important contexts. Indeed an object claimed to be the Grail now in the Cathedral of Valencia was allegedly in the Templars' possession,[60] and the Templars are essential to the modern Grail industry centring on the town of Rennes-le-chateau in France.[61] Such motifs can crystallise into a standard episode in which an old order is disrupted violently, but some secret object/information is preserved and passed on via an elite whose mission is to guard the object and carry the message into the modern world. The dissolution of the monasteries in Britain provides a context both for disruption and mysterious continuity. The Nanteos cup is by no means the only object to be given into the hands of sympathetic believers and to appear mysteriously generations later. A Greek icon of Elijah and the Ravens, supposedly brought back by Crusaders to Talyllychau abbey and now in St David's Cathedral was also allegedly preserved from falling into the hands of Henry VIII by being entrusted into the safe keeping of the Johnes family at Dolaucothi, and later at Hafod Uchdryd.[62] Essentially the same story pattern involving the precious relic of a religious house set at the time of the dissolution is told in connection with a piece of the True

The 17th century icon of Elijah, now at St. David's.

Cross associated with Stanbrooke Abbey.[63] Nor is the cup at Nanteos the only candidate for the Holy Grail. Much the same story of peril, preservation and miracle is told about other objects, such as the Silver Chalice of Antioch (now in a New York Museum and no longer attributed to Antioch), two agate chalices, one in Naples and one in Valencia, and another Antioch Cup, a glass bowl in an ornate case said to be Roman, but probably medieval.[64] The doubts surrounding the origin and ownership of these objects reinforce both sceptical and sympathetic re-telling of these legends. The mystery can confirm or cast doubt depending on the perspective of the narrator.

Another mysterious object whose context can be compared with the Nanteos legend is the Luck of Edenhall, owned by the Musgrave family of Eden Hall near Penrith. It is a glass vase, probably made in Aleppo in the mid-thirteenth century, kept in an ornate leather case of European origin.[65] One version of its origin claims that a Crusader brought it back with him, the other that it was a gift from the fairies. The latter version is the subject of a ballad which recounts how a servant boy was given a glass of magic water by a fairy to cure the mistress of the house.[66] In any case the family's luck is bound up with the possession of the object. The link between a mysterious, or religious, object and the fortunes of a particular family is common enough, and such legends began to appear in family histories during the eighteenth century. This feature is reflected in the Nanteos cup legend in the story of one of the Mirylees daughters who suffered a dreadful accident, but survived because of the power of the cup.[67] These legends link the narrators with the past, perhaps a romantic past, but one which by sharing in these legendary narratives gives a shared sense of identity as well. Both the Luck of Edenhall and the Nanteos cup have features in common with other objects brought back from the Otherworld, and placing the legend in this broader context offers an additional point of reference from which to understand its function. Legends which involve contact with the Otherworld are often worked out in terms of conflict and resolution within this broad category. Narratives which involve the possession of Otherworld objects are a popular and widespread type. Such objects are a source of both power and danger whether they are seen in the context of fairy traditions (as in the Luck of Edenhall) or religious ones (as in the Nanteos cup).

A number of Otherworld object tales feature in Welsh tradition and they illustrate several possible solutions to the conflicts which possession of these objects entails. Perhaps the most famous occurs in the medieval poem 'Preiddeu Annwn' in which Arthur and his warriors are involved in a fierce battle for possession of a magic cauldron. The supposed skull of St Teilo, now in Llandaff cathedral, but once used for cures, is another. Gerald of Wales in his *Itinerary Through Wales* records a story about the boy Elidyr who steals an object from the Otherworld only to lose his ability to return there. Similarly there are tales about someone who visits a cave in which Arthur and his men are sleeping, but loses the power to find it again if he attempts to steal its treasure. These narratives imply that interfering with the Otherworld is a dangerous activity, but sometimes humans do retain possession of an Otherworld object, and very often this object is a drinking vessel of some kind. The Luck of Edenhall is one example and there is a comparable tale from Wales collected by William Williams of Llandegai. The Nanteos cup seems to fall in this class although the context is that of religious relics rather than fairy objects.[68]

A number of mazer bowls survive as valued objects, some with traditions attached to them. The only other one known in Wales is in St Beuno's church, Clynnog. It is made of maple, with a silver gilt rim, central boss and dates from about 1485, but no specific traditions seem to be attached to it. Durham Cathedral has a mazer bowl, called the Judas Cup which was formerly used during the Maundy Thursday services.[69] Mazer bowls were not usually used for ecclesiastical purposes but were valuable objects which figure frequently in wills and monastic inventories. The *frater* at Canterbury at one time owned 138. Often they were fitted with a silver lip to protect the rim from wear and were adorned with pious inscriptions. The Clynnog inscription is a Latin invocation for Christ's mercy.[70] The Nanteos example has lost its metal lip and this may be why it is in such poor condition and has given rise to the story of having been nibbled away by pilgrims. One strand of tradition suggests that a metal rim was once fitted to protect the cup from borrowers who chewed off pieces, but that this destroyed its effectiveness and it had to be removed.[71]

Romantic traditions are not limited to mazer bowls. A cup supposedly concealed in a secret compartment in the statue of the Virgin in a Devon church was said to contain the blood of Christ.[72] A pottery three-handled cup at Abergavenny is called 'the leper cup', presumably because of its long handle, since no leper hospital is recorded in the area.[73] Stories such as these are impossible to prove or disprove, but their lateness and similarity suggest legend rather than historical fact. They do however acknowledge both the importance and the singularity of the object and can reveal much about the contexts in which such legends were told. Unfortunately they were frequently regarded as nothing more than superstitions and the context, especially when they appear in archaeological descriptions, is not always recorded. Newspapers are another important means of transmitting modern legends. An examination of the newspaper accounts of the Nanteos cup reveals a certain consistency in how they approach the problem of credibility and in which features of the legend are highlighted. On the whole, these accounts adopt a positive and reasonable position, either by taking a sceptical attitude to some feature of the legend or by presenting some concrete detail. The accounts then use this moderate and rational stance to validate more imaginative aspects of the legend. An article in the *Western Mail* for example, first cites 'antiquarian opinion' that the cup belonged to Strata Florida, then summarises the story of the Grail and Joseph of Arimathea and refers to the cures linked to the cup, finally concluding that it must have been used as a healing cup by the Abbey during the Middle Ages.[74] History and tradition are ostensibly distinguished, but then conflated, as there is no documentary evidence for the cup being at Strata Florida or used to effect cures there. A relatively brief response to this article gives a version of the legend which includes all the most romantic features:[75] the Grail,

Joseph of Arimathea, the Stedmans and the monks, Lionel Smithett Lewis's interest. This account points out that the cup could not have been at the Stedman's Staffordshire home, but accepts that it is made of olive wood and by implication genuine. Similarly an account in *Country Life* repeats the story of a cup 'reputed to be the Grail', the flight of the monks to Strata Florida where the Powells granted them asylum, and Joseph at Glastonbury. So enthusiastic was the veneration of the local people that the family had to protect the lip with a silver mount to prevent further destruction.[76] Here again the nibbling pilgrims provide a means to rationalise and perpetuate the legend.

A particularly dramatic cure was witnessed by the last hereditary owner of Nanteos, according to the *Sunday Express,* when an elderly rheumatic priest was cured after drinking from the cup.[77] This account seems to blend together several of the sources for the Nanteos legend. Besides the priest, it mentions an epileptic and cures for deafness, blindness and a request to return the cup to Glastonbury. The only record mentioned specifically, aside from the account of the rheumatic priest from the owner's confidential journal, is the Powell family correspondence, which contains a request for an epileptic boy to visit, although with no indication whether the visit occurred or its outcome. The cures for blindness and deafness do not appear in any extant Nanteos source, but they are mentioned in Arthur Machen's short story 'The Great Return'.[78] The request for the return of the cup suggests Lionel Smithett Lewis's attempts to induce Mrs Powell to present the cup to Glastonbury. The effect of this narrative patterning is to create a seemingly neutral position, appropriate to a newspaper, which, by implication at least, invites the reader's belief in the legend. Two other accounts, both published in America, repeat these elements with a greater emphasis on the Arthurian aspect, something which is almost completely absent from the Welsh accounts.[79]

Most of the printed accounts are in English. A Welsh description of *Cwpan Nanteos* appears in *Ysten Sioned,*[80] which is contemporary with the description of the cup in *Archaeologia Cambrensis* after the Lampeter exhibition. The

THE NANTEOS CUP

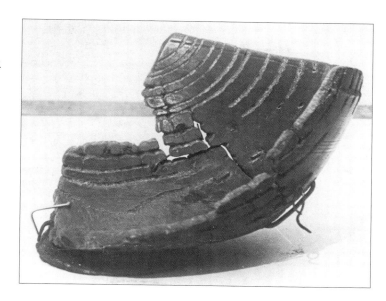

emphasis is on local use and local importance, including much the same details about its use in cures, and the belief that it was made from the Cross. An article on Strata Florida in the journal *Cymru* in 1907 also mentions the cup and its supposed association with the Last Supper. There is a photograph in which the rivets and wires joining the pieces are very clear, as is its decidedly incomplete state, and there is a summary of the Joseph of Arimathea story and the monks' flight to Nanteos. The account was written two years after Ethelwyn Amery published her booklet *Sought and Found*, and this account refers to that publication as a 'charming novel'.[81] During the first decade of this century, the legend developed from being merely a healing cup to the much more elaborate Holy Grail form. A short article appeared in *The Church Times* in 1906, and its conclusions were challenged by the influential Arthurian scholar Jessie Weston.[82] The actual source for the story of the monks fleeing to Glastonbury and the prophecy about the church claiming its own may never be identified, but it is more probable that antiquarian rather than oral sources lie behind it. Its elements recall Stow's writing on the fate of the Catholic Church after the dissolution, and the statement about the church claiming its own echo Archbishop Ussher's prophecies.[83] Two hints in the Powell correspondence give some support to this and suggest that Mrs Powell herself may have been influential in this particular development. Her correspondence with Smithett Lewis refers to John Stow and she received a rather cryptic note from the British Museum identifying a book as Ussher's prophecies.[84]

George Powell first allowed the object to be exhibited in 1878. It may be that it came into his possession not long before that time. Such an object discovered during repairs to the Abbey would easily attract the kind of tradition which has been discussed. Other factors too may have come into play. During this period the economic fortunes of the family declined. A pattern begins to emerge in which mundane experience is being contrasted with the colourful vagaries of this gentry family. George Powell's role in the first archaeological discussions of the cup and its legends, Mrs Powell's role in the development of the Grail aspect, the selling of the house in 1967 and its subsequent chequered fortunes provide contexts in which amusement, sympathy and even criticism can be expressed through re-telling the traditions surrounding the Nanteos cup.

We have seen that the first account published linking the Nanteos cup with the Grail appeared in 1905. It clearly signposts the location of the house and the identity of the owner without giving concrete details.[85] Written by an American visitor, Ethelwyn Amery, it combines an interest in a romantic past, such as is presented in sources like John Stow, with unabashed sentimentality. Amery was a member of the British Chatauquan Movement, which had its origins in the search for spiritual well-being. About the same time, Wellesley Tudor Pole 'discovered', as a result of a mystic experience, a mysterious blue glass bowl near Glastonbury, and this too attracted interest as a possible Grail.[86] The Nanteos cup is mentioned in a short story written by Arthur Machen sometime between 1910-1920 in which three relics, St Teilo's Bell, a miraculous altar and the Grail return mysteriously to a fictional village called Llantrisant (located somewhere in Pembrokeshire).[87] A sceptical young journalist hears rumours about the appearance of mysterious lights during a Revival Meeting at Llantrisant. When the journalist begins to investigate, he hears of a dying girl who suddenly recovers, the smell of incense in a Protestant church, three mysterious beings called the

Fisherman, a deaf woman cured by the sound of a saintly bell and a rose of fire on the sea which later appears as a mysterious jewelled object in the chancel of the church. These rumours coalesce in the vision which restores the dying girl who sees three men, one holding a bell, one a glowing object like an alter, and a third a cup. These are of course the three saints (i.e. the fishermen) commemorated in the name of Machen's fictional church. Traditions about the Methodist Revival often mention the appearance of mysterious lights. Machen, in the persona of the journalist, does not explain these, but rather drops hints, such as references to the Healing Cup of Nant Eos and the Healing Cup of Tregaron and a reference to an incident which allegedly took place in 1888 of a harpist who scoffed at the Cup but repented. Machen mixes tradition and fiction, a device which he used to good effect elsewhere, to create a sense of seemingly real journalistic reporting. The Grail image here is not a single object, but three, and thus consistent with Machen's theory expanded elsewhere that the Grail was originally a holy relic of one of the Celtic saints.

Machen's was an odd intellect. Together with his friend and onetime associate, A.E. Waite, he was interested in the origin and meaning of the Grail. For him it represented the real and ecstatic Celtic Christianity which existed prior to the advent of the Latin Church and he suggested that its origin lay in some religious object belonging to one of the early Celtic saints (a theory also put forward by Professor Mary Williams).[88] Machen's theories need to be seen in the context of a much wider interest in the Grail which linked it to both Gnostic mysticism and Celtic paganism. In 1874 the Reverend Sabine Baring-Gould suggested that the Grail was a survival of early paganism.[89] Alfred Nutt published a more extensive study in 1888, giving special consideration to possible links with Celtic tradition, and a popular version of his thesis appeared in his series on mythology and folklore in 1902.[90] A.E. Waite's book on Christianity and the Holy Grail was published in 1909, stressing its links with mysticism.[91] Jessie Weston commented unfavourably on the Nanteos cup itself, but her study of the Grail Romances culminated in the publication of *From*

Ritual to Romance, an influential statement of the supposed origins of the Grail in an ancient secret fertility ritual.[92] Theories of Celtic and of Gnostic influence still have their proponents, indeed through the work of Nutt and Weston, they have been influential in academic Celtic studies. Waite and Machen had great appeal for popular investigators, particularly those who were anxious to make the Grail relevant to contemporary British life. It is interesting that the Rev. Smithett Lewis offered to send Mrs Powell a copy of Waite's book, and Waite himself subsequently visited Nanteos.[93]

This fin-de-siècle fascination with the Grail in which academic and quasi-academic approaches intertwined is important for understanding the legend of the Nanteos cup. Some like Nutt, Weston and Baring-Gould focused on the Grail's origin, development and meaning, but others were concerned to apply the legend to a contemporary situation. This highlights another important aspect of these legends, the belief that their survival has consequences for contemporary society. Since the publication of Amery's book, the Nanteos cup has been associated with an ambiguous and evocative prophecy that 'the church shall claim its own'. Lionel Smithett Lewis's attitude reflects this, although his emphasis on a British church is nationalist in tone. Wellesley Tudor Pole's suggestions about the Sapphire Glass bowl have a similar millennial cast. He saw it as appearing at a time when civilisation needed it and was entering a New Age.[94] Tudor Pole was dismissive of the Nanteos cup and Arthur Machen had a decidedly negative view of Tudor Pole's 'Bristol Grail'.[95] Another group with an interest in the origin and relevance of the Grail were the neo-druids, whose concern with the origins of Christianity in Britain anticipates some of the attitudes of New Age religion. Owen Morgan (Morien) published a substantial book entitled *The Light of Britannia* which claimed to elucidate not only the mysteries of ancient British druidsim and determine whether Jesus was a druid, but also to reveal the secrets of the court of King Arthur, the creed of the Stone Age and the discovery of the Holy Grail in Wales.[96] His argument is a variation of the neo-druidic tendency to link all megalithic monuments with druidic worship. For Morien, stone circles reflected the 'druidic' symbols of the sun and the sacred apple, and of course the Grail, and since he considered that druidism survived in Wales, then Wales itself he argued was the Holy Grail. This was the kind of environment in which links between the Nanteos cup and the Holy Grail were formed.

An interesting pattern emerges if one looks at the range of traditions linked to the Nanteos cup in terms of a legend process rather than as a set of real or false traditions. It is not clear why Mrs Powell seems to have been keen to foster the reputation of the cup as the Grail but unwilling to endorse it publicly. No satisfactory study of her exists, but her letters and the testimony of people who knew her suggest she was interested in both High Anglicanism and Roman Catholicism. Other legends associated with relics include many of the elements found in connection with the Nanteos cup. Typically the relic is linked to some saint or famous person. Its early history is dubious and usually contains as least one perilous or miraculous escape. The object becomes associated with a particular family or church, the sphere of influence is likely to be co-extensive with that of the family or church who hold it in custody. Another important factor in the Nanteos legend is its relationship to the more general study of the Grail. There is currently a revival of interest in Grail studies. The speculations surrounding the town of Rennes-le-chateau had produced numerous theories in which Templars, Cathars, mysterious treasure and conspiracies abound.[97] Interest in the Shroud of Turin has suggested a link between the Grail and the Shroud, with the Grail being equated with Christ's tomb.[98] The Grail has found its way to the New World, via the Templars, a conspiracy and a secret Scottish society.[99] Modern UFO theory offers an explanation of its meaning,[100] and even the alleged suppressed 'female' aspect of religion enters the equation.[101] Victorian folklore scholarship regarded these traditions as confused and fragmented survivals which could be decoded by scholarship into historical material on the one hand and superstitious elements on the other. The former constituted a genuine core of information, while the latter could be further interpreted as pertaining to some myth or ritual in a remote age. The idea that the pagan world survived, often in secret, into the Christian Middle Ages, and that modern scholars could understand and recapture this link, is both a romantic and flattering view of the past. It reflects both the romantic and quasi-academic interest in the meaning of the Grail romances, which were popular in the latter half of the nineteenth century and the beginning of this one.

The legend process is complex and the relationship between a particular group and its legendary past is less a matter of whether a particular belief is true and more a question of how it functions within a complex cultural envelope. There has been a marked shift away from the search for confirmation of 'the folk' as somehow encapsulating the past, to a view of society as a closely integrated social organism. This less fragmented approach allows us to extend our understanding of the Nanteos legend, taking into account even the versions which take a sceptical view. Certainly the past is used to validate the legend, but the indications are that this is a romantic rather than a real past. The core of the legend appears to be a relatively modern development starting in the middle of the nineteenth century. Increasing interest in the archaeology of Wales, as evidenced by the accounts in influential journals such as *Archaeologia Cambrensis*, was clearly an important factor, as were popular and scholarly interests in the meaning of the Grail. However the legend remained surprisingly local in its geographical scope maintaining a connection with the family, the estate, even in those accounts which appeared in national newspapers.

The study of a legend such as this can never be fully concluded. Even sceptical re-telling perpetuates it and continued study contributes to its dissemination. The aim of the current work has been to explore facets of the development of the Nanteos legend which have not previously been considered. What emerges is a legend still much talked about, still linked to the Nanteos estate and to the Powell family and to Cardiganshire itself.

THE NANTEOS CUP

NOTES

1 Deborah Crawford, 'St Joseph in Britain: Reconsidering the Legends: Part I' *Folklore* 104 (1993) 86-98.

2 R. Osborne Jones (Ystrad Meurig) 'Recent Excavations at Strata Florida' *Transactions of the Cardiganshire Antiquarian Society,* 9 (1936) 23-26.

3 Ethelwyn M. Amery, *Sought and Found: A Story of the Holy Graal.*[sic.] (Aberystwyth, 1905); Anonymous: 'Account of Cup coming from Glastonbury to Strata Florida during the time of Abbot Richard Whiting'. N.L.W. 3297B n.d. 3 paper leaves hand-written.

4 John Stow, *The Annals of England faithfully collected out of the most authenticated Authors*, (London, 1605) f.572a.

5 Amery, *op.cit.* N.L.W. 3297B, 'Archaeological Notes and Queries: The Cup at Nanteos Cardiganshire' *Archaeologia Cambrensis* 5 (1888) 5th ser. 170-71. (hereafter *Arch. Cam.*)

6 Bruce Rosenberg, *Custer and the Epic of Defeat*, (Harrisburg: Pennsylvania State University Press 1964) 217-50.

7 Crawford, *op.cit.* 86-98; R.F. Treharne, *The Glastonbury Legends, Joseph of Aramethea, the Holy Grail and King Arthur* (London: The Cresset Press, 1967) chap 2.

8 Samuel Rush Meyrick, *The History and Antiquities of the County of Cardiganshire*, (London: Longman 1809) xli, 261-62.

9 Sidney Wright, *Up the Claerwen* (Birmingham: 1948) 61; S. M. Powell, 'Pilgrim Routes to Strata Florida' *Cardiganshire Antiquarian Society Transactions* 8 (1931) 9-24; R. Osborne-Jones (1936) *op.cit.* 22-23.

10 T. Jones Pierce, 'Strata Florida Abbey ' *Ceredigion* I, 1 (1950) 31.

11 Glanmor Williams, *The Welsh Church From Conquest to Reformation* (Cardiff, 1962) 365.

12 R. Isgarn Davies, 'Old Roads in the Parishes of Cardiganshire' *Cardiganshire Antiquarian Transactions* 9 (1936) 10-13, 22-23.

13 'Catalogue of the Local Museum Exhibited in the Hall of St David's College 1878' *Arch. Cam.* 10 (1879) 4th ser., 66, ; 'Report of the Lampeter Meeting *Arch. Cam.* 9 (1878) 4th ser. 336-39; Stephen J. Williams, 'The Cup at Nanteos' *Arch. Cam.* 5 (1888) 170-71.

14 *Arch. Cam.* 5 (1888) 170-71.

15 ibid., 170-72.

16 Douglas Hague, 'Report on Nanteos Cup 16/3/85' (N.L.W. ex 720).

17 N.L.W. N.L. 4624, 4631-35,4656, 4665 etc.

18 Ethelwyn M. Amery, op. cit; George Eyre Evans *Cardiganshire Antiquarian Transactions* 12 (1937) 29-30, another descriptions of the *Cwpan Nanteos* occurs in the folklore section of the same number p.58.

19 N.L.W. N. L. 4778-4793; S.W. Gentle-Cackett, *The Antioch Cup* (London, 1935) 7, 23-27.

20 N.L.W. N.L. 4778-4793.

21 Rev Lionel Smithett Lewis, *St. Joseph of Arimathea at Glastonbury*. (London: James Clarke and Co. 1955, rpnt 1964) 13-24.

[22] A.E. Waite, *The Hidden Church of the Holy Grail* (London: Rider 1909)

[23] W.R.Gilbert, *A.E. Waite: A Magician of Many Parts* (Wellingborough: Crucible 1987) 159.

[24] Bob Danvers-Walker, 'Is the Holy Grail in Wales? The Chalice of Nanteos' photocopy n.d.; John Cottrell, 'My Search for the Holy Grail' photocopy n.d.; Peter Bloxham 'Is this the Cup that was used at the Last Supper?' *Sunday Express* 1/8/1961.

[25] Treharne, *op.cit.* p.7.

[26] Meyrick *op.cit.* 254-65.

[27] James Stedman's probate inventory is printed in *Montgomeryshire Collections* vol.31 (1900) 73.

[28] Thomas Nicholas, *Annals and Antiquities of the Counties and County Families of Wales.* Vol. I & II (London, 1872) p.168; Meyrick *op.cit.* 265.

[29] H.M. Gillett, *The Story of the Relics of the Passion.* (Oxford: Basil Blackwell 1935) 102-05.

[30] ibid., 103.

[31] S.M. Powell (1931) *op.cit.* 9-24.

[32] Personal communications to author from residents and former residents in and around Aberystwyth 1991-1993.

[33] Personal communication to author in an unsigned letter.

[34] Personal communications from Aberystwyth University students; Emily Pritchard Cary, 'In Search of Noah's Ark, Mary's Grave and the Holy Grail' *Y Drych* September 1995, 14' 'More on the Nanteos Cup' *Y Drych* March 1996.

[35] 'A Welsh Relic' by JJB, *The Church Times* no. 2247 vol. LV, 16 Feb. 1906, 195.

[36] See above, n.24; A.G. Prys-Jones 'The Healing Cup of Nanteos' *Western Mail* 17.3.53.

[37] N.L.W. ex 720; Douglas B. Hague 'An Object of Romantic History' *Cambrian News* May13, 1988.

[38] David Salmon 'The Nanteos Cup' 26 Oct. 1940, 295, *Notes & Queries*.vol. 174 (London: Press Rd 1940).

[39] Wright, *op.cit.* 61; E.R. Horsfall-Turner, *Walks and Wanderings in County Cardigan* n.d. 25; Eyre Evans, *In County Cardigan* 1937, 25; *Arch. Cam.* (1888) 170-71.

[40] Frederick Blight 'The Nanteos Cup' *Western Mail* 21.3.53; 'The Future of the Nanteos Cup' *Country Life* 12.11.67.

[41] Horsfall Turner, *op.cit.* 25, illus., 26.

[42] Meyrick, *op.cit.*, 254-65.

[43] Gentle-Cackett *op cit.*, illustration between 20-21; 25-27.

[44] Oliver G. Villiers, *Wellesley Tudor Pole, Appreciation and Valuation* (Canterbury: Hardcastle, 1968) 26-29; Rosamund Lehmann, *My Dear Alexias, Letters from Wellesley Tudor Pole to Rosamund Lehmann* (Sudbury: Neville Spearman, 1979) 13-24.

[45] Samuel Williams, *The Aberystwyth Guide* (Aberystwyth: Baker Street 1816) 126-28.

[46] John E. Lloyd, *A Guide to Walks and Places of Interest Around Aberystwyth* (Aberystwyth, 1885).

[47] *Aberystwyth, Official Guide and Souvenir*, issued by Aberystwyth Corporation, Gloucester, 1923) p. 89; 1924, 80.

[48] ibid., 1934, 47-48.

[49] *Nanteos Historic Monument* (Aberystwyth: Cambrian News:1966) 7-8.

[50] ibid., 5-8.

[51] See footnotes 24,36,37,41.

[52] Based on letters and interviews.

[53] The hand-written slips are perhaps the most tangible form of authentication, although past owners, and even other informants, mention the existence of 'numerous' testimonials.

[54] These descriptions appeared in *Archaeologia Cambrensis* and *Cardiganshire Antiquarian Society Transactions* see above footnotes 5,13,18.

[55] E.L. Barnwell 'The Carnarvon Talisman', 'Bronze Vessel' *Arch. Cam.* vol 10 fourth series(1879) 99-108;140-42.

[56] 'Report of the Forty-Ninth annual Meeting held at Launceston . . .' *Arch. Cam.* 15 4th series (1896) 251-2.

[57] Charles R.Beard, *Lucks and Talismans; A Chapter of Popular Superstition.* (London: Sampson Marston and Co., 1934).

[58] Ian Wilson, *The Shroud* (London: Penguin, 1979) 73-95, 109-127.

[59] *Church Times* Feb. 16, 1906, 195.

[60] Gillett *op.cit.* 97-98.

[61] Michael Baigent, Richard Leigh and Henry Lincoln *The Holy Blood and The Holy Grail* (London: Corgi, 1984); Lionel and Patricia Fanthorpe, *Rennes-Le-Chateau, Its Mysteries and Secrets* (Middlesex: Bellevue Books, 1991).

[62] W.J. James 'Some Notes on the Painting *Elijah and the Ravens* in St David's Cathedral' (published by the author 1992).

[63] Gillett, *op.cit.*, 108-12.

[64] Fachim Kouchkji, *The Great Chalice of Antioch* (New York, 1933); Gillett, *op.cit.* 97-98; Gentle-Cackett, *op.cit.*, 25-34.

[65] 'The Luck of Edenhall' Masterpieces Sheet 6 (Victoria & Albert Museum, 1976).

[66] Beard, *op.cit.*, 98-114.

[67] Cottrell, *op.cit.*, 144.

[68] Mary Williams 'Some Aspects of the Grail Problem' *Folklore* 97: 83-103. Dr Williams considers both St Teilo's Skull and 'Preiddeu Annwn' in this article; 'Elidyr's Sojourn in Fairy Land' 42-49, 'Arthur in the Cave' 12-17, in W. Jenkyn Thomas, *The Welsh Fairy Book* (Cardiff: University of Wales Press 1995); Dafydd Glyn Jones, 'Stori Dylwyth Teg o FÙn' *Anglesey Antiquarian Society* (1995) 83-86. See examples of the tales listed as variants of 'Drinking Cup Stolen From the Fairies' *A Dictionary of British Folk-tales*, 2 vols. Katharine M. Briggs (Bloomington: Indiana University Press 1971) vol.1 214, 217, 223, 304-05, 333, 339.

69 D. R. Thomas, 'On Some Sacramental Vessels of Earthenware and of Wood' *Arch. Cam.* 6(1906) 4th ser. 47-60.

70 'Caernarvon Meeting Report' *Arch. Cam.* 26(1895) 4th ser., 144-45; *Arch. Cam.* (1926) 428-29; *Arch. Cam.* 6 (1906) 58 .

71 *Church Times*, 16 Feb. 1906, 195; Bloxham, *op.cit.*

72 Thomas, *Arch. Cam.* (1906) 62n.

73 Thomas, *Arch. Cam* . (1906) 70.; E.L. Barnwell, 'Supposed leper cups and bronze vessels shown at Abergavenny Meeting 1876' *Arch Cam* 10 (1879) 4th ser. 283-86.

74 A.G. Prys-Jones, *Western Mail* 17.3.1953.

75 Blight. *Western Mail* 21.3. 1953

76 'The Nanteos Cup', *Country Life* 12.11.1967.

77 Peter Bloxham, *Sunday Express* 1.8.1961.

78 Arthur Machen 'The Great Return' in *Holy Terrors: Collected Short Stories* (London: Penguin 1946) 108-40.

79 John Cottrell, Bob Danvers-Walters *op.cit.*

80 D. Silvan Evans and John Jones, *Ysten Sioned* (Aberystwyth: 1882) 83-85.

81 E.B. Morris, 'Ystrad Fflur' *Cymru* (1907) 85-90.

82 *Church Times*, 16 Feb. 1906 op. cit; Jessie Weston 'The Nant Eos Healing Cup', *Church Times* no 2,248, Vol. LV, 23 Feb. 1906.

83 *Strange and Remarkable Prophecies and predictions of the Holy Learned and Excellent James Usher, late Lord Archbishop of Armagh* (London 1681).

84 N.L.W. N.L. nos. 4784-4790. Mrs Powell's copy was probably the later edition, *The Remarkable Prophecy of Archbishop Ussher concerning the Roman Catholic Church to which is prefixed a letter addressed to His Present Majesty . . .* by John Phillips. (London, 1924).

85 E. Amery, op. cit. This reticence about location and ownership adds a further level of mystery to the narrative and was a feature in a recent television piece on the Nanteos cup, which filmed the present owner in silhouette and withheld details about its present whereabouts. Fortean TV, Channel 4 broadcast March 1997.

86 Lehmann, 1979 *op.cit.*, 32-52; 67-68; 71, 83, 183, 195, 199.

87 Machen, *op.cit.* 108-40.

88 Arthur Machen, *The Secret of the Sangraal, A Collection of Writings* (East Sussex, Tartarus Press 1994) 1-40;142-150, 228-232; R.A. Gilbert, 'Arthur Machen and A.E. Waite: A forgotten collaboration', *Antiquarian Book Monthly Review* vol. 11 no. 4 (April 1976) 7-8; *Arthur Machen: Selected Letters*, edited by R. Dobson, R.A. Gilbert (Wellingborough: The Aquarian Press 1988); Mark Valentine, *Arthur Machen* (Bridgend: Wales Poetry Press, 1995) 85-96.

89 S. Baring-Gould, *The Holy Grail* (1887, reprint Llanfynydd: Unicorn Press, 1976) 16-22.

90 Alfred Nutt, *Studies in the Legend of the Holy Grail with Special Reference to the Hypothesis of its Celtic Origins* (London: David Nutt 1888); *The Legends of the Holy Grail*, Popular Studies in Mythology, Romance and Folklore no. 14 (London: David Nutt 1902).

[91] Waite, *op.cit.* 1909, Introduction.

[92] Jessie Weston, *From Ritual to Romance* (1925, reprint Princeton University Press, 1993); Janet Grayson, 'In Quest of Jessie Weston' *Arthurian Literature XI* edited by Richard Barber (Cambridge: Boydell and Brewer, 1992) 1-80; Jessie Weston, *Church Times* 23 Feb. 1906.

[93] N.L.W N.L. no. 4790.

[94] Lehmann, *op.cit.* p. 183; Villiers, *op.cit.* 26-29.

[95] Lehmann, *op cit.* p.135; Dobson, *op.cit.* p. 38.

[96] Owen Morgan (Morien), *The Light of Britannia* (Cardiff: Daniel Owen, 1894) chap. v.

[97] Baigent, Fanthorpe see above note 62.

[98] Noel Currer-Briggs, *The Shroud and the Grail* (New York: St Martins Press, 1987).

[99] Andrew Sinclair, *The Sword and the Grail* (New York: Crown 1992)

[100] John F. Michell, *The Flying Saucer Vision: The Holy Grail Restored* (London: sidgewick and Jackson 1967).

[101] Graham Phillips, *The Search for the Grail* (London: Century 1995); Margaret Starbird, *The Woman with the Alabaster Jar: Mary Magdelen and the Holy Grail* (Santa Fe New Mexico: Bear & Co, 1993).

NANTEOS.CUP.COM

Since Dr Juliette Wood planned and wrote this chapter, the internet has given new life to the Nanteos cup and the myths associated with it. Enter Nanteos+cup in a search engine, and the screen will fill with websites, many of which are virtual duplicates of each other. Most of the material is based on the Glastonbury-Strata Florida tale, dealt with above by Dr Wood, and needs no repetition here, except to note the embellishments which so many love to add to the basic – and baseless - legend. For example, one site (in Seattle) claims to have been shown the cup at Nanteos 'in a maze of exceedingly ancient cellars' in 1983, though the cup has never been kept in the cellars, and in 1983 was safely in the care of the Mirylees sisters in England. Another site claims that the cup is in 'the museum at Aberystwyth'. A site associated with Adrian Wagner repeats the groundless claim that Richard Wagner visited Nanteos, and that the cup inspired his opera 'Parsifal'.

Two websites will no doubt extend the cup's reputation. One, again based in Seattle, offers you 'a free prayer/healing cloth, which has recently touched water from the Holy Grail... Also, a free pamphlet on "The Church that Jesus Built", a mystic and mysterious church recorded in history as being built by a young Jesus Christ and on whose grounds the actual Last Supper Grail was found (known as the Nanteos Cup).' Another site offers a similar service, provided by a 'Rev. Griffiths' of Glouchester (sic). The most useful sites are those which list the cup along with other artefacts also claimed to be the holy grail, including those referred to in the preceding chapter.

Gerald Morgan
Caroline Palmer

APPENDIX

APPENDIX 1: NANTEOS HERALDRY

Michael Siddons

The coats-of-arms attributed to the Powell family do not lend themselves to easy interpretation. The best surviving evidence for the heraldic practices of the Powells are a funeral hatchment now hanging in the entrance hall of the mansion, and the magnificent shield crowning the Llanbadarn Fawr church memorial to Sir Thomas Powell (d.1703). This shield is difficult of access; some of its colours may have been obscured by dust or incorrectly restored, resulting in some of the anomalies referred to below. It is not known which member of the family was commemorated by the hatchment.

The hatchment: (now at Nanteos)

Quarterly of four:
Argent, a cross flory engrailed Sable between crows (some late manuscripts say choughs) close Sable, legged Or. These arms are attributed to Edwin of Tegeingl [Englefield in

The Powell funeral hatchment at Nanteos

Flintshire], a well-known ancestor-figure. The Powells claimed descent from Edwin through Llywelyn Gaplan of Anhuniog, but the descent is probably fictitious. This coat is charged with a canton Sable, a chevron Argent between three spear-heads Argent, embrued Gules. These arms are usually attributed to Bleddyn ap Maenyrch, a Breconshire chieftain, but in the collection of Cardiganshire pedigrees by David Edwardes (d.1690), it is said that Cadwgan ab Iorwerth, who is given as the grandfather of Llywelyn Gaplan, gained this coat with the chevron Or at the winning of Cardigan. The fact that this coat is here borne on a canton suggests that this is the coat which was intended. Earlier sources do not give this coat.

Azure, a lion passant Or between three fleurs-de-lis Argent. This is probably intended for Einion ap Seisyll, lord of Meirionnydd, whose attributed coat is usually blazoned Argent, a lion passant Sable between three fleurs-de-lis Gules.

Per fess Or and Sable (so far unidentified).

4. Argent, three boars' heads couped Sable, armed Or (?). These arms are attributed to Elystan Glodrydd, from whom the Joneses of Nanteos claimed descent.

Crest: On a wreath Argent and Sable, a talbot's head erased Argent, collared Or.

Sir Thomas Powell's memorial.

Quarterly of twelve, in three rows of four:

A chevron [Or] between three spear-heads [Sable]. The coat on the canton in quarter 1 of the hatchment, i.e. probably Cadwgan ab Iorwerth.

As quarter 1 above, without the canton. (Edwin of Tegeingl).

A chevron [Or] between three roses [Sable]. Probably intended for Owain ab Edwin, to whom were attributed the arms Gules, a chevron between three roses Argent.

A gryphon segreant [Or]. (Llawdden or Llowdden, said in some manuscripts to have been descended from Uchdrud ab Edwin). Gules, a gryphon segreant Or.

A lion rampant in an orle of roses [Or]. The arms attributed to Gwynfardd Dyfed: Azure, a lion rampant in an orle or roses Or. He had many descendants in south-west Wales.

A chevron [Or] between three quatrefoils (?) in outline [Sable]. These may be 'Bowen knots', which would make this the coat of the Bowens of Pentre Ifan, Llwyn-gwair, etc., descended from Gwynfardd (quarter 5): Gules, a chevron between three Bowen knots Argent.

A gryphon segreant [Or], probably the same as quarter 4.

A chevron [Or] between three fleurs-de-lis [Sable]. This is probably the coat attributed to Collwyn ap Tangno, whose descendants include the Vaughans of Trawsgoed: Sable, a chevron between three fleur-de-lis Argent.

Per sinister semée of ermine-spots, a lion rampant [Or]. The coat attributed to Tudur Trefor: Per bend sinister Ermine and Ermines, a lion rampant Or. As 1.

A dragon's head erased, in its mouth a human hand couped at the wrist and bloody. This coat is often attributed to Tegau Eurfron, wife of Caradog Freichfras, another important ancestor-figure, as Argent, a dragon's head erased Vert, holding in its mouth a human hand couped at the wrist proper, bloody. According to the pedigrees Tudur Trefor was descended from Caradog Freichfras..

A lion passant between three fleurs-de-lis Sable. Einion ap Seisyll as in quarter 2 of the hatchment.

Heraldic shield of Sir Thomas Powell, Llanbadarn Church.

APPENDIX

APPENDIX 2:
OUTLINE GENEALOGIES OF LLECHWEDD DYRYS AND NANTEOS[1]

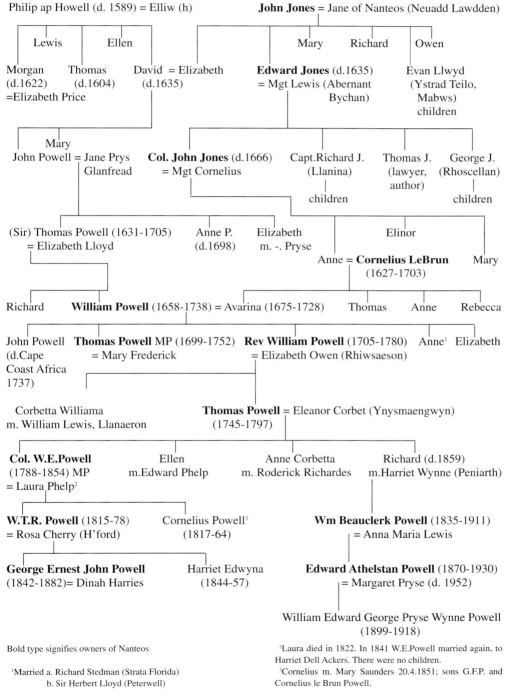

Bold type signifies owners of Nanteos

[1]Married a. Richard Stedman (Strata Florida)
    b. Sir Herbert Lloyd (Peterwell)

[2]Laura died in 1822. In 1841 W.E.Powell married again, to Harriet Dell Ackers. There were no children.
[3]Cornelius m. Mary Saunders 20.4.1851; sons G.F.P. and Cornelius le Brun Powell.

CONTRIBUTORS

Dr. Richard Moore-Colyer is Professor of Agrarian History in the University of Wales, Aberystwyth. He has published extensively on the agricultural, social, cultural and landscape history of Wales and England.

Captain J. Hext Lewes R.N., O.B.E., (1903-92) was owner of Llanllyr. He was Lord Lieutenant of Cardiganshire 1956-74, and Lieutenant of Dyfed 1974-78. His father was a first cousin of Mrs Powell and he was closely involved in the destiny of Nanteos after her death.

Gerald Morgan teaches local and Welsh history at the University of Wales, Aberystwyth. His latest publications are *A Welsh House and its Family: the Vaughans of Trawsgoed*, and *Helyntion y Cardi*.

Dr. Caroline Palmer is a garden consultant, and writes on Welsh gardens. Her recent publications are *Cuttings - A gardener's pot-pourri from Wales*, and *Prigs*. She edits the *Bulletin* of the Welsh Historic Gardens Trust and teaches Biological Anthropology at the University of Wales, Lampeter.

Anthony J. Parkinson was the Head of Architectural History for the Royal Commission on the Ancient Monuments of Wales until 1995. He has lectured and published articles on many aspects of the architectural history and rural industries of Wales.

Dr Michael Siddons is Wales Herald Extraordinary, the leading authority on Welsh heraldry and historical genealogies, and author of the definitive study, *Welsh Heraldry*, published by the National Library of Wales.

Dr. Juliette Wood is an American-trained folklorist who studied Celtic at Oxford and Aberystwyth. She is past-president of the Folklore Society, and lectures in folklore at the University of Wales, Cardiff. Her latest publication is *The Celts*.

INDEX

(Since all members of the Powell, Jones and Phelp families are included in the genealogy on p. 259, references to the genealogy are not included below, nor to the summary genealogies on pp.8, 19, 23. There are no separate references to chapter end-notes. References to pictures related to individuals are in **bold** type; pictures of other subjects may be found in the list of illustrations.)

Abbey estate 34
Aberbrwynen 19
Abermaed 5
Abermarlais 4
Aberystwyth: Assembly Rooms 62-63
         castle 10
         Castle House 62
         council and art gallery 108-111
         Nanteos interests in 34, 84
         riots 84
         Swinburne at Aberystwyth 101
         university: see University College
               of Wales
Antioch, Silver Cup of 239, 240
Apperley, Newton Wynne 209-10
Appleyard, Robert 53, 55, 61, 122-23, 128, 195
Amery, Ethelwen 226, 243
Armstrong, Adam 127-28
Arnason, Jón 95

Bayreuth 106
Bliss, Mr & Mrs Geoffrey 151-52
Bonsall, George 62
Brackenbury, Augustus 84
Breconshire, lands in 34
Brown, 'Capability' 187
Brown, Major-General Sir George Brown 87-88
Burne-Jones, Edward 111
Bwlch-gwyn lead mine 28-29

Calais 71, 126
Cardigan 85, 87
Cardiganshire police force 89
Castle Howard **161**, 161-62, 164, 190
Ceffyl Pren, Y: 85
Cherry, Eleanora (née Phelp) 59-60, 70
Cherry, William George 59-60, 62, 66, 67, 70,
         128-29, 134
Civil Wars 10-13
Cockerell, Samuel Pepys 169
Committee for Compounding 12
Corbet, Edward Maurice, of Ynysmaengwyn 36,
         57, 59, 62, 67, 121-22
Cornelius family of Freemantle (Hants) 9
Cornwallis, Francis 25

Coultart, W.R. 156, 158-59, 169, 170, 171, 206
Cox, John 93
Crawford, William 201
Cwmystwyth 13, 38-39
Cymmrodorion, Society of 31

Davenport, John 36, 193-95, 201, 205
David ap Philip ap Hywel 8, 17
Davies, John 185-86, 189, 190
Deio ab Ieuan Du 2
Dieppe 71
Dolaucothi 5
Doré, Gustav 105
Dyffryn Llynod 163

Edward ap John ap Ieuan Goch 3
Edwards, John 128-29, 196-98
Elijah and the Ravens, icon 238
Elvey, Sir George 106
Emerson, Ralph Waldo 104
Emes, William 187, 195
Esgair-mwyn lead mine 28-30
Etretat (Normandy) 102-4, 113-4
Evans, George Eyre 226

Fountain Gate, Tregaron 23
Franco-Prussian War 104
Frederick, Thomas 24, 185

Gennet, Mary Selina 67, 75
Glanfread 18
Glastonbury Abbey 221-22, 228, 229, 230
Gogerddan, *see* Pryse family
Goncourt brothers, 102-3
Graham, Sir James, of the Home Office 86
Griffiths, Thomas 205
Gwarnant Park 86
Gwyn-Jones, Timothy 152

Hall, Edward Crompton Lloyd 86
Hawkstone 47, 48, 195
Haycock, Edward 132, 158, 160, 164, 165, 170,
         171, 172, 173, 174, 175, 203, 207
Herbert family of Hafod Uchdryd 18
Hesp, Gary 152

Hill, John, of Prees 48, 51, 119-20, 195
Holy Grail, legend of 221ff
Hughes, Hugh 52, 53
Hughes, James, of Glanrheidol 70, 122, 127, 130, 195

Iceland 95, 96, 98
Icelandic legends and literature 93-4, 97-98, 112

Jamaica 133
Jane, heiress of Nanteos 3
Jochumsson, Matthias 98
John ab Edward ap John 4
Johnes, Thomas, of Hafod 4, 83, 195
Jones, family 4, 5, 6, 14
Jones, Anne (wife of Cornelius Le Brun) 14-15
Jones, Edward of Nanteos 6-9
Jones, Edward, of Llanina 20-21
Jones, George, of Rhoscellan 9, 21
Jones, (Col.) John 9-15, 37
Jones, John (of Derry Ormond) 62
Jones, Richard 9
Jones, Thomas, of Llanbadarn 4
Jones, Thomas, of Nanteos 9
Jones, Thomas, of Aberystwyth, entrepreneur 84

Kent, William 187
Kumpel, Wilhelm 110,111

Laura Gardens 72
Le Brun, Cornelius 13-15, 37
Lead mining 37-40, **37**
Legends of Iceland 95, 98
Lewes family of Llanllyr 7
Lewes, Captain J.Hext 147-48, 150
Lewis family of Abernant Bychan 7
Lewis, Sir James, of Abernant Bychan 7, 9
Lewis, John of Llanaeron
Lewis, Lionel Smithett 227-28, 236, 246
Lewis, Margaretta 99
Lewis, Sylvanus 99, 136
Lisburne, viscounts *see* Vaughan
Liszt, Franz 105
Llanbadarn Fawr (and church) 6, 10, 18, 77, 132
Llanbadarn-y-Creuddyn 8, 17
Llanbrynmair 129
Llangoedmor 85
Llanina estate 9
Llanllyr 86
Llan-non 86
Llechwedd Dyrys 8, 15, 185, 192
Llety'r Cynydd 2
Lloyd family of Ystrad Teilo, Mabws 6

Lloyd, John, of Peterwell 26
Lloyd, Sir Herbert, of Peterwell 26, 28
Lloyd, James, of Mabws 33
Lloyd, Richard, of Mabws 25
Lloyd, Walter, of Peterwell 25
Llwynymwyn lead mine 30
Longfellow, Henry W. 93, 95
Lovesgrove 123-24, 129-30
Lozon, Victor 130
Luck of Edenhall 239

Machen, Arthur, 235, 242, 244-45
Mackworth, Sir Humphrey 24
Magnusson, Eirikur 95, **96**, 98, 104
Mathafarn 9
Maupassant, Guy de 102-4
Mazer bowls 240-41
Merton College, Oxford 9
Metropolitan Police 87
Meyrick, Samuel Rush 230
Mirylees family 151, 221, 229, 231, 239
Mirylees, Mrs Betty Garnons (née Williams) 149-51
Mjolnir 93
Montgomeryshire, lands in 34
Morgan ap Philip ap Howell 16-17, 18
Morgan, Owen ('Morien') 246
Morgan, Thomas 48, 49
Morris, Lewis 28-31
Morris, Richard 31
Morris, William (artist and poet) 98
Murray, Adam 126
Murray, Sir George 49-51

Nash, John 170, 197-99, 201, 202
Nanteos: (see also under various Powells)
    contents in 1666 13
    cup 2, 105, 219-48, 253
    demesne & gardens **184**, 185-215
    dog kennel eyecatcher **188**, 188-89
    estate 23, 33-6, 48-50, 134, 136-38
    game 209-212
    genealogy 259
    ghost stories & legends 235-36
    heraldry 255—57
    mansion **2**, **7**, 27, 76, 155-78
    politics 24, 25-26, 31-33
    situation 2
Neuadd Lawdden 2-3
Newman, Reg 214

Offenbach, Jacques 93, 105
Ouseley, Sir Frederick 106, 107, 112

Owen, Athelstan, of Rhiwsaeson and
Ynysymaengwyn 28

Parry, Joseph 107, 112
Parry, Stephen, of Noyaddtrefawr 25
Parzifal 105, 236
Pencarreg farm 10
Penglais estate 5
Penglanowen farm 10
Penparcau Schools 160
Penson, D.Kyrke 178
Pierce, T. Jones 224
Plascrug 'castle' 189-91, **191**, 213
Phelp family 47, 53, 55, 57
Phelp, Cecil 72, 74
Phelp, Edward Tufton 57-58, 60, 71, 74, 77
Phelp, Mrs Ellen (wife of James Phelp) 55, 59,
65-66, 77
Phelp, Ellen Elizabeth (née Powell; wife of
E.T.Phelp) 52, 53, 57-59, 65-66, 71, 74, 121,
124
Phelp, Fanny 69-70
Phelp, James 55, 57
Phelp, Julia 69-70
Phelp, William Edward 77, 99, 134, 211
Philip ap Howell 16-17
Pocock, Captain Samuel 49-50, 52, 120
Pole, Tudor 246
Politics *see* Nanteos: politics
Powell family of Llechwedd Dyrys & Nanteos
throughout
Powell, Anne (wife of Richard Stedman & of
Herbert Lloyd) **26**
Powell, Anne Corbetta 124
Powell, Athelstan John 74
Powell, Mrs Avarina (née Le Brun; wife of
William Powell) 21-22, 185
Powell, Cornelius 61, 65, 69
Powell, Cornelius le Brun 74, 134
Powell, Mrs Dinah (gwraig George Powell) 108
Powell, Edward Athelstan 137-140, **138**, 214
Powell, Mrs Elizabeth (née Owen; wife of Rev.
William Powell) 28, 30-31
Powell, Eleanor Laura 74
Powell, Mrs Eleanor (née Corbet; wife of
Thomas Powell II) 36, 47-49, 51, 52, 57,
59, 119-21, 123-25, 129
Powell, Ellen Elizabeth *see* Phelp, Mrs Ellen
Powell, George (d.1882) 73, 74, 75, **92**, 93-114,
94, 136, 213, 224, 236, 237, 244
Powell, Mrs Harriet (née Wynne; second wife of
W.E.Powell) 74, 75, 76, 132, 206
Powell, John 22-23

Powell, Mrs Laura (née Phelp, wife of
W.E.Powell; d.1820) 47, 55, 60-67
Powell, Mrs Margaret (née Pryse) **147**, 147-151,
221-47 *passim*
Powell, Mrs Mary (née Frederick; wife of
Thomas Powell I) 24, 185
Powell, Morgan *see* Morgan ap Philip ap Howell
Powell, Richard 20-21
Powell, Richard Owen 73, 213
Powell, Mrs Rosa Edwyna (née Cherry, wife of
W.T.R.Powell) 75, 95
Powell, Sir Thomas (d. 1705) 18-22; **22**, 255-57
Powell, Thomas I (d. 1752) 24-30, 162, 170, 185
Powell, Thomas II (d.1797) 33, **35**, 48, 83, 119,
192-93
Powell, William (d.1738) 15, 20-24, 185
Powell, Rev. William (d. 1780) 28-33, 170, 171,
185, 186
Powell, William Beauclerk 74, 99, 114, 136-37,
213-14
Powell, William Edward (d.1854) 47-89, **50**
army career 52, 58, 59
building in Aberystwyth 56, 71-72, 75, 84
conspicuous expenditure 54, 84, 122-24
death 76, 132
education 49, 51-52, 120-21
estate & demesne management 119, 127-32,
195-207
extra-marital affair 67-68, 75
family relationships 124-26
Lord Lieutenant of Cardiganshire 59, 84
marriages: 53, 55, 56-57, 75
Member of Parliament 59, 83, **87**
military and public service 61, 121, 131-32
Rebecca Riots 83-88
sheriff of Cardiganshire 54
Powell, William Edward George Pryse Wynne
139, 140, 139-40, 147-51, 214
Powell, William T.R. (d.1878)
artistic interest **72**, 73, 209
childhood 59, 65, 69
conspicuous expenditure 133
death 77
demesne and garden 208-13
education 72-73
father of George Powell 95, 99-101, 108
marriage & marital problems 9975
Member of Parliament 100, 134, **135**
military enrolment 73, 133
other 77
Pryse family of Gogerddan 4, 6, 18, 25
Pryse, Lewis 24
Pryse, Pryse 62, 83, 141

Pryse, Richard 10
Pryse, Thomas, of Dol 25
Pugh, Rowland, of Mathafarn 9, 21

Rebecca Riots **82**, 83-89
Repton, George Stanley 62-63, 198-99
Repton, Humphry 202
Richardes family, of Penglais 4
Richardes, Alexander 126
Richardes, Mrs Anne (née Powell) 67, 71, 125-26
Richardes, Roderick Eardley 67, 71, 125
Rhoscellan estate 9
Rhoslawdden 3
'Rhyfel y Sais Bach' 84
Ring opera cycle 102, 106
Roads 186
Robson, Thomas 48, 51, 194-95
Rossetti, Dante Gabriel 111
Royal Cardiganshire Militia 58, 65, 84

Sade, the Marquis de 93, 102
Schumann, Clara 93, 106
Shroud of Turin 238, 247
Sigurdsson, Jón 96-98, **97**
Solomon, Rebecca 105
Solomon, Simeon 105, 111
Stainer, John 106
Star Chamber, court 6-7
Stedman, family, of Ystrad Fflur (Strata Florida) 27-28, 222-23, 230
Stedman, Richard (d. 1744) 27-28, 234
Strata Florida Abbey 222-23
Sunny Hill, Tregaron 74, 77
Swinburne, Algernon **92**, 93, 100-106, **103**, 114, 115-7

Tabernacle chapel 36

Tenbury 106
Thomas ap Philip ap Howell 17
Tregaron 25
Tŷ Mawr, Ysbyty Cynfyn 16-17

Ucheldre Mill 17
University College of Wales, Aberystwyth 107, 111

Vaughan family of Trawsgoed 2, 4
Vaughan, (Sir) John 11, 19
Vaughan, John (first viscount Lisburne) 24
Vaughan, John (second viscount Lisburne) 25
Vaughan, Sir Robert, of Hengwrt, 123
Vaughan, Wilmot (third viscount Lisburne) 30-32
Vaughan, Wilmot (fourth viscount and first earl of Lisburne) 32-33, 83

Wagner, Cosima 106
Wagner, Richard 93, 102, 105, 106, 236
Waite, A.E. 228, 234, 245
Welsh School (Ashford Welsh Girls' School) 36
Weston, Jessie 243, 245-46
Wernddu farm 10
Wesley, S.S. 106
White, George **131**
Whitelock, Bulstrode 10
William of Malmesbury 230
Williams, Sir Glanmor 224
Williams, Nathaniel, of Castle Hill 62

Ysbyty Cynfyn 16,17, 18
Ystrad Fflur estate 27
Ystwyth, Lord (Matthew Vaughan Davies) **140**

Zwecker, Johann Baptiste 95, 101, 105,111